# Torn From the Homeland

## Unforgettable Experiences During WWII

## Czeslaw Plawski

authorHOUSE®

AuthorHouse™
1663 Liberty Drive
Bloomington, IN 47403
www.authorhouse.com
Phone: 1-800-839-8640

First published by AuthorHouse     3/11/2011

ISBN: 978-1-4567-0128-4 (hc)
ISBN: 978-1-4567-0127-7 (sc)
ISBN: 978-1-4567-0126-0 (e)

Library of Congress Control Number: 2011903423

Printed in the United States of America

This book is printed on acid-free paper.

# Acknowledgments

This book was originally written and published in Polish. Marta Zieba and Diane Mechlinski accomplished the very difficult literal translation. I appreciate their skills and thank them for their efforts.

I also wish to thank Ruth Mathieu, Elizabeth Novitsky and Lynn Mathieu for a respectful and thorough job of editing this manuscript. Their work was done with dedication and zeal.

Above all, my wife, Teresa, deserves my thanks and gratitude. Theresa supplied much of the integral information and offered countless valuable suggestions to enhance the completion of this odyssey. She was with me every step of the way.

This book is dedicated to our grandchildren. During moments when they may experience difficulties and disappointments in life, may they take strength from the struggles we have endured, and gather the support they need from God's care as well as from their own inner selves.

Czeslaw Plawski

# Foreword

*Torn From the Homeland* relates the actual sequence of events in the lives of two Polish families during the course of World War II. It recalls the many happenings and hardships faced by the families of Czeslaw (Chester) Plawski and Teresa Bajorski Plawski. It is based on recollections of both Teresa and Czeslaw, as well as many of their friends and family members.

The author recalls his early life from the time he was physically incapacitated and forced to continuously battle for his existence. At an early age he could only dream of regaining his health and being able to work and compete proudly and equally with his peers. Since he lacked physical strength and prowess during the early years of his life, he was compelled to use his mind and wits to achieve his desired goals. He developed within himself an animal instinct for survival, which served him well during times of war and misfortune.

During the difficult and depressing times after the onset of the first battles of World War II in September of 1939, the author's family fought in a variety of ways against the German occupation and Russian invasion of Poland's soil. Their lives were in constant danger, and that condition persisted until the end of the hostilities.

The family of the author's wife, Teresa, was uprooted from its home and driven into the depths of the USSR to a work camp in Siberia.

They spent many years in misery and hunger, doing slave labor. They were then forced to roam over three continents, with the single goal of survival and the hopes that they could return to their homeland and become a reunited family.

# Contents

# Mlynowa No. 9
## (Czeslaw)

On Mlynowa Street in Wilno, Poland, stood an old three-story house, built before the First World War but untouched by the passage of time. Viewed from the street, its walls covered with white plaster and set on enormous foundations resembled a closed and inaccessible fortress. This was an apartment building owned by Father Michniewicz, a former Bernardine parish priest.

Mlynowa Street was named for a mill whose remains could still be seen in the water at the bend of the swift-flowing Wilenka River. The twisting bed of this small, stone-bottomed river divided the old district of Zarzecze from Wilno's city center. Fed by springs in the far southeast, the Wilenka flowed freely through green fields and meadows until she came to a stop, checked by the French Mill's Dam. She waited only until the overflow from her rising waters was drained. Released, she sluiced headlong over innumerable stones, so polished they shone, and rushed on. She swam beside the road at the foot of the Belmont pine forest before hurtling into the city. Her course taking along Bernardynski Park, skirting Trzech Krzyzy Mountain on the other side. On the mountain's summit, against the blue of the sky, rose enormous white concrete crosses. They were built in memory of three monks brutally murdered by Budionny's Cossacks during the First World War.

Above the green crowns of the riverside park, the sandy yellow mountain slope, overgrown with soaring pine trees, created a wonderful panorama. Wilenka neared her mouth, finishing her run between the mountain and the ruins of Prince Gedymin's castle on her left bank. This massive old fortress, built on a high hill between rivers, had been unconquerable for hundreds of years. The remains of the thick walls and tall red brick bastille atestament to Lithuania's power in the 13$^{th}$ century. It was there that Wilenka ended her independent existence, swallowed by the larger river Wilja.

From the top of the palace ruins, one could see greenly forested hills surrounding a valley traversed by two blue ribbons of river. In this valley lay the old and beautiful town of Wilno. Red tile roofs stood out richly against the white walls of the city's buildings. The whole was interlaced with a labyrinth of narrow streets and city parks, creating a colorful mosaic. From the soaring towers of forty-two churches, scattered throughout this old town, came the sound of bells interrupting the evening hush. The bells reminded people it would soon be time to rest and give thanks to God for granting the faithful the opportunity to look upon and wonder at His works.

The Wilenka River, which seemed so calm and friendly in summer, changed her face in winter. With the coming of the first frost, the stones at her bottom covered themselves in ice, looking like giant white pearls under a transparent watery cloak. The surface of the river was the next to freeze, allowing a warmer layer of water to flow between the ice and the bottom. For five months, a thick layer of downy snow covered Wilno's neighborhoods. It enveloped the stony earth and the half-meter of ice on the lakes and rivers like a feather quilt. Inevitably, the seasons changed. At the beginning of April, a warm wind blowing to announce the approaching spring. Violet pasqueflowers emerged from under the snow in the forests. Melting snow turned into silvery streams and flowed down to the still, ice-covered river. Wilenka awoke from her sleep. The force of the swollen water caused the thick ice to crack with the sound of cannon fire. Its surface fissured with lines like a great map. In one abrupt moment, the river threw off her winter coat and hurled herself into the dance of spring.

Giant ice floes heaped into moveable hills, whirling and surging in a dizzy rush. Nothing stood in Wilenka's way. She took wooden bridges with her, raising them in to the air under pressure from the rushing floes, and then dropping them like toys into her swift rapids. She was hurrying to fall into the arms of her mightier sister, Wilja, so together they could slip into the sea. The rising, troubled waters overflowed her banks. She carried away trees, cattle and houses with people still desperately clinging to their straw roofs, and swept clean the property of riverside villages and hamlets.

The city was also awakening. Groups of people began to gather in the squares, delighting in the rays of the spring sun. Students enlivened promenading crowds with laughter and songs, and by playing various musical instruments. On the streets, children with overflowing baskets of blossoms, looking to earn ten groszy (cents), pressed bouquets of forget-me-nots and pasqueflowers into the hands of passersby. Trees sprouted young leaves and city lawns grew green with new grass. Bands of colorful early blooms tempted throngs of bees and butterflies with their fragrance and sweetness. Lovers, embracing on park benches, reveled in the perfume of flowers during spring evenings. Warm gusts of wind announced the coming of the summer, which was a time to rest after a hard winter. Warm clothing was now being exchanged for colorful summery garb.

Fishermen waited on the riverbanks for hungry fish to take the bait they had cast into the water. While gazing at their floats, they forgot about the rest of world. The murmur of the water temporarily banished their daily cares. The beauty of the spring stupefied people and the scent of the cherry flower on a warm May night was mesmerizing.

The short spring passed quickly, and after a few weeks came the hot, dry summer with its cool nights. On holidays, the riverbanks swarmed with people. Rowboats, sailboats and kayaks sailed up the river to the town of Werki, seven kilometers from Wilno. There among the pine trees the city's inhabitants rested from the hardships of daily life.

After the First World War, Poles, Byelorussians, Lithuanians, Russians, Jews, Tartars and Karaites populated the province of Wilno. The diversity of faiths, customs and languages was never an obstacle to a friendly coexistence at school, work, or shared places of recreation. Churches, minarets and synagogues stood side by side, and for hundreds of years the inhabitants of this border city had thronged to them to pay their homage to God.

Nevertheless, there were minor incidents sometimes resulting in the loss of few teeth or someone spending the night in the hospital with a broken nose. Such occurrences were routine, especially around Easter, when men walked the streets on legs made unsteady by liquor. Wilno had always been a happy, friendly and good-humored place, but one had to respect certain customs such as not escorting girls back to unfamiliar neighborhoods. The girls were considered property of the jealous young men who lived in those neighborhoods and were therefore under their protection.

It is in this city that my story begins. Bored with my mother's womb, and eager to see the beautiful world full of life and exciting sensations, I was born. This took place on September 15, 1925, at Mlynowa Street No. 9, in a three-room apartment on the second floor. It was a very difficult period in young post-war Poland. Unemployment and the cost of living were high. My father, Roman Plawski, a typesetter by profession, made what was then considered a fairly good salary, though it proved rather modest for a man with a young family and two old mothers to support.

Due to limited living space, the two grandmothers were forced to share a room. This often gave rise to small misunderstandings that lasted the entire day. The old women were eloquent and voluble speakers, and Mama couldn't take their shouting for long. Heroically, she would try to reconcile them. Then the war front would change, and the two women would take on even greater verve and turn on the lady of the house. The prodigious battle would last until the moment father returned from work. Seeing his wife in tears and guessing the reason for her distress, he would join in the general chaos. However, thanks to his years in the choir, he could use his voice to draw his mother's attention to himself. Mama's mother would then fall silent, frightened by father's baritone. A momentary quiet would descend on the house, but the cold war continued. One grandmother would stealthily stick out her tongue; the other retaliated by lifting her skirt and thrusting out her rump. This was the battle's final phase. Father would separate the bellicose women between two rooms. These skirmishes repeated themselves frequently and became unbearable. Finally the warring ladies had to be permanently separated. My mother's mother went to live with her other daughter. A comparative peace descended on our house, and Mama was left with just one opponent – her mother-in-law.

Luckily for me I was young and oblivious to the mayhem. My mother would recall these times to me much later. From my earliest days, I was curious, and desirous of adventures and new sensations. I was forever crawling into forbidden places, creating a mass of trouble for myself and compounding the worries of my parents. I am told that when I was a year old I tried out my first steps setting off on unsteady legs to explore the kitchen. I teetered along, and by supporting myself against the wall, managed to crawl over to the oven. Curious about its red-hot doors, I reached out for them. The result was that I glued myself to the doors and left behind the burnt skin of both hands. The stench of scorched flesh alerted my mother that something was wrong. She was just coming up the stairs as she returned from a short visit to the store, where she had gone to buy necessities for dinner. Mama had left me locked in my room in the care of my four-year-older brother, who had grown tired of my crying and opened the door to the kitchen. This practice of leaving children at home while the mother did outdoor chores was very common. In no way was it considered a sign of neglect, but of necessity. The damage to my left hand was severe. The palm and finger muscles were burned along with the skin. Soon a short red line going up my hand indicated that I had blood poisoning.

At the hospital the doctors examined my wounds and announced that my left hand would have to be amputated at the wrist to save my life. My despairing mother could not reconcile herself to this diagnosis. It was more than she could bear. The thought of amputating a small boy's hand just as his life was beginning, drove her into a state of frenzy. I am told that for three days and three nights my mother carried me in her arms unceasingly, while I howled with pain, not sleeping for a moment. She made wet compresses with herbs for my burnt hand, on the advice of an elderly Russian woman who lived in the same building. The old woman was a professed soothsayer, and also collected herbs, which she dried and offered to the tenants at a modest price. Using these folk treatments my mother saved my hand. To this day I have an ugly scar, a memento of my first independent foray into forbidden territory.

Soon after my hand healed, I fell ill with scarlet fever. To protect the other children in the building, my parents were forced to leave me in a hospital that dealt with infectious diseases. This was my first, never-to-be-forgotten, moment of parting from my family. I was not quite two years old. Held in the arms of a hospital nurse, I saw my mother leave the building. I watched, terrified, as her beloved silhouette receded in the distance. To this day I can still remember her tearful face looking in through the window. At any given moment, I can summon up the sight of the red hat on her head. Crying with despair, I was left alone in a strange place among strangers. A few weeks later I developed a new illness and was transferred to another hospital. The scarlet fever damaged my kidneys and left behind chronic nephritis.

It is not clear to me how long I was away from home; but the moment of my return has remained in my memory. Upon release from the hospital my mother dressed me for the first time in a pair of blue trousers with white buttons on the legs. When I came home I refused to let them be removed, even when I went to bed. I was also shy, feeling strange among my own family after such a long separation.

My newly acquired illness returned rather frequently; the smallest cold was enough to put me back in bed for a few weeks and sometimes even for up to a month. I was required to observe a strict diet without a grain of salt, leaven, meat or protein. The illness also necessitated that I lie quietly. Any violent movement increased the bleeding in my kidneys. It was difficult to make a small boy understand the urgency of staying in bed for such a long time. I took advantage of every moment of my mother's inattention to slip out of bed and stand on a chair to look out the window at the other children playing in the courtyard.

For several years I was disabled with kidney problems a few times annually. I ate only fruit and vegetables. This inadequate nourishment made me thin and weak, resulting in extended periods of convalescence. I was still too young to understand the gravity of my state of health. I balked at unsalted, unsavory foods. My mother used a variety of methods to encourage me to eat. She told me I was eating for my grandmother's health or my father's, or my brother's, or even for the health of the cat. Every spoonful was for somebody else. After a time I wised up and demanded to be paid to eat my meals. I put the coins in a piggybank and kept it by my side as a plaything. When my father was short of money I would often lend him some at a ten-percent weekly profit, keeping the transactions absolutely secret from my mother.

Most of my winters were spent at home. My parents hesitated to take me for walks for fear I would catch cold and cause a recurrence of my illness. My mother was so concerned about my health that she often summoned the doctor to the house. I listened to their conversations about my kidneys and my future. I played and pretended to ignore their conversation. The doctor was pessimistic. According to him my illness was very serious and incurable, and cautioned my mother to expect the worst. He recommended the house be kept warm, that I behave calmly, and that I maintain a low-salt diet. Keeping a small boy quiet and under constant surveillance was an almost impossible assignment.

Once, after the doctor had left, I set a woolen thread on fire and watched the flame climb, waiting for it to extinguish. When my mother questioned what I was doing, I told her I was divining how long I would live. She cried, telling me that everything would turn out alright, that I would outgrow my sickness, and that I must be strong and full of hope. She said this with tears in her eyes, which were full of despair and motherly love.

Since early childhood, I had always been industrious and full of new ideas. One day I was sitting on the chamber pot eating some fresh cherries. After consuming the fruit, I decided to put the pits up my nose to block the odor. After I had finished my business, I tried to remove the pits, which were now unnecessary. This was an apparently uncomplicated task, but not easy to execute. By digging around in my nose with my finger, I only managed to push the pits in deeper. I began to have difficulty breathing. My mother was alerted by my cries and lacking the proper surgical tools at home, called on our neighbor, Mrs. Narkiewicz, for help.

Mrs. Narkiewicz was the mother of my friend Janek. She possessed a head of very long hair which was held in place by large hair pins. Mrs. Narkiewicz considered herself a medical expert. She quickly removed one of her hairpins and began to use it to dislodge the embedded cherry pits. Blood started pouring from my nose and I began to choke. There was no solution to the situation but to get medical help as fast as possible. I was taken to the hospital by horse-drawn cab, and after a painful extraction, became famous for discovering a method to prevent odor inhalation during moments of stomach disturbance.

Time passed quickly, and it was impossible to keep a sickly but lively boy at home. I was lured outside by the desire to play with the other children who lived in the building. In order to join my friends, I walked down steep stairs to the first floor balcony surrounding the stone paved semi-circle courtyard. The balcony was built out of thick, solid planks and railings through which we could watch the interesting lives of the ground-floor tenants. For a few hours each day, immediately after breakfast, the housewives took their place on the balcony, enjoying the sunshine that illuminated and warmed their meeting place. Behind the backs of the gossiping mothers an indescribable commotion transpired. The younger generation was also enjoying the fresh air.

My brother Tadek and I lived on the top floor. On the next floor below lived our closest neighbors Wicia and small Wladzia. Wladzia was a very capable girl. She would make round balls from the material in her snub nose. These she used as a handy substitute for chewing gum. At the end of the balcony on the first floor lived Witek and Jozek Liminowicz. Nicknamed "Pickle" by the tenants, Jozek had an oblong head and a very powerful voice. He yelled his head off all day long until every window in the building rattled, and the tenants despaired. His tenor voice turned out to be very useful to him as an adult. Although he went into the army, he was never sent to the front, but successfully sang on the stages of the Polish Army Theater. Edek and Janek Narkiewicz, along with Bolek Ploski, occupied the apartments on the other side of the first-floor balcony. This group of "adored" children whirled about the women like a hurricane, while secretly eavesdropping on their conversations.

One day, I was chased by a friend on the balcony unaware that a casement window had been opened into it from the Narkiewicz apartment. The pane must have been extremely clean, as I ran directly through it, though naturally a bloody face resulted. Once again it was off to the hospital. The surgeon put stitches in my split nose, and beside my eye. He told me I was lucky. I do believe I was truly very fortunate; I could easily have lost my sight.

From the balcony, one would walk down winding, twilit wooden stairs, past the doors of the apartment occupied by the widow Esmunt and her daughter, Marysia. Plump Marysia had great, big, black, calf eyes. In the dark, one-room apartment beside theirs lodged an old maid, crazy Jadwisia. She made her living by helping neighbors wash their linens and floors. A giant, red gate stood at the exit from the stairwell under the concrete ceiling arch. The gate separated our fifteen-family apartment building from narrow Mlynowa Street. Beside the gate were the entrance doors. They were massive, squeaked incessantly, and locked precisely at ten o'clock each night. Whoever returned late had to ring Mr. Antoni Korwiel, the house supervisor, and wait patiently for him to come and open the doors. To avoid listening to his complaints, interwoven with Russian curses, it was necessary to appease him with a payment of fifty groszy (cents).

Jadwisia often stood near these doors, smiling at the men as they passed by. If one of them was intrigued by her flirtations and started chatting, she would open her bathrobe to reveal her naked charms. She would then run off laughing to the darkened cellar, whose entrance lay by the stairs leading up to the first floor. Her lover would quickly follow her, encouraged by her wooing and happy with the promise of a free amorous adventure. After one such visit an abandoned cigarette butt caused a fire. A cloud of black smoke began to spew into the courtyard. The fire brigade came but the heat and the thick smoke prevented them from going down into the cellar. Two firefighters lost consciousness, poisoned by gases from the burning rags and black coal. The fire was eventually contained, and the building was saved. The old bricks that made up the cellar's thick ceiling prevented the fire from penetrating to the first-floor apartments. The excited housewives on the balcony had something to talk about for a long time, but poor Jadwisia lost her trysting place.

The gate was also a frequent meeting place for men who liked to spend their free time in pleasant conversation while watching both the horse-drawn and pedestrian traffic. The setting of the house was sometimes dangerous. It stood on a sharp turn at the end of Zarzeczna Street, which climbed steeply uphill. Sometimes the men, engrossed in conversation, had to flee in a panic to avoid a collision with a horse's head. Heavily laden wagons traveling down the street took on speed, the drivers vainly tried to check their horses, whose shoes slid across the cobblestones, the vehicles lurching violently toward the apartment walls. Most often the jutting shafts of the wagons landed in the window of the barbershop beside the gate. The sound of breaking windowpanes caused a panic among the men sitting inside waiting to be shaved. After such an accident, the Jewish barber could be heard complaining about bad horses and stupid drivers.

Mr. Antoni Korwiel, the house superintendent, had been somewhat wronged by fate; his leg had once been hideously broken at the knee and never properly set. He limped heavily. He lived with his wife and his son, Gienek, in the second part of the courtyard, which was reached by walking under the ceiling arch that divided the yard. In the annex behind his apartment, lived the owner of the previously mentioned barbershop.

A nearby apartment was occupied by a short, thin shoemaker, his daughter, two sons, and a most formidable wife. She was a huge woman who towered over the rest of the family. This family followed a weekly routine of hosting a party which lasted from Friday afternoon through Saturday evening. The strumming of guitars and the loud crooning of Russian ballads emanated throughout the area. Much vodka was consumed, and the party was often rowdy. By Saturday evening, the tipsy guests dispersed, usually after rigorous brawling and shouting.

For much of Sunday, quiet prevailed. The serenity did not last throughout the day, however. With many neighbors in quiet observance, the usual Sunday brouhaha erupted at the shoemaker's abode. After many loud arguments and much name calling, the fracas climaxed by the man of he house being tossed through the front door by his wife. He was soon folowed by the children, who were grabbed by the seats of their pants and flung outdoors by their mother. The door was then slammed shut and peace and quiet again prevailed. This was not a serene or boring environment in which to live.

Time passed and I grew up, just like every other child in the tenement house. I was increasingly tempted to play with the band of teenagers who cavorted in the large courtyard. Anyone descending the stairs from the balcony entered this courtyard, where a basin with running water had been installed in the wall. A large sign announced that the water was only for use in the kitchen and that the washing of dishes and linens in the basin was strictly prohibited. The sign was clear and legible, but the rule was difficult to enforce. The housewives did not enjoy carrying buckets of water up to their apartments and then down again to the drain at the far end of the building.

Every moment of Mr. Antoni's absence was used by the women to wash the linens in this basin, saving time, work, and the effort of climbing the stairs. The water discarded after such a wash gurgled away in the gutter to our amusement. The current seized the paper boats we made and carried them away under the arch of the first floor ceiling to the second section of the courtyard, more spacious than the first, and planted with large trees. The boats sailed with the stream to the end of the courtyard, where they fell into the catch basin and ended their long journey. To the right of the gutter was the playground, and directly behind it a flower and vegetable garden planted by the tenants. The high walls of neighboring apartment buildings surrounded our entire kingdom and concealed our childhood adventures from the world.

The most important building in the courtyard stood behind the printing press workshop. It was a large outhouse, painted white with lime. Its entrance led to a spacious room with a canal into which the men urinated. A strip of wall a meter high from the floor had been painted black with pitch to protect the white walls from the shorter citizens, who sprinkled them rather frequently. Evidently not everyone had served in the army and mastered the art of hitting the target. From the antechamber, men walked into four cabins that contained wooden platforms with holes cut into them for more serious activities. A sign admonished: "Please don't put your feet up on the planks." This suggestion was easy to write but harder to follow, especially during the long freezing winters. After two weeks of frost, towers of excrement loomed above the holes. How could people be expected to sit on their neighbors' frozen refuse? Mr. Antoni was forced to imitate a miner and disintegrate the mountains with a pickaxe. While he worked he cursed the innocent architects of these pylons in an eastern accent, calling them "sons of a b----s."

Directly behind this repository stood a substantial wooden receptacle for food waste. Painted black, it looked impressive. A large tin flap covered the stinking interior with its collection of rats, big as cats, which stampeded away when the flap was raised. This is where we hunted, enthusiastically pegging stones at all moving targets. The older children used homemade rubber slingshots. The missiles from these weapons also easily reached the windows of neighboring apartment buildings.

The older inhabitants of the building considered the twelve children both a joy and a torment. They enjoyed our vivacity and mischievousness, while being concerned about our future. At the time we couldn't understand why our games were always being criticized;

evidently they clashed with the sensibilities of the building's supervisor and other inhabitants. According to the adults, climbing tall trees was dangerous, hiking on the roof damaged the tiles, and walking in the garden trampled the vegetables and flowers.

In the evenings, the children frequently activated the electric bell on the gate. Mr. Antoni came along to see who needed his help. If no one was at the gate, he knew who had sounded the alarm. He would swear and shout at us, calling our mothers women of easy virtue, and more than once woke the sleeping tenants with his ranting.

Since we were the youngest, Janek Narkiewicz and I were usually put on guard duty or sent on reconnaissance missions to give the other children a safe and unobstructed escape route once a prank had been played. Naturally, the supervisor blamed us and complained to our parents. This usually ended with a bribe to calm Mr. Antoni's fury. But sometimes the poor man became frustrated and tried to capture us himself. This usually ended in a fiasco due to the hobbling of his broken leg.

Years of lighthearted games on the grounds of the apartment building slowly passed. The gate was no longer a boundary separating Janek and me from that other world which increasingly awoke our interest. There was a river at the end of Mlynowa Street whose bend created a deep cove, glorious for swimming. Wading in the water and jumping around on the slippery rocks in our wet clothes, we would head downstream to nearby Trzech Krzyzy Mountain. On its slope, covered with loose yellow sand, our imaginations took over. We were no longer Janek and Czeslaw but wild Indians, heedless of meals and the hour. We dug tunnels in the sand. With warlike cries, we jumped from the steep slope, experiencing the sensation of birds in flight. The mountain's summit was full of World War I trenches, now covered in sand, in which we played soldiers with the other boys. We quenched our thirst with water from a small stream that flowed from the depths of the earth, and sated our hunger with green gooseberries and apples from neighboring private gardens. Sometimes we had to flee an attacking dog or the owner of one of the orchards. Nevertheless these were the most joyous and adventure filled moments of the day. The setting sun called us back to reality and reminded us it was time to go home. We returned exhausted and prepared for our parents' admonitions and complaints about our muddy, wrinkled clothes.

The seasons changed quickly; leaves fell from the trees and the first snows announced the coming of the holiday season. This was vacation time, time off from school and time to look forward to all of mother's homemade delicacies. On one particular Christmas Eve our father distributed the presents and gave my brother and me two silver zloty (dollar) coins. After eating a substantial supper, we ran to empty our distended stomachs before bed. Neither of us felt like going to the fetid public toilets. It was much more pleasant to sit in the bushes on the bank of the Wilenka and take care of our needs by the light of the moon and the murmur of the water. My brother, Tadek, put the money in his coat pocket. As he threw the coat over his head, he heard a quiet plop that told him the coin had landed in the river. We returned home distraught, saying nothing of our loss to our parents. The next morning before church we ran to the river, took off our boots and waded in the icy water in search of our lost treasure. The coin was found. We were lucky that it had landed on the sand between the stones. Our legs, frozen to the bone, warmed up in the run back to the house.

Among the toys I received for Christmas was a pair of ice skates. I waited impatiently for the first opportunity to test them. The moment finally came with the first big frost. A thin layer of ice formed over the river's quieter waters. I donned my new skates and eagerly set off on the glistening icy surface. The skating was fantastic. Unfortunately, I skated out onto a thinner stretch and found myself up to my waist in water. I dragged myself out, took off my boots and pants, and wrung them out. Then I skated long and fast around the hole in the ice with the hope that the water in my soaked clothing would evaporate. I said nothing about my adventure at home, afraid my skates would be confiscated and hidden away until the public skating rink opened in the park. As it turned out, I had to wait a long time for the pleasure of skating on a real rink. Once again I landed in bed for a few weeks with kidney infection and a high fever. While I was sick I urinated into a bottle and visually checked for the levels of blood and protein in the urine. This more or less indicated how far the sickness had advanced. This was always a depressing time. I despaired at being imprisoned in three rooms, far away from my friends and my beloved river, Wilenka.

While at home, I devoured the books my father brought me. He was an avid reader and volunteered his evenings in the Printers' Union library. My reading was very diverse; I would read books about the Wild West and then secretly borrow my father's Tolstoy, Orzeszkowa, Zeromski, Mickiewicz and other serious writers. I was enchanted by Sienkiewicz's trilogy. Kmicic from "The Deluge" was my hero. At the time I was weak and sickly and therefore I delighted in reading about courageous people and long journeys into unknown lands. In my imagination I became the strong, brave hero of whatever narrative I was enjoying. More than once I complained about my fate to my mother, who was the only one who could raise my spirits. She would often tell me that when I grew up I would do everything I now only dreamed about, if I only had faith and resolve. She would say this with tears in her eyes, but convinced that with determination and the will to live, I would be able to conquer my chronic illness.

Every Saturday our father gave my brother and me a weekly allowance of fifty groszy (cents) each. My brother, Tadek, would disappear from home immediately, and would not be seen again for some time. He would only come back when he had spent all of his money on chocolate, ice cream and sweets. Sunday, he would politely propose that we go to the cinema together, with the condition that I pay for the tickets because he didn't have any money. I wanted to get out of the house with my older brother, so I agreed to his proposition, but I laid down my own condition that he had to carry me to the cinema. I crawled onto his back and rode as if on a horse through the city streets, happy that I was at least partly taking advantage of the power of money. At the cinema, I had to buy him some sweets or a soda so I wouldn't have to listen to his complaints about being tired. By the time the screening finished, the situation had changed. The horse balked and didn't want to take me on his back. I had to give up on my ride and march all the way home on foot.

While I was growing up, I dreamed that I would equal or even surpass my friends in physical ability. In time, as my sickness passed, I would try to win their esteem and respect by climbing the tallest trees or promenading on the roof, to the horror of the neighbors, when my parents were absent. I developed the undeserved reputation of being possessed by the devil, and all the mischief done by other children was laid at my door. Unjustly accused, I sometimes had to bear the punishment for deeds I had not committed.

From my earliest childhood, I was a fervent fisherman. In this I emulated my father, who spent days on the same spot at the river's edge. He often took me with him, to where Wilenka emptied into the Wilja, creating whirlpools that deepened the sandy bottom. This was his favorite fishing spot. Not wanting to disturb him, I would wade into the shallow water from the sandbank that the river had deposited. One time as I played, I grabbed a floating branch and drifted downstream with the current. The shallow water came to an end, and I found myself in Wilja's rapid waters. I let go of the treacherous branch and started digging in the sand with both hands, trying to reach the bank of the river. I could not call for help; water filled my mouth, and the fine sand slipped away under my fingers. By a miracle my hand found a large rock buried in the sand, allowing me to pull myself back into the shallows. My father, busy with his fishing, saw nothing of my precarious situation, which so nearly ended in tragedy. It was only when I returned in my drenched clothes that he asked what had happened, calling me a numskull who couldn't be left alone for even a moment.

My fishing required supplies for which I sometimes did not have the funds. Here initiative and resourcefulness were required. My fishing rod was cut from a hazel bush in the forest, stripped of its bark, and hung in the attic to dry. I attached a weight to one end of the branch to straighten it. The line was made at home out of horsehair. I would go to the town-square on market days. When the wagon driver's attention was elsewhere, I would yank hairs from the tail of an appropriately colored stallion.

A mare's tail hairs were not useful. Urine made them fragile and difficult to weave. More than once the wagon's owner had to calm an unexpectedly kicking horse, which evidently didn't enjoy this kind of tweezing. From the hairs I obtained, I would weave a line that could now be part of an exhibit for a cottage industry. I would start with five hairs, separate them into two or three sections, and then repeat the process with four, three and two hairs until I ended up with one strand matching the color of the water in which I was to fish.

Once a peasant drove into our courtyard with a beautiful horse harnessed to his wagon. He spent the night with friends and in the morning went out to give the animal its oats. The horse was there, but its beautiful gray tail was gone. Naturally the blame fell on me, though I swore, with hand on heart, I was not involved in the mysterious disappearance of the horse's tail. There were other fishing enthusiasts in the building but I was the youngest, and so it was no surprise that I was unjustly blamed. I can only imagine how the villagers greeted the peasant when he returned from the city with a horse missing its tail.

The young fisherman's one unavoidable expense was the purchase of small hooks adapted to fishing with flies for bait. For these hooks I spent some of my meager savings. The flies were easily captured on the doors of butcher shops. I would choose ones with yellow bellies because the local fish liked them best. I twisted the flies' heads off and put them in a matchbox, where they would remain until it came time to go fishing. For deep-water bait I dug up red worms from the garden, or used large, fat maggots picked off a dead cat or dog found in the fields. I covered the carcass in dry sand and patiently waited. Moments later the maggots would come up onto the surface, evidently in need of a bit of air. After this kind of operation my hands might stink a bit but who cared about such minor details?

Fishing with homemade equipment was not always successful, but just lazing on the bank of a favorite river was reward enough for any troubles. On warm and sunny days, I would put my rod aside and wade through the water, frightening the fish. When they tried to escape and find shelter under the rocks, I would dive and pull them from their hiding place with my hands.

Sometimes it wasn't easy to find carcasses with insects. At the butcher shop where my mother bought our meat, I asked for a calf's head. I hid the head behind the chimney on the roof and waited for the insects to hatch. After a few days the results were excellent, and I collected most of the maggots and went fishing with my father. The calf's head, forgotten, ripened in the sun. A fragrant stream from the rotting meat began to ooze across the roof. The tenants wrinkled their noses and called for Mr. Antoni to help find the source of the odor. After a long search the supervisor noticed a swarm of flies circling the chimney, and thinking that some dead animal could be lying there, climbed onto the roof. He was greatly astonished to find a calf's head at such a height. Suspicion once again fell on me. Mr. Antoni came to complain to my parents, and in order to restore peace my father once again had to pay a few zloty (dollars). This time I escaped punishment, my father having unwittingly become my accomplice when he used the same bugs for bait.

During summer vacations, grandmother would often take us to a home on the Poholsza estate, which lay sixty-five kilometers from the city of Wilno, and belonged to my father's cousin, Lucjan Plawski. Loaded onto a horse-drawn wagon with the house cat tied up in a bag, we would set off eastward on the daylong trip. The goal of our journey lay between the city of Oszmiana and the smaller city of Holszany. The horse pulled the brimming wagon over ruts that ran alongside the paved road. From under his tail, blew the smell of digested oats, and this mixed with the aromas of the forest and the passing fields. Occasionally, when we had gone a dozen or so kilometers, the driver would stop to give the horse a moment to rest. Grandma would hand out the sandwiches she had prepared. The cat got his share of food and drink, also. The remaining time we spent running around to stretch our legs, which had become cramped by sitting in the wagon.

In the late evening, we reached our journey's end. We were met by the barking of the household dog and kisses from two old maids, Julia and Helena, my father's relatives. The two spinsters managed the estate and lived there year round. Their brother, Lucjan, rarely made an appearance. He spent his time, free from care, in Warsaw or abroad. Evidently someone had to spend the money made from the sale of grain. And, when the money was exhausted, Lucjan sold wood from the estate's forests. The sisters opposed his wasteful and exploitative lifestyle. They categorically forbade him to sell the beautiful Oak Forest, visible from the main house, which lay two kilometers from the estate. Though they were already too old to walk there, they took pleasure in gazing at the lush forest when they sat on the balcony and rested from the day's labors. Lucjan was resourceful, and ordered the middle of the forest cut down and left a few old oaks on the periphery. The money was gained, and some of the view remained. The beautiful Laluszki forest, for that's what it was called, ceased to exist. All that remained of it were memories, and a large pasture.

These were the kinds of vacations that today's children cannot imagine. Grandmother was old and only concerned about making enough food for the hungry holiday-makers. She spent the entire day not knowing where we were and happy for the relative quiet. The large surrounding forests full of berries were our playgrounds, and the small stream that crossed the estate was the place where we swam and caught fish, frogs and crayfish.

On the other side of the stream, in the fields of the neighboring Piotrowicz estate grazed a fine herd of cows ruled over by a great, bronze bull. The bull had an aversion to strange children. Upon seeing us, he would lower his head, armed with huge horns, and steams of breath would escape his nostrils. Pawing the sod with his front hoof, he would angrily prepare to charge. We teased him, coming closer a few steps at a time until he charged, and we then fled rapidly, jumping across the stream to the other side. Apparently the bull respected the fact that the other meadow was not his territory, and gave up the chase at its border.

With friends from nearby villages we grazed their horses in forest pastures, sometimes spending the entire night by a cozy fire. There was no better taste in the world for me than potatoes, still in their jackets, roasted over this fire.

Grandma knew about our escapades but considered them normal for boys our age. This woman, a widow, had raised twelve children, eleven boys and one girl. She was never oversensitive or worried about the fate of her absent grandsons. She was our caretaker, doctor, and cook, and that was sufficient. Our parents, on the other hand, were uninformed about the summer's adventures and excursions. The moment always came when we had to say goodbye to the vast forests, fields and green meadows. The responsibilities of school beckoned. Despite our sadness we were required to leave this beautiful place and return to the city and our parents.

One summer morning, on May 12, 1935, the bells rang out loudly. Their ringing was despairing, full of sorrow and lamentation. This sound, coming from the towers of Wilno's many churches, announced that something serious and tragic had occurred. Mama dressed quickly and went to the bakery for bread and news. Why the alarm? After a few minutes absence she returned with tears in her eyes.

I remember her prophetic words as if it was today: "It is the end of Poland. Marshal Jozef Pilsudski has died." An indescribable sadness enveloped us all. We had been brought up to love our country and its leader, *Dziadek* (grandfather), for that is what the entire Polish nation had called him.

A few weeks later, crowds of Wilno's inhabitants thronged the sidewalks along the streets where the funeral procession was to pass. Tearful eyes watched out for the first glimpse of the army columns and the flower-covered cannon carrying the urn that contained our leader's heart. The urn traveled the streets of his beloved city and came to rest forever in the earth of the cemetery at Rosa. It lies there, next to the body of his mother, covered with black marble, in a place now given over to Lithuania. Millions of Poles, those who remained in their homeland, and those who were scattered throughout the world by the hurricane of war will never forget him.

Sometime during 1936, we moved into a new home on Mostowa Street, not far from river Wilja's bridge. The bow of this bridge, hung high on both banks, dividing the center of the city from the neighborhood of Kalwaryjska Street. A change in surroundings, a different school and better living conditions were the reasons for this decision. I sadly left behind the old walls of the tenement house, the children with whom I had spent my early life, and my beloved Wilenka River with its nearby Trzech Krzyzy Mountain.

My new school was on Zeligowska Street, in the very center of town and I had to walk about an hour to get there. It was an unforgettable time; with my schoolbag on my back I marched alone through the city streets, a proud, independent, eleven-year old boy. Soon I became acquainted with other boys from the same neighborhood and the whole troop of us would make the journey together, chasing and pushing each other all the way. We were growing up. The school's rigors slowly began to produce results. Our teachers instilled in us a love of our country, respect for our elders, and an interest in the world around us. Our childish games turned serious and military, and books acquainted us with the history of our country's rise and the lives of her heroes.

In 1937, the school arranged a trip throughout Poland. I signed up for this trip and paid for it with money I had diligently saved. It cost me thirty-five zloty (dollars), which had taken many years to accumulate. We traveled the entire country in a rented train compartment where we also ate and slept. We admired our country's beauty, its development, and what we believed to be its might. It was the best investment of my funds I could have made, one that I appreciated and remained proud of for many years.

In 1938, after finishing six grades of primary school, I passed the exam for the Mechanic's High School on Kopanica Street, in Zarzecze. On my way to this school I had to cross Mlynowa Street, near the house of my childhood. Memories of the pleasant years I had spent there flooded back with irresistible force, and I would often drop in to chat with old friends.

At this new school, practical training followed the first year of study. Part of every second day was spent in the locksmith workshop, learning the basics of the mechanic's trade. In my second year, we worked with machines and in the forge. This was my favorite assignment. There I enthusiastically pounded red-hot steel with seven kilogram (14 lbs.) hammers until my hands hurt. Our instructor chose me, along with two of my friends, to forge the larger and more serious pieces, seeing how we had progressed in the rhythmic beating of the hammers. Time passed. The muscles in my arms hardened, my back straightened, and that year I gained considerable height and weight.

At school I met a new friend, Mietek Fijalkowski, with whom I would enjoy long years of brotherly companionship. Inseparable as Siamese twins, we spent all our days together. We were interested in sports and so, full of enthusiasm, we signed up at the Falcon Club. Five days a week, for two hours at a time, we practiced wrestling, boxing, and exercising on the trapeze. I changed beyond recognition, gaining confidence, muscle, and at the same time the condition of my kidneys strengthened. The nightmare of sickness passed, and I never had any serious problems with my health again.

The moment came when Mietek and I set off for our first school dance, an event I remember to this day. Not knowing how to dance, we spent the night standing against the wall, scuffling our feet and daring each other to find a dance partner. That, unfortunately, is all that resulted from our first encounter with the fairer sex.

This was probably the happiest time of our lives in our native land, which had begun to develop under the government of President Ignacy Moscicki and Army Marshal Rydz Smigly. New industries were arising, cadres of professionals were being trained, and new police and officer schools were turning out throngs of patriotically educated young leaders. The civilian population was optimistic about the future, both their country's and their own. The radio and newspapers assured us about the might and readiness of our military. Our army parades were splendid. The cavalry rode on beautiful mounts with their swords unsheathed, and the infantry marched proudly with rifles on their arms. Teams of six horses drew heavy artillery on stone-paved streets. The sounds of the orchestra resounded everywhere, and with it the powerful chorus of the army:

*Jak to na wojence ladnie (how beautiful it is at war)*
*Kiedy ulan z konia spadnie (when the uhlan falls off his horse)*

Unfortunately, from the west came more and more news about the expansion of German industry. Adolf Hitler ranted louder and louder about the German need for more living space. War psychosis began to trouble our nation. Finally, in 1939, the Germans demanded the opening of a channel through Poland to Eastern Prussia. Our government categorically refused. The conditions for the arrangement were unacceptable. We won't budge an inch, we're ready to fight, our leader Rydz Smigly assured us. The reserves were mobilized and conscription announced. And here the naked truth about administrative incompetence and inadequate transport and communication began to be revealed. In vain, the new soldiers gathered at the barracks, waited for weapons. These were to be distributed from warehouses, but no one knew which ones or when.

The order went out for the civilian population to hand in their radio speakers and all firearms and vehicles, including bicycles, at designated collection points. My brother, Tadek, with eyes full of tears but believing in the usefulness of his sacrifice, took in his brand new "Kaminski" racing bicycle. He had purchased this with the first money he had earned at the printing house where he was an apprentice. I stood in line, bent down with the weight of a twelve-lamp Cosmos speaker, waiting for it to be collected, only to see it brutally thrown down in the corner on a pile of junk. We never understood for what purpose this collection had been ordered.

Students were being prepared to direct traffic, dig anti-tank ditches and build anti-aircraft shelters. In the city enthusiasm prevailed, after all, we thought we had a powerful army in active service that would be able to check the enemy's incursion until all the conscripts had been armed. The speakers that had been hung up in the streets broadcasted patriotic military songs, interrupted every few moments by secret command codes. Finally the terrible day came.

On September 1, 1939, at five a.m., Polish radio reported that the Nazis had brutally attacked a radio station in the city of Gliwice. Then it was announced that a motorized German armored division had crossed the Polish border. The invasion came from three sides: from Czechoslovakia in the south, the Third Reich from the west and Prussia from the north. On the following day, German planes attacked our army columns on the road, bombing factories, electrical plants and train junctions.

Three weeks previously, the leadership of the Polish army had predicted the possibility of a German invasion and prepared a plan of defense. The mobilization of our active army was nearly complete. The reservists in the barracks were only waiting for their allotment of arms and uniforms. Unfortunately this equipment never reached the patriotically minded soldiers of the mass levy.

The German army, having crossed our nation's border, engaged in battle with divisions of the Frontier Defense Corps and subdivisions of the Polish Army, garrisoned near the border. Unfortunately, the German armored columns had already wedged deep inside the country and were rapidly streaming east. With this maneuver they cut off the communication lines between our units, which were on their way to meet the enemy. From the first day of war, a two hundred-person force at the Westerplatte garrison continued to defend itself against enemy attack. This small defensive fortress was situated on a thin strip of Polish land between the Baltic Sea and the Martwa Wisla Canal that crossed the Free City of Gdansk. In spite of massive bombardment from the Schleswig-Holstein armored war ship, heavy air attacks from diving planes that dropped masses of bombs, and being besieged by massive infantry attacks on the ground, the fortress's small garrison, under the command of Major Henryk Sucharski, remained stubbornly at its post. Only after seven days of heroic battle were they forced to capitulate, having run out of ammunition, water, and medicines for the large numbers of wounded.

The Gdansk post office also defended itself for a few days. When it surrendered, the Germans shot all the surviving postal workers. Under the pressure of the approaching armies from Eastern Prussia, bombarded from land and air, our capital city of Warsaw held out bravely, resisting the enemy's overwhelming force for nearly a month. Receiving no help from the outside, she had to capitulate.

We first heard the rumble of planes over Wilno as we were digging anti-aircraft ditches in the courtyard of the house on Mostowa Street. Against the blue of the sky, we could see the white smudges left behind by the planes as they flew over. The rattle of machine guns, set up throughout the surrounding hills and church steeples, greeted them.

It was like trying to shoot God in the foot, since the planes were far beyond the reach of bullets. Every few moments the missiles fired from cannons flew up like tossed oranges into the air, only to arc and fall somewhere into the neighboring fields. It was a spectacular sight, interrupted every now and again by the powerful tremors of distantly falling bombs. In those first days of war, Germans bombed army buildings, airports, and train junctions.

War was still exciting; no one in Wilno had come in contact with blood or corpses. The traffic on the streets was unbelievable, with army columns and civil defense vehicles it resembled a parade. Unsurprisingly, it proved impossible to keep a growing boy at home. I snuck out at every opportunity, until one day I was taken by surprise by an anti-aircraft alarm on Wilenska Street. The scream of the factory sirens announced the coming of enemy planes, and the police and the anti-aircraft defense started to herd people into the nearest shelter in the Helios cinema. I was swept by the crowd into the theater lobby, disappointed that I would lose my chance of seeing the war up close. I dashed under the outstretched arms of a policeman and ran onto the street, right into a speeding army car. The bumper hit me in the right thigh and I flew into the air like a stone from a slingshot. I heard the screech of brakes and two soldiers jumped out of the car and ran toward me. That was all I needed to see. I tore myself up from the road, terrified, and bolted like a rabbit down the street, feeling no pain. I don't know whether or not I was chased. Fear is a great motivator and energizer. After a moment my leg cramped from the pain and I hobbled home. For a few days I was completely uninterested in either the war or the air attacks, and bore a souvenir in the form of a huge bruise on my leg.

The war continued. The radio still announced that our army was bravely retreating to new and better positions. It said we were preparing a strong defense on the east bank of the river Bug, and that Warsaw was still defending itself and waiting to be relieved by our army. On the streets, martial tunes still blared from the speakers, inspiring us to fight and die a hero's death in defense of our country. We were cheered by the news that, General Franciszek Kleeberg, the leader of the independent operational group, Polesie, had won a victory over the Wehrmacht's 13th motorized division.

The charge of the cavalry brigade against the enemy's tanks around Kock was an exercise in futility. Lack of communication with the rest of the army, a dearth of ammunition, and news of the army's unfortunate state forced General Kleeberg to capitulate. After Warsaw fell, any hopes of resisting the enemy disappeared. Who was to be believed, why was the truth obscured? Why didn't the radio ever broadcast that the Red Army had knifed us in the back by crossing our country's eastern borders?

On September 17, our sleeping family was awakened by the sounds of violent shooting coming from neighboring streets. The rattle of tank treads shook the houses. Windowpanes vibrated from the frequent cannon fire. Terrified and not knowing what was happening, we anxiously waited until morning for news about our city's situation. In vain we tried to imagine what was happening. As far as we knew the front was still far away, beyond the new line of defense on the river Bug. We didn't know that what we were hearing were sporadic attempts at defense against the approaching Russian Army. A few army units and civilian youths were heroically attacking the enemy's tanks. Near the Wilja Bridge, the Officer's Legion, led by First Lieutenant Edward Swida, resisted the Soviet invaders and damaged two Soviet T-34 tanks in the process. One tank attempted to force its way across the river and became stuck, submerged in water up to the tower. Right before dawn, silence fell over our neighborhood. In the morning, after a sleepless night, we dressed and went outside to assess the situation.

At the intersections, we saw massive tanks with red stars on their turrets. Unfamiliar soldiers in Soviet uniforms, and already drunk, stood on the sidewalks. They were drinking cologne from a destroyed pharmacy. "*Oto charoszaja wodka* (what good vodka)," they were saying to one another, "*Charaszo waniajet* (smells good)."

Not a single Polish soldier was in sight, and the police had disappeared as if swept away. The broken windows and decimated store interiors were sad evidence of our defeat. When we inquired about the state of affairs, we were politely told that the Soviet army had come to liberate us from the capitalists.

I didn't return home at that time, but instead ran to the barracks of the 6th engineer regiment to search for any abandoned weapons. The rooms were deserted; evidently there hadn't been any weapons there since the beginning of the war. Nevertheless, I returned home with pockets full of machine gun bullets and a bayonet in my belt. You should have seen my mother's and father's expressions when they saw my war loot! My father ordered me to go to the devil and throw all my stuff into the Wilja. But I didn't obey his orders, and hid my stash under the roof of the outhouse in the yard.

The days that followed were sad, filled with disbelief at such a swift and unexpected defeat. Poland was torn in two. The Germans stopped at the western side of the river Bug, and the Soviet Union captured the territories to its east. At the same time, the Red Army conquered the Baltic countries. Estonia, Latvia and Lithuania lost their independence, and became Soviet republics.

In Wilno, food grew scarce. There were no supplies; everyone ate the last of the stores they had prepared for the war and the approaching winter. Masses of Soviet soldiers were stationed on the town squares, badly dressed but well armed.

The terrified city population, expecting fearsome and hostile Cossacks, was faced instead with the Soviet Army's quiet, well organized rank-and-file. Conversations were initiated. The Russian language was well known in Wilno and there were no difficulties in communicating. The soldiers didn't swear or accept gifts, except for the smokers, who exchanged food for cigarettes. When questioned about living conditions in the Soviet Union, they replied that they had everything in abundance and food transports were coming to our aid. Their words contradicted the visible reality. Their wasted faces, meager and unlined army coats, tarpaulin shoes stinking of tar, and machine guns hanging from strings, gave us a very different picture of their country's prosperity. Yet Stalin's orders were sacred to them; the army tried to maintain the best possible image in order to win over the working class and communist sympathizers.

A few days after the arrival of the army came the NKVD (Soviet Military Police) units. They began to carry out an invisible purge among the groups they believed to be hostile to the USSR. Familiar faces began to disappear from among representatives of the clergy, the Polish officer class, the intelligence services and the state police. These being the groups considered most likely to organize and constitute armed opposition in the future. Temporary power was taken over by cadres of criminals freed from jail, local communists, and workers enlisted into the civil militia. Offices and schools reopened, and portraits of bearded leaders of the proletariat, Marx, Lenin and Stalin replaced the crosses that once hung on the walls.

Although the weather was already cold, the lack of food forced us to fish the river. Anchored by its bank were rafts, bearing wood cut down farther upriver, and waiting to be treated at the local sawmill. We sat on these rafts, cast our rods, and waited for the fish to bite and for our mother to bring some food to us hungry fishermen. With joy, I saw our mother bringing us a meal and ran to meet her, jumping on the moving logs. At that moment my right leg slipped on the wood's wet surface and my foot came down on a thick, crooked nail protruding from a beam submerged in the water. I felt something push into the middle of my sole, looked down, and saw a piece of iron sticking out near my small toe. Without thinking, I instinctively jerked my leg up into the air, tearing my wounded foot from the trap. I felt no pain; it was a lightning fast moment that saved me the pain of having the nail sawed down and removed.

I had to forego my meal and, leaning on my mother's arms, limped to the nearest doctor's office. Iodine was poured on my wound, and on that note my day of fishing ended. Luckily there was no infection, and after a few weeks I was once again able to run. The souvenir of this event would long make itself felt when I bathed in cold water. The toe that had been pierced by the nail would go stiff and then the entire leg would cramp. More than once this happened in the middle of the river, and I would have to swim to shore on my back. The pain in the cramped leg would be unbearable. I would rub it vigorously with my hands to revive the circulation, and only then could I once again go back into the water.

After a few weeks of Bolshevik rule, we heard with a certain relief and joy that Wilno was to become part of the Lithuanian Republic and made its capital. At least the church, we thought, might have a hope of surviving in Catholic Lithuania. A short time later a few divisions of the Lithuanian Army entered the city followed by the new authorities, police in light blue uniforms with red edging and gold plumes in their caps. They were imposing. Tall and well built, these men with their high caps were like giants from fairytales. Armed with infantry rifles and long clubs in their belts, they proudly walked the streets of Wilno, once the capital of the Great Kingdom of Lithuania. In appearance they resembled a flock of puffed-up turkeys, galakutas in Lithuanian, and the nickname stuck. They refused to speak to the population in Polish. The language was well known in Lithuania, mainly due to intermarriage, but the hostile authorities didn't want to accept this.

In the reopened offices, Russian and Lithuanian systems were introduced straightaway. Polish money was exchanged for Lithuanian litas at a rate of two to one, and in the workplace, salaries were paid out in the new currency. Farmer's wagons loaded with food began to arrive in the city squares from beyond the neighboring Lithuanian border. At the newly opened cooperatives the most pressing necessities could now be bought with coupons. Lithuania was a small state, but superbly organized. This predominantly agrarian country had set up cooperatives that bought grain, meat and dairy products from farmers and in exchange supplied them with the fertilizer and equipment they needed to cultivate their land, thus eliminating the middlemen who usually made most of the profit.

Many new pupils came to our school. They were Lithuanians from Kaunas and other cities. Lithuanian was made the language of instruction and Russian became compulsory. Learning these languages was not easy, and sometimes we just sat there as if at a Turkish sermon. My last name was changed, against my will, and I was re-baptized from Plawski to Plauskas. Nevertheless, I had to make peace with this if I wanted to finish my studies.

At first the relationships between students were tense and distrustful, but with time they began to stabilize and life on the school grounds became bearable. We were united in our shared hate for the oppressor who had deprived us of our independence, and was now forcibly imposing the doctrines of communism and reverence for its leader, Stalin. Insidious was the system that tried its utmost to foster the new spirit in the young people. Their propaganda, their rewriting of history books, their criticism of Poland's pre-war government and clergy, and their propagation of sport through free access to equipment did not yield the expected results. The propaganda and coercion rebounded from our young minds like a ball thrown against a wall. We took as much advantage as possible of the free opportunities for sports and games in the houses of culture, but thought only of our future retaliation.

The winter of 1940 was unbelievably difficult. With the Soviet horde came terrible and unprecedented cold spells of minus forty degrees Celsius. Such temperatures lasted for weeks. Trees split with the sound of gunfire, burst open by their frozen sap. Chimney smoke rose high in the air like candles, undisturbed by any wind during these almost Siberian frosts. Breath froze on whiskers and eyebrows, and noses went white, frostbitten by the cold air.

Through our streets marched the ranks of a foreign army, Mongol soldiers with songs on their lips. Their words spread through Mickiewicz Street, rebounding from the walls of houses and flying into the distance, offending the ears of an ill-treated nation. Soviet officers promenaded on the sidewalks with wives in silk nightgowns under their army coats. The women, proud of their booty, thought they were wearing ball gowns. Such clothing was unknown in the land of socialism. We joke about it now, but at the time it was a sad reality. The truth that had until then been hidden in the Soviet Union was now being revealed. Stalinist terror could no longer conceal the secrets of the workers paradise.

That summer I made my first appearance in a boxing ring. My pride at winning the bout against an older and more experienced middleweight was indescribable. I had been weak and sickly in childhood and by sheer willpower and stubbornness had managed to accomplish what I could only dream of, as I had lain exhausted by kidney disease. My memories of those years of powerlessness and infirmity were slowly effaced, and along with my physical development came self-confidence, ingenuity, and courage.

In my third year of practical training in school, I began making wedding rings from brass pipes. These were sought after in the surrounding villages and eagerly exchanged for food. Given the lack of gold, the brass rings were quite acceptable. Kitchen knives were also in demand, and these I made from metal saws and mounted them in aluminum handles. They were easy to sell, and brought a good profit. With the money I earned I bought myself a wristwatch. I also contributed at home with cash for provisions.

Though difficult and full of discomfort, life under foreign occupation proceeded without any great excitement. Then, on a night in the spring of 1940, the rumble of trucks and the pounding of rifle-butts on doors awakened the city's terrified inhabitants. Hordes of NKVD with bayonets on their rifles burst into the homes of supposed enemies of the communist system and chased entire families out into the streets. These unlucky citizens, gathered under the watchful eyes of huge dogs and surrounded by guards, were hurried to the train station. There they were quickly loaded into cattle wagons readied for a long voyage to Siberia. This action had been superbly organized. In the course of one night, those who the Soviet Union considered inconvenient were removed from the city. This was the second purge of the Polish intelligentsia, destined for slave labor in Soviet camps.

Sadness and doubt enveloped the remaining population; no help seemed forthcoming, the situation was hopeless, and the only thing left to think about was how to preserve ones Polish heritage under the boot of the Soviet and Lithuanian communists.

At the beginning of 1941, there was a new war developing. London radio informed us that Russian-German relations were on the verge of armed conflict. This was the moment for which the general public had been waiting, and there was hope of some kind of change. We were completely disgusted with so-called Soviet friendship and the rule of their devoted Lithuanian flunkies. Slowly, those who had served Moscow for their own ends began to disappear from the city; they were returning to Kaunas to await the coming change and to resurface elsewhere under another banner. Transports wound through the city streets on their way east, loaded down with furniture taken from offices, machines looted from factories, and works of artistic and historical value. The city was brazenly looted of everything that testified to its Polish character. The frightened faces of recent government representatives were everywhere, as they hurriedly fled into the depths of the USSR.

# From Nehrybka to Siberia
(Teresa)

Wojciech and Katarzyna Maselek and their younger daughter, Jozefa, lived on a farm four kilometers from the city of Przemysl. They were enjoying a visit from their older daughter, Emilia, and her two children, eight year old Edek, and four year old, Teresa. The family believed that during these days of war, the young people would be safest far from the city.

Emilia's husband, Jozef Bajorski, was a professional noncommissioned officer in the Polish Army. He had been mobilized and sent to the front, and since then all trace of him had vanished. The September 1939 defeat, inflicted by the modern German army, was unmitigated. While retreating from the enemy, some Polish soldiers crossed the border into Hungary and were interned. The Bajorski family still hoped that Jozef was among the mass of escapees. The situation was tragic. The Red Army had invaded Poland without first declaring war, and occupied the territories east of the River Bug. Przemysl and its surroundings found themselves at the mercy of the Soviets and terrorized by Ukrainian populations hostile to Poland. Despite this disaster, for the time being, life on the Maselek farm continued without disturbances or difficulties.

Then came the freezing winter of 1940. On February 10th, the sudden barking of the courtyard dog awoke the sleeping family.

Moments later they heard rifles pounding against the door. Frightened, Wojciech still in his underwear, quickly jumped out of bed and opened the door. A group of Soviet soldiers forced its way in. Wojciech was pushed against the wall with his arms in the air and could only look on, stunned, as the soldiers prowled the room. When the patrol leader arrived he ordered that everyone in the house must dress and go outside. *"You have one hour to pack,"* he said. When they asked him where they were being taken he replied curtly, *"Malczac ne razgarywac." (Shut up, don't talk.)*

Panic overwhelmed the family. They did not know where to start or what to do. The children crouched in a corner and cried, while the women frantically ran back and forth, picking up and putting down the same things again and again, not knowing what to take with them. The sergeant, now calm, and seeing their shock and fear, took pity on them and advised them to quickly pack as many necessities as they could, because they would need them for the long journey ahead. All the while Wojciech stood against the wall and looked at his wife, Katarzyna, with reproach in his eyes, blaming her for the family's fate. Wojciech had returned to Poland from the United States unwillingly; having succumbed to the persuasions of his determined young wife.

Before coming back to Poland, he had lived in the United States near Bristol, Connecticut. As a teenager, Wojciech had emigrated from Poland to the United States in the hope of making a better life. He had been quite successful, and after working at various jobs, had managed to acquire many acres of land. He was gainfully employed as a butcher in a slaughterhouse. He liked his new home, lived alone, and knew his own mind. Wojciech was quite content. It was his luck, good or bad, that while at a party, he met the nineteen-year-old Katarzyna, newly arrived in America. The poor man fell madly in love, and in the normal course of things, the young lady led him to the altar.

Shortly thereafter, Katarzyna became pregnant and gave birth to their first son, Janek. But there was something about her new country that did not appeal to her, and Katarzyna kept insisting to her husband that she wanted to return to Poland. She ignored his refusals and continued to badger him, relentlessly revisiting the topic. Finally, already pregnant with their second child, she left her husband behind in America and went back to Poland with their young son, Janek. Even then she gave Wojciech no peace, showering him with letters full of love and longing and calling for him to join her. After giving birth to their second child, Emilia, and seeing her husband had no desire to leave America, she entrusted her children to a neighbor, packed her things, and returned to her husband in the United States. Katarzyna's will finally prevailed, and Wojciech sold his land, boarded a ship with a bag of gold dollars in hand, and found himself on his way back to Poland.

Soon after arriving, Wojciech bought a large farm and exchanged his remaining gold dollars for paper notes, which he deposited in the bank. Shortly before World War I erupted, he was conscripted into the Austrian army. It was not what he had in mind. He did not want to fight for foreign interests, or leave his young wife alone with what were now four young children. So he deserted and came home, straight into the arms of his beloved spouse. Gendarmes hunted him intently, and the desperate man was forced to hide. He made a hideaway in the chimney and concealed himself there in moments of danger. Meanwhile, the money in the bank depreciated, until all that remained was a regretful memory.

The war ended. Poland regained her independence and life on the farm returned to normal. Wojciech cultivated the fields with the help of his daughters, Emilia and Jozefa, while his son, Tadek, became a dentist. The young doctor lived in Przemysl and had his own practice. Wojciech maintained an ongoing correspondence with his oldest child, Janek. Janek had been born in America, and, at eighteen years of age, had returned from Poland to work for relatives in Connecticut.

Everything seemed to be proceeding smoothly. The farm was well managed and profitable. His oldest daughter, Emilia, was married, and he lived to see the birth of two beautiful grandchildren. But events did not unfold as he might have wished. The good times did not last, and a new disaster came in the shape of another war. Now, he thought, all I can do is stand nearly naked against the wall of my own house, waiting for the next humiliation. Katarzyna, his wife, was busy throwing an assortment of necessities into various trunks and baskets, and didn't sense his reproachful glances. The Bajorskis' things, still packed from their arrival, were easy to assemble. Everything was loaded into waiting sleighs. At the last moment, Katarzyna ran into the house and grabbed four huge loaves of bread from the oven. The children were hoisted on top of the bulging wagons, and the sleighs set off toward Przemysl.

The horses moved quietly over the snow and away from the farm. The barking of the dog and the lowing of the cattle, which sensed the moment of parting, bid them farewell. The despairing animal voices were audible for a long time. The lights that still shone in the windows of the abandoned house receded and finally disappeared over the horizon. Fear and despair choked the sixty-five year old Wojciech, and tears froze in his moustache. The women prayed out loud, giving themselves up to the protection of the Virgin Mother of Lezansk.

Little Teresa cried. Every tremor of the speeding sleigh drove a large trunk into her leg, wounding her painfully. No one paid attention to the child's discomfort. The adults were occupied with their own thoughts, afraid for the future and grieving the loss of their country, their home, and most of their earthly possessions.

From the direction of various neighboring villages and farms, came other sleighs filled with despairing deportees. The line of wagons grew longer as they neared the Przemysl train station. Anguished cries of greeting resounded all around. "Mrs. Maselek! What am I going to do with four small children and no husband! I didn't have time to take anything! I've got no food or clothing for the children!" cried the policeman's wife, whose husband had died at the front. Moved to pity, Katarzyna caught hold of two loaves of bread and two blankets and threw them onto the passing sleigh. The macabre journey was relatively short. Just before dawn, the deportees saw a long train of cattle cars standing off to the side, their opened doors ready to receive their share of unfortunate exiles.

Men, women and children were loaded into the cars at lightning speed and they hurriedly found a place on the tiered plank beds inside. They pressed down on top of one another like herrings so the entire family could have a place to rest. Those who moved too slowly were prodded with rifles. No compassion shone in the eyes of the convoy guards, soldiers from the Soviet Asian republics. In the last moments before departure a small group of people who had gathered at the station tossed packages of food through the still-opened windows. Some acted spontaneously, others at the behest of a local parish priest.

A moment later the doors banged shut. The soldiers slid the steel bolts across with a screech and the long train, made up of dozens of cars, shuddered and set off on its journey, puffing heavily with the steam of two locomotives. The whistle of steam engines and the monotonous rattle of wheels drowned out the human lamentations and cries. From then on, the deportees would share the fate of vagrants without a country or a home. Bound by common misery, shut up in a cold, dark cage, they gave themselves up to their only consolation and prayed ardently to God, asking Him to protect His suffering people. Slowly, the exhaustion born of too many sensations took its toll. An uneasy sleep enveloped everyone. Curled up in various positions on the bare wooden planks, they were temporarily able to tear themselves away from reality.

The deportation of Polish populations from lands occupied by the Soviet Union had been superbly organized. In accordance with long drawn-up lists, elements hostile to the communist system were removed from territories that were being prepared for a change in their social structure. In the course of one day, from the Romanian to the Latvian border, thousands of families of higher government officials, the intelligentsia, farm owners, army officers, and policemen were collected and loaded onto waiting trains. They were meant for life and work in Siberia. There, scattered throughout numerous camps, they were to forget their nationality, their native tongue, and their religious denomination. In the future, they would share the fate of those deported there by first Tsarist and then communist authorities. People who were never heard from again. A sad chapter of history was repeating itself. Siberia was waiting to receive the sweat and blood of exiled Poles.

After a few hours of nightmarish sleep, little Teresa's voice roused the dreaming family. "Mama, I need to pee," the shivering child cried. Emilia climbed down from the overcrowded bed with great difficulty, holding the girl in her arms. What is there to do now? Like it or not, she had to sit the little girl against the wall and let her relieve herself on the floor. The serious problem of the lack of toilet facilities for everyone became manifest. Someone seized an axe and made a small hole in the floor near the wall opposite the bolted doors. One after the other the passengers relieved themselves onto the passing railway tracks. It was unpleasant business, especially for the younger girls, and the older women made a screen out of their own bodies to hide the humiliation of the young ladies who crouched there. A freezing wind from the rushing train blew on their naked buttocks, stinging like the prick of a thousand needles, and urine sometimes spattered whoever stood nearby. The strong wind blew in through the large air spaces, and piercing cold tormented everyone.

The train car originally contained nothing but a round stove in the center and a pile of coal in one of the corners. A fire was started in the stove and suitcases were stacked in an attempt to block some of the cold air. All of the other belongings were neatly organized, and the travelers prepared for a long journey in their moving hotel.

The first meal consisted of whatever bread they had managed to take from their abandoned homes. For water, the passengers reached up through the windows broke off the ice that had collected on the roof, and melted it on the hot stove. In this way the distraught passengers passed the first day of their journey through occupied Polish lands, which slipped away from them before their eyes. With sad gazes, they bade goodbye to undulating hills, green fir forests, straw thatched huts, and small village churches lying picturesquely among vast, snow-covered fields. These sights would remain forever lodged in their memory, snapshots of a beloved country seemingly lost forever.

The train rushed on remorselessly, stopping only for military transports coming from the opposite direction. No one was allowed off the train for even a moment. A soldier would thrust a bucket of hot water through a slightly opened door and straightaway slam it shut. The deportation was conducted in the utmost secrecy; the Soviet authorities did not want knowledge of their disgraceful behavior to spread among the inhabitants of lands they had taken by force. The transport passed Lwow without slowing down, and continued northeast towards Rowno. The train flew by the larger cities, maintaining the same speed as it barreled toward the former Polish-Soviet border. Finally, with a long whistle and a screech of brakes, it slowed and came to a stop. The ice-covered bolts were thrown back. In rushed cold fresh air, and the soldiers of the border patrol.

Bayonet wielding soldiers encircled the train and guards with huge mastiffs patrolled both sides. The soldiers peered in everywhere. They looked under the wheels, on the roof, between cars, thoroughly searching every inch of space. They should have known no one would be stupid enough to want to enter their Soviet paradise voluntarily. Inside they counted people, taking down all their names, dates and places of birth, and then moved them to the side with those who had already been counted. After a few hours, the senseless roll call finally ended - the doors closed, and the train moved onto some sidetracks.

Time dragged on unbearably for the deportees, who were expecting the worst. Once again the doors screeched open, and the snow's daylight glare hurt eyes accustomed only to the dimness of the cars. A soldier's commanding voice rang out: *"Wsie wylizac na dwor."* (Everbody out.) He didn't have to say it twice. All of the captives jumped out into the deep snow, happy to be able to stretch their legs, wash their travel stained faces, and seek relief in the open air. This last activity was especially unpleasant for the young women, who had to crouch beside the train cars in clear view of the surrounding soldiers. The soldiers did not take their eyes off their victims for even a moment, standing with their guns aimed and ready to fire. The prisoners had no choice. Some things could not be delayed, and it was necessary to get acclimated to the new conditions. The short moment of comparative freedom ended with the locomotive's whistle and the order *"Wlizaj abarotno w pojezd."* (Get back inside the cars.) At the last minute, people grabbed all handy receptacles and filled them with snow so that they would have water when the snow melted. The doors slammed shut. With a huge shudder and the rattle of metal the two-kilometer long train set off on its unknown way.

As the oldest woman in the car, and a person who had survived many vicissitudes of fate, Katarzyna Maselek took it upon herself, with the agreement of the others, to organize a system for living in the overcrowded space. Because there was only one stove for heating the train car and cooking their modest meals, it was decided that food would be prepared communally. Everything they had managed to take with them was collected and counted. Their supplies had to last for at least a month, which was how long, they roughly calculated, it would take them to reach Siberia at their current speed. Once this was done, Katarzyna assigned the women their cooking rotations. The men would be responsible for keeping the fire going in the perpetually burning stove by adding fuel when necessary. After that, there was nothing more for anyone to do. Trapped in a small room, cold and hungry, the deportees huddled together on the bunks.

The detainees passed the time praying, telling stories about their former life in Poland, and discussing the destruction of the army. The Maseleks took the lead in these conversations; they had lived in America, after all, and therefore, had interesting stories to tell. Afterwards, bored and perpetually hungry and thirsty, the travelers would fall into a deep sleep. A new day would dawn, the same as before, enlivened only by the sound of the wheels against the rails and the hunt for the enormous lice that hatched in their dirty, unwashed clothes and heads. This plague, combined with that of the bedbugs lodged in the wooden beds, gave no one any peace. The entire company scratched until they bled. They had no recourse but to endure.

The length of time spent standing on the sidings waiting for the military echelons to fly by grew longer and longer. The travelers never knew when the transport would start. One time the train shuddered so violently that the burning stove was knocked over, along with a full pot of bubbling soup. The hot liquid drenched the legs of a woman standing nearby burning her badly. Coal scattered all over the floor and smoke and ash filled the car. By the time the men had cleaned up the floor and secured the stove they were black with soot. The children laughed at them, unaware of the tragedy of the situation. That day there was nothing hot to eat.

Through the high windows just under the roof, the passengers saw vast snow covered fields, and from time to time, poor, straw-roofed huts and the dirty neglected train stations of the cities they passed. The days dragged. People looked forward only to the stops when they could take care of their needs, stretch their cramped legs, and get their bucket of hot *"kipitku" (water)*.

Three weeks passed. Slowly the views began to change. On either side of the railway tracks spread impassable fir forests. The terrain became more mountainous and snowy, with long, continuous turns over which the train wheels flew with a frightening screech. Sometimes the train plowed into snowdrifts so large that the entire crew had to get out and shovel before they could go on. More and more often they plunged into long tunnels, and traveled in complete darkness. Smoke from the coal locomotives crept inside the trains poisoning the air. A few days later they crossed to the other side of the Ural mountains and across the border separating Europe and Asia. After one more week of nightmarish travel, the crew began to detach a pair of cars at each of the small stations where they stopped, shortening the train. This was the beginning of the distribution of exiles among the camps located throughout the Siberian taiga. One after the other, the deportees reached the places where they would live and work as slaves.

One morning the train groaned to a stop at a squalid station. It could go no farther. Beyond, the tracks stopped. The doors opened and they were ordered to *"Soberajsia z wieszczami na dwor" (Take your things and get out).* People joyfully jumped out of the filthy cars into the clean, deep snow. Everyone had had enough of traveling in the stinking, lice-ridden compartments. Whatever happened to them next could not be any worse than living in that overcrowded cage.

Beside the neglected train station stood a long line of wagons and sleighs ready for the onward journey. Harnessed to the sleighs were small, wild looking Siberian horses with long coats and fringes covering their eyes and foreheads. Next to the sleighs stood the equally hirsute Siberians. Their thick caftans, pelt caps and felt-soled boots protected them from the cold. Smoking pipes and cigarettes made from cheap tobacco rolled in newspaper, they waited patiently for the "Polish sirs" to jump out of the wagons. They observed the new arrivals with concealed curiosity.

All of the belongings were taken off the train and loaded onto sleighs, the children and the elderly were wrapped in blankets and settled on top. With a shout, the entire column rushed forward along a narrow, snow-covered road. The adults walked beside the sleighs, holding on with one hand so as not to deviate from the road by even a step.

As time went by the column stretched out slightly, the distance between the vehicles grew longer, and it became possible to strike up a conversation with the Siberian driver. To the question "Where are we being taken? Where are we going to live?" came the quiet, frightened answer "Don't worry, you'll have a place to live. It was built long ago. No one lives there now. You'll work in the forest, cutting down trees. You'll like it here in the Soviet Union." The poor exiles floundered in the knee deep snow kilometer after kilometer. They walked like wraiths beside the untiring horses. There seemed to be no end to the winding road, through snow-covered virgin forests, that stretched for hundreds of kilometers. From time to time, there was the despairing and frightened cry of some unfortunate, who had stepped forward carelessly and fallen up to his armpits in downy snow. Pulled out of the abyss he would march on, stumbling and looking forward to a moment's rest.

At night, the column reached a small village and the horses stopped beside an empty school where people were to sleep. They fell down onto the bare, wooden floors, utterly exhausted, and there spent a cold winter's night. Huddled together, one on top of the other, they had only each other to keep them warm. The second day was no different than the first. The exhaustion was terrible. The deportees walked like robots, tripping from fatigue and lack of food. Dozens of kilometers later, at nearly nightfall, a large meadow appeared before the eyes of the bone-tired travelers. On it, in a half circle, stood three large barracks, a small barn for the horses, and an office with quarters for the commandant and the guards.

This was a deserted camp built in the 1920s by deported Ukrainians who had been torn from the fertile lands of Ukraine and flung into the wasteland of the Siberian taiga. Cast into the middle of the forest without any means to live, they waited out the winter in shanties made from spruce branches. Most died of cold and hunger. The survivors built the barracks with their own hands and spent years of imprisonment there, in the land of socialism, on the orders of the almighty tyrant Stalin.

The camp administrator assigned a few dozen families to each building. The following day was set aside for cleaning and settling down in the abandoned buildings. The snowdrifts that had collected in front of the windows and doors had to be scraped away with bare hands. When the door was opened it revealed a long, dirty room with plank bunk beds along both sides. A brick oven for heating and cooking took up a great deal of space in the middle. The remaining furniture in the room consisted of rough wooden tables and benches. Each family moved into a living area and crammed the things they had brought with them under the tables and beds.

The first task in their new place was to light the oven and sweep the dusty barracks floor. Windows were opened to let in the fresh, cold air and drive out the mustiness of a closed up building. Now utterly exhausted, everyone fell down on his makeshift bedding and was asleep in moments. Healthy Polish snoring interrupted the nocturnal quiet of the Siberian taiga. It would seem to be one of the shortest nights these poor people had ever spent.

The new arrivals were awakened at dawn by a terrible noise. The camp guard was pounding an empty gas can with a wooden club, shouting *"Wychaditie na dwor" (Everybody outside).* A moment later the commandant came out of his house with his uniform still unbuttoned. He climbed up on a pile of sawed lumber and addressed the sleepy crowd.

In a booming voice he declared that the great and hospitable Soviet Union had taken them in as exiles, and would give them work and a place to live in the beautiful Molotowska Gubernia. *"You will be employed in cutting down trees and receive compensation in the form of a portion of bread and soup from the camp kitchen. You'll only get food if you fulfill the designated work norms. Everybody must work. If you don't work you won't "kuszac" (eat). School-age children will go to school a few kilometers away. The elderly will work in the camp and the kitchen. Forget about Poland, which you'll never see again. Don't think you can escape. The forests and wild animals bar your way. You'll live in these barracks here, work there, he said, indicating the forest, and sleep there, he said, pointing to the cemetery that lay on a small hill beyond the barracks. You are not allowed to leave the camp without my permission. If you do, you'll be imprisoned. Go back to your barracks. Tomorrow morning you'll start work in the forest."* With this he finished his speech, stepped down from his platform, and went back to finish his interrupted rest.

The disheartened group returned to the barracks in silence, depressed by their sad reality. There was no alternative but to settle down as best they could in their new surroundings. Frightened by the mere sight of the huge impassable taiga, the thought of escape never crossed their minds. Grandma Katarzyna, Mama Emilia and Aunt Jozefa rolled up their sleeves and started washing the family's filthy clothes. They rinsed years of dust from tables and benches with the water that Grandpa Wojciech brought in from the courtyard well. When the cleaning was finished, they bathed Teresa and Edek and fished clean clothes from their unpacked suitcases. Then it was the adults' turn to throw off their sweaty, lice-ridden undergarments and scrub their dirty hair and worn out bodies. They held up blankets to shield the women who took their place in the basin one after the other, delighting in the luxury of a bath.

Only after they had managed to remove both the dirt left behind by the previous inhabitants, and that acquired during the journey, did their thoughts turn to a hot meal, which they deeply craved.

Dinner was a sad affair. The food stores were already nearly exhausted. Emilia took what flour and tiny bits of fat and salt she had left and made dumplings, which, when cooked, satisfied the family's famished stomachs. After this modest meal the family prayed fervently to God, thanking Him for His protection on the road, for their health in such terrible conditions, for this primitive place to live and the roof over their heads. It was night, and time for sleep. Everyone was dropping from exhaustion. The children, wrapped in clean bedding and not fully understanding the misfortune that had befallen them, fell asleep straightaway. The adults followed their example, preparing themselves for the following day's work in new, unprecedented conditions. Cutting down trees in a snow-covered forest was unimaginable to people unacquainted with that kind of activity. In the end, physical exhaustion overcame their unsettled minds and a salutary sleep enveloped everyone, erasing the cares of the previous day.

Children's restless fidgeting aroused Emilia. As she awoke she began to feel itching on her face and all exposed parts of her body. She got up from her bunk and lit the candle she had placed nearby for such contingencies. The sight that met her in the weak light was indescribable. With horror she saw a mass of insects, swollen with blood, moving over the bodies of her children. The bedding undulated with thousands of starving bedbugs rushing to escape the movement and the light. Dismayed and disgusted, Emilia ripped the blankets off her sleeping family and shook their contents onto the floor. Sleep was interrupted, candles were lit throughout the building, and the old people, who didn't have to work in the forest, sat up until dawn protecting their families from another bedbug invasion.

When the new day dawned, Grandmother and Grandfather declared open war on the red plague. They boiled buckets of water on the stove and then flooded every chink in the wooden bunks, benches and tables, scalding bedbugs that had been hiding there for years. Grandfather carried and boiled the water while Grandmother and her neighbors poured the bubbling liquid over all the visible nests of these smallest citizens of the Soviet paradise. Steam from the water filled the building and turned it into a sauna. They carried out their repellent work with dogged enthusiasm. It was a war between Polish exiles and the red army, or at least that's how they imagined it to themselves with amusement. But despite massive casualties the war was only partially won. Every night, until the end of their stay, they would be attacked by troops of Russian bedbugs thirsting for Polish blood.

There was no time to rest. Right after this purifying operation, the floor had to be washed again and a modest meal prepared for the children and Grandfather. It was difficult to make a decent meal with what was left of the meager supplies. As usual, Grandma cooked barley in water with a little salt, and after the children and elderly had eaten, the remaining was left for other members of the family who were still at work.

On the following day, the guard's pounding on the empty can once again signaled it was time to leave the barracks. People dressed quickly in their warmest clothes and came out into the darkened square. There the foreman assigned them to the various tasks involved in felling trees. The youngest and strongest would chop down the firs and pines, and after these were hewed, another group would cut off the branches and prepare the trunks for transport to a nearby riverbank, where they remained until the ice broke in the spring. At this time they would be lowered into the water and floated to a faraway port, and from there be transported to a sawmill for further treatment.

Carrying an axe and accompanied by a man with a handsaw, Aunt Jozefa stumbled through the forest, falling up to her knees in snow. She was on her way to do something she had never done before. The towering trees with their snow-topped crowns greeted her with reluctance. They didn't want to be cut down and end their life in the wonderful Siberian taiga under the blows of axes and saws. There could be no pity and no other outcome. Workers had to carry out their orders if they wanted to get a piece of brown bread in payment for their ungodly deed. After stamping down the snow around a tree, workers used hatchets to cut a crevice into the trunk on whatever side the tree was to fall. Then, kneeling in the snow, they sawed into the fissure of the hard, frozen trunk to prevent the saw from jamming. Slowly, with a uniform back-and-forth movement, the saw burrowed into the bulk of a virgin tree. After a time the tree would shudder and begin to bend, first slowly and unwillingly, then faster until it fell with a crash, its weight throwing clouds of powdery snow into the air.

Aunt Jozefa had to work slowly and steadily. She tried not to tire herself out or sweat. In that climate, with frosts of up to minus fifty degrees Celsius, wet underclothes meant the chance of inflammation of the lungs and a wretched death. One after another these colossuses, which had grown for so long, toppled under the foreigners' hatchets. Other men armed with sharp axes descended on the now supine and defenseless trees, and sawed off branches as thick as arms, which were then cut into small pieces and used as fuel in the barracks ovens. The day drew to a close. Slowly, dragging their tired legs, the workers returned to the camp.

They made their way back through a trench of snow that had been removed from the middle of the road and then drenched with water from a large, horse-pulled barrel to develop an icy surface. Emilia Bajorski drew this assignment. She would start the first thing in the morning, shoveling trenches that when dampened and frozen made rails for the sleighs that dragged trunks to the riverbank. This kind of work was considered light labor and assigned to women with small children.

Time passed. Everyone waited longingly for the spring and summer. The severe winter passed in hard fashion. Insufficient food and clothing sapped the last of the exiles' strength. Their gums began to bleed from lack of vitamins, their teeth came loose in their mouths, and the children coughed, cold and undernourished, on their diet of bread, flour and barley.

Every day, eight-year old Edek would march two kilometers to school, where he was fed the slogans of communist propaganda. On his return home, he would question his dismayed mother. *"Is it true that God doesn't exist? – Is it true that father Stalin is the protector of all working people? – Was grandfather really an exploiter who lived off rented labor?"* This was the kind of nonsense the poor child was forced to listen to while surrounded by portraits of the bearded leaders of the proletariat hunging on the classroom walls.

To get to school the boy walked through the forest, a meadow, and then through a village field divided into unplowed strips of land thickly covered in bushes. It was a journey he made in perpetual fear, peering uneasily to check if a horned head was poking out from among the thicket of shrubs. That area was where the large male village goat was put out to pasture, and since a goat will eat anything that falls into its snout it was always loitering among the roadside foliage. No one knew why it felt such antipathy against poor Edek, but it definitely did. When the goat saw the boy it would come out of the bushes and follow him step by step. Edek's nerve would invariably desert him and he would start to run, which is evidently what the goat wanted. It would give chase with its head lowered, choosing Edek's backside as the target of its attack. The assaulted boy would land in the wet, melting snow while the goat, pleased with its easy victory, sauntered proudly back into the bushes.

Every once in a while the camp would get a visit from Doctor Kowalska, a Russian of Polish descent, who was summoned in the event of a serious sickness or an accident at work. She greatly admired Mrs. Bajorski's gold wristwatch and took the first opportunity to examine the children and pronounce that they were anemic. She recommended they drink milk, which was not available, and mentioned she had a goat that she would be willing to exchange for the watch. That is how the Bajorski's acquired a new member of the family, a young white goat with a full udder of nourishing milk.

Edek was given the responsibility of taking the goat out to pasture, and foolishly chose the territory occupied by the detested ram. With the goat tied on a string, looking this way and that in fear, the poor shepherd set out on his way, dreading an encounter with his enemy. He didn't have long to wait. A moment later the bearded bachelor trotted out of the bushes. But, oh, wonder of wonders, he showed not the slightest bit of interest in Edek's backside. His entire attention was concentrated on the graceful moves of the little goat's tail. From then on a truce arose between the student and the combative village goat. The animal stopped its attacks and completely ignored the boy. After a certain time the little goat grew stout. The shrubs and the buck's attentions evidently had a vivifying effect, and the result was that two baby kids came into the world.

The long awaited spring finally arrived. Early flowers and young birch leaves emerged from under the melted snow, and the entire world awoke from its winter slumbers. Along with the greenery came a plague of insects. Clouds of mosquitoes and small black flies crawled into the eyes, noses and ears of the workers. It was impossible for them to protect themselves entirely. The insects penetrated the flesh and left behind itching, suppurating wounds. To shield their faces from attack, the forest workers made masks from what fabric they had, sewing horsehair nets in the holes they had cut out for their eyes and mouths. The warmth of the approaching summer also brought red juicy raspberries and wild fragrant strawberries to the forest pastures. During any spare time, the workers gorged on these until they were sated, collecting and drying the remainder to guard against the lack of vitamins during the next winter. After the berries came wonderful, fragrant mushrooms, which were salted in clay pots or spread out on straw and dried in the sun.

The work in the forest stopped and the brigades were sent to make hay on the banks of the Soswa River. The grass was cut, dried, baled, and then delivered to neighboring villages as winter food for cattle. At night, the exhausted workers slept in temporary sheds made from tree branches and covered in straw. Their nights were miserable. The land near the river was swampy and full of mosquitoes mercilessly assaulting the bodies of the sleepers. At dawn, their hands and faces swollen with bites, they would once again set to scything the dew-covered grass.

Such human activities were incomprehensible to the brown bear lazing about on the riverbank. He watched their actions with curiosity and then, having nothing else to do, laid his huge head between his paws and went to sleep, snoring loudly. Every once in a while he would awaken, heated by the sun's rays and the buzzing of insects, and walk into the river to cool off. At first people were afraid to work near such a huge beast, but after a time they saw that he was peacefully inclined and stopped fearing him. He was undoubtedly a great point of interest in their monotonous life.

The short summer passed quickly. Grandpa cut willow branches on the riverbank and taught himself to weave snowshoes, which he sold for a small profit. Most importantly, it made for easy work for Grandpa Wojciech, who was rapidly aging and failing in health. With the first blasts of freezing autumn winds, the poor man caught cold and became ill. He developed a very high fever and walked around nearly unconscious, bumping into walls and crying from pain. Doctor Kowalska was called and managed to produce some injections that saved Grandfather's life. She said he had suffered a heart attack, caused by blockage in one of his arteries, as well as inflammation of the lungs. The gold earrings that had been Emilia's wedding gift from her husband found their way into the doctor's ears. It was the best possible trade she could have made at such a critical moment. Grandfather never again recovered his full strength, and continued to cough and lose weight.

At the beginning of October, the white of the first snow again covered the earth, heralding the coming of a new winter. The Christmas holidays, observed in secret, were days of sadness and remembrance of a lost country, home, and family, whose fate was yet unknown. Instead of a consecrated wafer, they shared black bread and wished each other health, a return home, and a reunion with their missing father and husband, as well as with Grandfather's and Grandmother's son, Tadek, who had remained in Poland. The severe Siberian winter of 1941 was a dreadful repeat of 1940.

Exhausted by work and constantly undernourished, all of the families again waited for the warmth of the spring and the summer. One night a hungry bear wandered into the camp. Smelling the horses, it tried to break into the stables. The noise woke the guard, who managed to kill the animal. After its skin was removed and handed over to the commandant everyone received a piece of meat, the first they had eaten in a year. The tough bear meat made a wonderful feast.

A great surprise awaited the family in the spring. Grandmother received a letter from her son, Janek. He told about his life in America and said that he had sent fifty dollars to their camp address. A few weeks later, a notice arrived from the town of Gorki, thirty kilometers away, stating that the money had arrived and could be collected at the post office. Grandmother was now too old and weak to walk to the town, which lay beyond the River Soswa, so the commandant agreed to give Aunt Jozefa leave to go and authorized her to pick up the money.

The poor woman set off on her far and unfamiliar way through the still snowy forest along the icy river. She searched for a safe place to cross. She saw with dismay that the ice had cracked into enormous floes, now separated by thin streams of dark water. Stumbling along in despair, not knowing what to do, she walked up the river and prayed for help. The day was drawing to an end, and there was no time for her to go back.

Someone in heaven heard her prayers. A young boy came running out from a nearby hut and asked her what she was doing out there in that wilderness. After she had explained the situation, he pulled two long planks out of the fence surrounding the cabin. These were to be used to help them get back onto the ice if they fell into the water. Then, selecting larger pieces of ice that lay close together, he jumped from one floe to another in a zigzag manner, leading the frightened woman, who didn't even know how to swim, to the other side of the river. Having made the crossing, he advised Aunt Jozefa to ask to stay the night in a nearby hut, explaining that the people who lived there were a decent lot.

An exhausted Aunt Jozefa knocked on the door of the small, out of the way house, and asked the owners if she could sleep under their roof. The good people agreed, giving her a modest supper and a place to sleep on the straw-covered floor. She was asleep in seconds. At dawn she set off again. The owners of the house gave her directions and, pitying her misfortune told her she could stay with them again on the way back. The dollars sent to the post office were paid out in rubles, at a rate of one ruble for one dollar. For the first time in a year Aunt Jozefa ate her fill, with bread she bought from a local bakery. Her leave was for three days, and she had to hurry back if she was to return before the deadline. The day was exceptionally beautiful and warm. The way back offered no difficulties. In the evening Aunt Jozefa once again stayed with her kind hosts, giving them a few rubles for her bed and food.

On the morning of the third day she found herself on the bank of the wide river, hoping to cross in the way she had been taught. But what she saw gave her a terrible fright. Under the influence of the warm air, the water had risen and picked up speed, though for now the floes still swam rather slowly. Huge pieces of ice rubbed against one another gratingly as they moved downstream with the current. Aunt Jozefa did not have the courage to jump across the moving ice and instead ran up and down the bank praying, with no chance to cross to the other side. Evidently providence was still looking out for her. The same boy was on his way to school, saw the familiar silhouette on the other side, and again came to her aid. Aunt Jozefa jumped with him on the floes, praying to the Holy Mother all the while. She was so frightened that she did not even realize she had reached the other bank. The boy refused any payment for his help. Evidently not all Russians were hostile to Poles. Having experienced years of suffering, some of the citizens could understand and pity the suffering of others.

The rest of the journey along the river took place without great difficulty. By evening, Aunt Jozefa turned into the forest that led to the camp. Unfortunately the day was ending, and at night everything looked different. After walking part of the way she completely lost her bearings. She sobbed from despair, aware that she was lost, and not knowing what else to do, began to shout. She called out for a long time, until finally she heard her father's voice coming from afar. Grandfather, uneasy about the falling dark and sensing that Jozefa might lose her way back, had gone out to meet her. The joy and relief when they both walked through the door was indescribable.

Even with the piratical exchange rate into worthless rubles, the money collected from the post office added up to a significant sum. It allowed the family to acquire many of the essentials they lacked for the severe Siberian climate. They bought knee-length felt-boots for the entire family so they could be warm and comfortable outside even during the greatest frosts.

Despite the prohibition against trading with the village inhabitants, the articles that the family brought from Poland had disappeared one-by-one in exchange for food. When they ran short of flour, grandmother took a camera and a silk scarf and went to a nearby village to trade. This time the poor woman was unlucky. She ran into two policemen patrolling the road to the village who demanded her papers, which, of course, she could not produce. Grandmother was arrested and imprisoned in the village jail. The lockup had been built out of thick tree trunks. Her cell had no windows and only a wooden bunk on which to sleep. Police confiscated the camera and the scarf.

After Katarzyna had been missing for a few days, a worried Grandfather asked one of the guards for help in unraveling the mystery. At the guard's intervention, grandmother Katarzyna was set free, but neither scarf nor camera was returned. For a small reward in the form of a pipe and some cheap tobacco, the guard wrote a letter to the police commandant in Gorki, explaining that the arrested woman was not a prisoner but a deportee. The letter explained that the things she had been carrying were her own, and that she had intended to exchange them for food for her grandchildren. The guard asked grandfather to swear that he would not reveal who had written the letter, which was in Russian.

After a few weeks two high-ranking policemen came to the camp to investigate. Everything was explained. The requisitioned things found their way back to their owner. The policemen offered vodka to all concerned, and the unfortunate situation was resolved. In the end, the adventure ended happily. Now the authorities turned to Grandfather with the question of who had written the letter. Grandfather stubbornly maintained that he had done it himself. One of the policemen said, *"Ty stary duraka nie walaj."* (*Don't think that we are stupid, old man.*) They knew grandfather could not write in Russian. The intoxicated officials, happy that they had carried out their responsibilities to everyone's satisfaction, without having to write any difficult legal reports, were happy to forget who authorized the letter.

Soon after grandmother's adventure, Mama Emilia fell ill with inflammation of the lungs. She was taken to a nearby hospital with a high fever, and stayed there under the care of the now familiar doctor. There were no medicines, and her back was cupped in order to bring the blood to the surface. At the hospital she was also told, in great secrecy, of the tense political situation that had arisen between Russia and Germany. When she returned to the camp, she noticed a change in the way the authorities treated the deportees. The military guards were uneasy about the possibility of war and being sent to the front to defend their country.

Reports that the German army was massing on the border reached the exiles' ears with increasing frequency. The news was received with trepidation and fear. One wondered of the consequences of armed conflict between two nations hostile to Poland. Finally, on June 22, 1941, the camp commandant called all of the residents into the square, and announced that the Germans had invaded the Soviet Union. It was a turning point for the inmates, who had never thought they would leave the camp alive. Straightaway they felt the impact of the war. Food rations decreased and two hours were added to every workday.

The situation on the front was not positive for the USSR. The German army moved east at a rapid pace, occupying new territories and taking thousands of prisoners daily. In the camp everyone was exhausted and hungry. The goat milk was the only thing that kept the children alive. Mama put a certain amount of the already modest food rations aside in expectation of an even worse time to come. Along with berries and mushrooms she also dried scraps of black bread.

In August 1941, a high-ranking NKVD (Soviet Military Police) officer came to the camp and told the assembled company that in accordance with an agreement between General Sikorski, leader of the Polish army in England, and Russian Leader, Joseph Stalin, all exiles were amnestied and free citizens from that moment on. They could either leave the camp or stay and become Russian citizens. All of the residents were filled with indescribable joy. They cried with happiness and fell into each other's arms. The moment they had been waiting for, so long, was suddenly here. People already knew that there were intentions to create a volunteer Polish army to fight the Germans alongside the Soviets. Hope arrived that there might be a chance of regaining a free Poland, something for which the exiles would do anything – even march from Siberia to their homeland on foot.

Debates began on how and when to depart. No one knew where they could join forces with the army now being organized. People were frightened by the thought of another journey. Everyone's health had deteriorated. Nevertheless, the knowledge that they were free citizens gave them the strength and the will to live.

To find money to pay for the departure, the family had to sell almost everything they had. The task fell to Grandmother. Grandfather continued to weave snowshoes for a few meager rubles. Aunt Jozefa worked in the forest with Emilia so they would continue to receive food rations, and Edek continued going to school. Only little Teresa clung on to her grandmother's skirts, begging for a piece of sugar and a doll made out of scraps of torn clothing.

The goats were the biggest problem. They were considered members of the family, and there could be no thought of killing them. Besides, no one was willing to do the deed or even knew how to go about it. So the family took advantage of an offer to sell them. The goat and her kids passed into the possession of the village baker, who paid six hundred rubles for them, and he promised the children that he would take good care of the goats. The final preparations took two months. Winter came, but this time it was full of hope and anticipation for the moment of departure. The trip south promised warmth and a rendezvous with the long unseen Polish army.

Not everyone was happy to leave, however. Families whose nearest and dearest were already settled in the graveyard, and those who did not have money for the voyage decided to stay in the place of their exile.

At the beginning of November, a few dozen families left behind the place where they had worked, hungered and fought to survive and where the bones of their friends lay in the frozen earth of the Urals. Without looking back, they set off in rented sleighs to the train station many kilometers away. The steel rails would take them to the Kujbyszew or Saratow region thousands of kilometers away. There in a sun-drenched land the Polish army was rising, and the newly released exiles hoped to follow their army back to their beloved country.

# Joining the Resistance
## (Czeslaw)

The two-person kayak moved steadily through the river toward the city. My friend, Mietek, and I were on our way back from a sandy beach near the top of the Wilja River, seven kilometers from Wilno. We had taken a well-earned vacation after finishing our third year at the High School. The weather was beautiful and we had spent most of our time on the water in our favorite kayak, unconcerned with what the future might bring. Halfway home we heard the factory sirens begin to howl, warning of an air attack. Minutes later came the far-off roar of bombs falling on local military targets. The planes made an impressive sight, diving against the blue of the sky and dropping their deadly bombs on bridges, army barracks, train junctions and power stations.

It was June 22, 1941, the day war broke out between Germany and the Soviet Union. In my excitement at the news, I had neglected to put on a shirt and my back was burned red by the June sun. By the time I returned to the city, my arms were covered with blisters and I was forced to stay home, unable to move from the pain. When the howling sirens announced another German attack, my entire family was forced to flee to the cellars without me, while I, covered in vinegar soaked towels, couldn't even raise myself from bed. I would rather have chanced being killed than risk scratching my aching skin by trying to get to our provisional shelter.

The next day, we could already see Soviet soldiers marching east through the city streets, row after row of tired, frightened men fleeing in panic before the approaching Teutonic army. In a few days, the city was empty of the last of the Soviets and their Lithuanian lackeys. On the morning of the third day, columns of German trucks carrying neatly dressed soldiers of the armored divisions began appearing on Wilno's streets. The young, blond army with skulls on its collars was an intimidating sight. Gendarmes wearing green and blue uniforms took up positions at every crossroad. They directed the flow of motorized units, armed with detailed maps of Wilno and its surroundings. After a few days, the movement of the army subsided, and in its place came masses of captured Soviet soldiers being marched to the train station. It was horrifying to watch. Thousands of starving soldiers walked with their heads bowed and their uniforms torn, wounds wrapped in bloodied rags. Some townspeople took pity on them and began to throw them bread, but if any of the soldiers ventured to retrieve the bread, they were immediately shot by their convoy's leader.

Life in the city slowly returned to near normal. Schools and workplaces reopened under a new administration. Essential items reappeared in stores and could be bought using temporary ration cards. The city's government changed, and places once occupied by communist sympathizers were now taken over by fascists from Kaunas. Soon afterwards posters announcing the compulsory registration of Jews appeared on the city's corners. A few weeks later a ghetto arose in the old town center, and began to fill with Jews that had been driven from their homes by the Germans and Lithuanians. The next group of war's casualties now walked the city streets, carrying all their possessions in handcarts and suitcases. They were walking toward an uncertain future, their fate no different from that of the Poles at the hands of the NKVD just a few months earlier. The only thing that had changed was the nationality of the victims.

The new authorities also began to conscript young Poles for work in Germany. My brother Tadek was one of the first to find his name on the list. The day finally came when he had to leave Wilno for the Reich as one of a group of unpaid workers intended as slave labor for armament factories.

The conscripts were first taken to a bathhouse to shower and then herded to the Wilno train station, where they were packed into cars to wait for departure from the city of their birth and youth. Happily my brother found that two of his friends - Leon Birenczyk and Ryszard Traulolta, the son of the Lieutenant Governor of Wilno – were among the group in his car. It was much more comforting for him to go out into the unknown in the company of his two close friends. The train set off through Kaunas toward the German-Lithuanian border. In the afternoon it reached the border city of Eidkun, where everyone was given a modest cold meal. Once again they were herded into a bathhouse and their bodies and clothes disinfected. Afterwards the train crossed into Western Prussia and stopped in a small town. That night the deportees slept in the cars while the train stood in the station.

The next morning they set off once again across a land whose well-tended fields they could admire through the train's open windows. It was an unforgettable journey through enemy territory. The travelers passed vast stretches of earth belonging to another country. Before the war, train travel had been a luxury few could afford, and my brother and his friends now felt like foreign tourists. The transport moved, without stopping, through Prussia to the beautiful city of Torun. Here a change came over the German guards. They began to behave more strictly toward the laborers they were transporting, insisting on cleanliness and order in the train cars.

In Poznan, the train made a longer stop. Tadek remembered a young girl's fear at hearing the Polish anthem being played on a harmonica. She had been sweeping the platform, but when she heard the melody she came up to the train window and said warningly, "You have no idea of the danger you're in. Don't risk being sent to a concentration camp for a song." Her warning was appreciated and heeded.

After Poznan, the train crossed into the Reich at night and reached Frankfurt by morning. For the third time everyone was herded into baths and subjected to the same disinfection process as in Eidkun. They were then taken to a small suburban train station. From there on to a transit camp in Kelserbach, where a German commission was distributing workers among various farms and factories. Tadek was assigned to an artillery factory in Kassel. The factory stood on Betenhausen Street and belonged to a local landowner named Herr Schonberg, who had been a meat-grinder manufacturer before the war.

In the evening, the workers were taken to the canteen for dinner and then quartered in the barracks that stood on the factory grounds. The next morning Tadek was introduced to his job and taught how to use a lathe. For the moment he would work as an apprentice under an older lathe operator, who went by the Polish name of Smiech.

Soon afterwards the factory was flooded with Ukrainians and later the French, who took their place in the barracks with noise and laughter. They came loaded down with supplies of food from sunny France. But their high spirits lasted only as long as their provisions. Faced with a lack of food and the prospect of German cooking, all their humor vanished. They were overcome with depression. It was then that the physical and psychological differences between the Poles and the prosperous French became apparent. Despite being poorly treated, hungry, and deprived of their freedom, the Poles were always in a better mood. They bolstered their spirits with jokes and songs and waited hopefully for a better time to come.

In the fall, the Gestapo burst onto the factory grounds and screamed for the guards to bring every Pole into the yard. The Poles were made to stand in a square and were surrounded by machine-gun wielding Gestapo and furiously barking dogs. A translator, with the Polish name of Sikora, addressed the group. He ordered the members of a secret Polish political organization to step forward. There was a complete silence. No one moved. The Gestapo picked out eighteen Poles and took them away. They returned twice more in the middle of the night and arrested another ten. The arrests were based on a false report made by a laborer who had been caught stealing alcohol. Although it was never proven that any of those arrested belonged to a secret Polish organization, they all ended up in concentration camps in the German Reich.

A similar report foiled Tadek's and his friend, Piotr Pip's, plans to escape from Germany in the late fall. One night after they had completed their shift, a guard, accompanied by Capt. Lutz, told them their plans had been discovered. Their leave to go to town was revoked and their clothes and money confiscated. A colleague who had known their secret plan had informed on them to the Germans. A few months later, the authorities, surprisingly lifted the punishment and returned their things. Having learned from their betrayal, the boys kept any new plans to themselves.

In November, the two friends went to the city for a walk that ended with their buying two train tickets to Lipsk. By late evening, they had reached the first stage in their journey. To avoid going through Wroclaw, they chose a northern route in the direction of Cotbus. Because they had many hours before their train was due to depart, they sat down to rest on a bench in a square near the station. This brought them to the attention of a German, who told the police that two suspicious individuals were relaxing on a park bench, apparently waiting for a train. At the station checkpoint, a gendarme was already inspecting everyone's papers and travel documents. Tadek and his friend circled the station, climbed onto another platform, and waited there until the train for Cotbus was about to depart. As it began to move, they ran across the tracks and jumped inside, undetected.

From Cotbus, they took the train to Krolewiec, sitting in a compartment with three Wehrmacht soldiers on their way back from vacation. The presence of these soldiers proved to be very useful during the document check. When a German gendarme asked them why they didn't have vacation permits, the boys told him they were only going to be gone for two days, to visit a friend who worked at the train station in Krolewiec. One of the soldiers confirmed their story, telling the guard that the two had, in fact, spent the entire time discussing the upcoming visit. The gendarmes left, wishing them a pleasant stay. In Krolewiec, they had a meal at a restaurant and then found an air raid shelter before curfew began. The next morning, having spent the night on a sandy floor, they dusted off their coats and walked back out onto the street. Because they didn't want to make themselves conspicuous by asking directions for the station, they began looking for someone carrying a suitcase. They were in luck. A little while later they caught sight of a soldier with a yellow band on his cap. They followed him to the Ost Bahn, where they bought two tickets to Grodno.

In their train compartment, the two friends struck up an acquaintance with a woman going home for the holidays. She gave them some of her sandwiches and made their satisfied stomachs very happy. The train continued on toward Suwalki. Soon a soldier in a major's uniform entered their compartment and asked the boys in Polish where they were going. When they told him they were on their way to Grodno after visiting a friend in Krolewiec, he advised them to go through Kaunas. "Get out in Suwalki," he said, "if they catch you further on they'll clap you into a concentration camp." They could tell from his accent that he was a Mazurian (region in Poland) – a Mazurian with a good heart. But the two foolishly ignored his sensible advice and continued on the same train.

It was Friday, the day food merchants made their way to Grodno with their goods. Before they had reached Augustow the Germans raided the train, requisitioning foodstuffs and checking documents to flush out speculators. For the escapees, all was lost. They were arrested and arrived in Grodno as prisoners. There they were taken to a military post. After an hour's wait they came before a German officer, who scrutinized them carefully while flipping through a folder full of papers. He spent a long time studying the photographs, luckily without finding any that matched the two escapees. Calling in a gendarme, he began saying something quietly to him about Polish bandits. At that point, Tadek and Piotr had no choice but to confess that they had escaped from compulsory labor in Kassel.

The interrogation came to an end, the officer handed them over to the local police, and they were taken to prison. The head of the prison was exceptionally well disposed toward the two escapees and even gave them half a loaf of bread before having them taken to their cell. The same couldn't be said for the warden. He confiscated the prisoners' belts and gave them a kick to move them along.

That night they were awakened by the shouts of partisans being taken away for interrogation and torture. After a month's stay Tadek and Piotr were transferred to a punishment camp from which they were to be sent back to Germany. Tadek worked on the campgrounds alongside some local laborers, and this gave him the opportunity to send a message to our parents in Wilno.

Out of the goodness of his heart, a local man named Ulas sent my parents word that my brother was being held in the camp and would soon be shipped back to a factory in the Reich. Father Roman immediately came down to Grodno disguised as a railroad employee. With Ulas' help he made the acquaintance of the Arbeitsamt (German Labor Office) secretary, a young and sympathetic Polish woman. Using her charm and some money, she was able to persuade a German doctor that Tadek Plawski suffered from epilepsy and was unfit to work in an armaments factory. Tadek was freed from the camp but told to remain in Grodno, where he would be employed at a freight station. A few days later, father and son both dressed as railroad workers, snuck across the border to Wilno. It was a joyous day. My family was reunited after a long separation, and Mother shed tears of joy at having her son returned to her from Germany.

The summer of 1942 brought another unforgettable day. While sitting at the table over a modest supper, our father, a longstanding printer, showed signs of unusual nervousness. Finally he pushed his unfinished meal away and began to speak in lowered tones. "Listen," he said. "We have something very important to discuss, something that could determine the fate of our entire family. It is a matter of life and death." There was a momentary silence. Our father then told us that the Underground Bureau of Information and Propaganda had asked us to operate a secret press that would publish appeals and leaflets to the Polish people. These would be aimed at boosting morale and helping people endure the disaster that had befallen our nation. To preserve the utmost secrecy, the work would have to be done at our home. It would involve great danger, and if we were discovered we would face imprisonment, torture and death.

Silence fell on the room. The seriousness of this issue, and our pride at the task with which we had been entrusted, took our breath away. Our mother, Zofia, was the first to speak. She got up from her chair and addressed my father in a trembling voice. "Roman" she said, "There is nothing to consider, take the assignment. We have to fight for our country's freedom. Let God's will be done; with His protection we will help you to the last of our strength, and if disaster strikes we'll die together." Tadek and I readily seconded her decision. At our age danger seemed unreal, a factor that didn't enter the equation, and our desire to fight the enemy was overpowering.

Soon afterwards we were sworn in by Tadeusz Pazowski, an old friend of the family. He had been the police commissioner in Oszmiana before the war, and had fought as a legionnaire during World War I. My father, Roman, received the code name "Tonko," my mother became

"Kania," Tadek, the printer's apprentice became "Bak," and I, a student mechanic, became "Majster."

The materials needed to set up our press were stolen from the "Patria" printing house. The burglary was arranged beforehand with Patria's owner, Jozef Babiarz, another former legionnaire and friend of my father. This was done for safety reasons and to disguise the source of the type. Maciej (Jerzy Dobrzanski) became the publication's editor, Renata (Zofia Borkowska) acted as liaison between the editor and District Commander Wilk (General Aleksander Krzyzanowski), while Jelonek (Stanislaw Kialka) became the supervisor of the "Farba" press.

On the streets of our German and Lithuanian controlled city, leaflets, printed in Polish, began to appear carrying the latest news on the situation at the front and political developments in the West. They circulated widely among the population, advising it on how to respond to the edicts of the occupying forces and urging tireless resistance against the enemy. The leaflets were printed at our new home on Zwirowa Gora Street 13, near the Bernardine cemetery in Zarzecze. We laid out the texts in our damp basement, printed them on a mimeograph, and then dried and wrapped them in waxed paper. Thus finished, the small packages were ready to be smuggled to other underground cells.

While this difficult and monotonous work was being carried out, our mother would stand by the window and watch the street. Her job was to warn us if friends or neighbors stopped by unexpectedly. If she knocked on the floor it meant danger and we would have to interrupt our printing. Sometimes we sat for hours without moving, waiting for an unwanted visitor to depart. After we finished work, we buried the type cases, types, matrices, mimeograph, ink and paper under the basement floor and covered it with potatoes.

In the summer of 1942, with the agreement of the commander of the Home Army, we began to publish a regular newspaper, *Independence*, which appeared every two weeks. The paper was a great success. It provided wide-ranging information about the activities of the authorities at home and the government-in-exile in London. The Gestapo and the police conducted an intensive hunt for the source of the paper. Their nightly raids and searches of homes, belonging to former publishing employees, narrowed the circle of suspects. It became vital to move the press as quickly as possible to a safer location, in the home of someone not directly linked to publishing.

At the beginning of 1943, a modern portable press was brought in from Warsaw, and installed in Maria Kosmowska's apartment on Filarecka Street in Zarzecze. The ground-floor kitchen was divided in two by a double wall, creating a narrow space. It's entrance was through a trap door that lay under the protective tin plate of the kitchen stove. From there we walked down the stairs and through a small tunnel to a secret room with no windows and no other kind of ventilation. It felt like being buried alive. The owner of the house, a former Polish Army soldier known as "Pen," would then screw shut the steel cover over the entrance to mask its purpose.

After a few hours of working in this room, the heat and lack of oxygen would become unbearable. Sweat ran into our eyes and drove us into a state of physical and nervous tension, with tragically comic results. My father and brother were both professionals and frequently disagreed on the layout of the text. This would lead to quarrels, during which my father would usually pull out his ancient Russian pistol and threaten to shoot us both if we didn't defer to his opinion.

Amused by the situation, and to stop the fighting, I would propose that we take the poison pills we had been given to swallow if discovered. These pills constituted our only means of defense against the Gestapo's tortures. When we finished working, "Pen" would undo the screws and release us. Understandably, mother was very anxious while we were gone. She kept her tearful eyes fixed on the clock and counted the minutes until our return. Her ears strained to hear the footsteps of the three dearest to her heart. When the moment finally came, our greetings were brief, masking our feelings of happiness and fear.

The leaflets we had brought from the press would be packed away in a basket under a pile of fresh vegetables. On the following day our mother, wrapped in a scarf and pretending to be an old woman, would set out to meet "Lonek" (Leokadja Blazejewiczowna), who would then transport our publication to an unknown cell. Mother always maintained that despite the extreme danger involved in carrying the leaflets through the city she was very proud and happy to do so. She always expressed relief at having disposed of the incriminating bundles, which minimized the risk of discovery. Realistically though the danger was only deferred for another two weeks.

Months of nerve-wracking, suspenseful work passed. We kept hoping for a change for the better. When that change did come, however, it was painful and frightening, with the potential to destroy all the families familiar with the workings of the resistance. During a street raid, the Gestapo arrested "Renata" while she was carrying some compromising literature. On the first night of her interrogation, the hapless girl was tortured to death. Despite her dreadful sufferings she refused to reveal the identities of any of her co-conspirators. A few days later, her mother was shot to death in the Ponary forest near Wilno. "Farba" Press was immediately moved to another hiding place in the town of Snipiszki. On the orders of General Aleksandr Krzyzanowski, "Renata" (Zofia Borkowska) was granted posthumous Silver Cross of the Order of Virtuti Military on July 14, 1944.

I was not mentally or emotionally suited to the work of publishing a secret newspaper. Monotonously turning the printing press crank gave me no satisfaction. I asked to be transferred to another cell. "Farba" continued with my father and brother at the helm. Soon afterwards my friend Mietek and I were once again sworn in, this time by Jan Czerechowicz a former Polish Army sergeant.

By this time we had finished our studies and were working at a German military garage, repairing Opel cars that came in from the war front and needed an overhaul. Due to the scarcity of oil, trucks intended for local use had to be refitted with charcoal burners. My job was welding and installing steel pipes about six centimeters in diameter. That size pipe also happened to make ideal grenade heads. I would take a piece of pipe that had been cut down to the right size, and weld a nut for the fuse on to the bottom. During our lunch break, Mietek and I would throw these unfinished grenades through an open window into the garden of a neighboring courtyard, taking advantage of the time when the Germans were eating Polish bacon in their rooms. A member of the Polish underground would be waiting in the garden to collect the heads.

To safeguard our activities, we used a few pieces of pipe to make a carbide lamp, the kind used to light homes when the electricity failed. One tank functioned as a container for the carbide and the other held the water, which dripped through a small valve to create a flammable gas. The burner involved pressing together two thin wires inside a copper pipe. After the wires were removed and the gas was lit, the resulting flame could illuminate the inside of a house. We always carried the lamp with us so that if we were caught at our secret work, we could explain why we needed all those bits of pipe.

After we had made about eighty pieces of grenade, we were ordered to stop. Someone from the organization had been arrested while carrying the grenades through the city. By examining the pipes used to refit cars in all the workshops in Wilno, the Gestapo might be able to trace the pieces back to their source. We expected a raid at any moment, and lived in fear of being arrested.

Around this time, someone in the resistance told us that a partisan unit led by Lieutenant Gracjan Frog (pseudonym Goral) would soon be going out into the field. The decision was simple. We had dreamed of armed combat against the occupier. We wanted to take an active part in the army, prove ourselves men in night marches and ambushes against an enemy army. This would also allow us to avoid having our role in the making of the grenades discovered.

In order to protect our families from Gestapo reprisals for deserting our work, we made it known that we were voluntarily going to Germany to work in the armaments industry. We were not taken seriously. The Germans laughed, thinking this was nothing more than a youthful joke. One evening toward the end of September 1943, Mietek Fijalkowski and another friend from school, Janek Piwcewicz, met at my house. I said a brief goodbye to my tearful mother and father. "You're biting off more than you can chew," my father told me.

When we left the house, the darkness of the peaceful cemetery surrounded us. Wilenka murmured from afar. I knew my way, as I had spent my childhood on the river's banks. We were to meet up with the partisans in the Czartowski Jar (Devil's Ravine), beside the road to Nowa Wilejka, which was at the foot of the mountain adjoining the Belmont forest. After marching for an hour, in the darkness along the riverbank, we crossed the highway and reached our destination.

"Stop, whoever you are!" called a voice from the roadside bushes. We spoke the password and found ourselves among a group of people huddled against the mountainside. The first order given to us was to keep silent. We waited for other volunteers to arrive. Some time later we heard steps, then the same password and reply, and several more people quietly joined our group. "We're waiting for a few more," our commander told us, "they're bringing weapons." We didn't have to wait long. Two boys – distant relatives of our leader, as I later learned – appeared out of the darkness of the ravine. They were pushing a bicycle weighed down with a huge sack that apparently contained enough weapons for the entire unit. In the silence of the night, the commander told us that he required absolute discipline from us, and that in this unit he was the master of life and death.

He distributed the guns. I was given a small lady's revolver with a six-bullet chamber. Not knowing what to do with this six-millimeter piece, I stuffed it into my coat pocket. Our commander explained to us that we had to keep the safety on our guns at all times in order to prevent any accidents. He was so agitated that before he had even finished speaking, he inadvertently fired off his own pistol, nearly shooting one of us in the knee.

He immediately rallied us to march, putting the bicycle and its enormous sack into my care. I was proud to have a whole store of weapons at my side. But my pride quickly passed. I followed the rapidly climbing column along the steep side of the thickly overgrown ravine, slipping over the rain-dampened earth and constantly struggled with the bike as it caught on the bushes. I began to sweat profusely. The sack and the bicycle grew heavier and heavier. After a while my nose began to bleed. I undid all the buttons of my coat, shirt and pants so that I could cool off. Covered in blood, I must have looked like a war-weary partisan after a savage hand-to-hand battle. Finally, gasping and weak, I asked Mietek to help me with the heavy sack that hung from the bicycle's frame. My friend didn't let me down. He tied his belt to the steering wheel and helped pull the bicycle uphill while I pushed on the seat with all my strength, digging my feet into the wet earth. Between us we managed to reach the mountaintop. We stepped onto the flatter forest floor with relief. From here it would be somewhat easier to transport my mysterious load.

The next morning we hid in the forest, exhausted after an all-night march, and listened to our commander talk on the subject of future battles and our sphere of operation. We were given code names – I became "Sosna" (pine), Mietek "Jodla" (fir) – and assigned to the forest squad. The commander announced that he had been a lieutenant in the Polish Army and in that organization he was known as "Goral". As the leader of our unit, he required unquestioning obedience from his subordinate soldiers. All criminal or military infractions would be severely punished, including execution. He repeated that he was now the master of life and death, and that we would do well to remember it.

After hearing this memorable speech and eating the sandwiches our farsighted parents had prepared for us, we spent the rest of the day reclining on the mossy forest floor. In the evening, the lieutenant sent me off to find a dirt road that lay one kilometer away from our hiding place. There I was to wait for a few more people who would be joining our unit. Walking through a thicket of young spruce, I was able to find the road with the help of a compass. I sat down under a roadside bush and wondered why I had been given this assignment. I didn't know if I should be proud or if it was another in a series of misfortunes. I already had great doubts about being able to find my way back to the camp. There were obviously no sidewalks or lights, and soon it would be so dark I wouldn't be able to see my hand in front of my face.

I waited. Darkness fell and I continued to wait, hoping someone would eventually arrive. The light drizzle that had started around midnight made my wait even more unpleasant. After a few hours, disappointed, I set off on my way back. I groped forward in complete darkness, tripping over the tree roots that stuck out of the earth and bumping my nose into the trunks of thickly growing pines. I searched blindly for the group of partisans that slept hidden somewhere in the bushes. After covering what I thought was the correct distance I failed to find the camp. I turned back and stumbled through the pathless forest as before. Despite strenuous efforts I still couldn't find the sleeping soldiers anywhere in that damned forest. I couldn't call out, because the master of life and death had ordered complete silence. I walked in circles, close to despair. Only near dawn, did I hear the loud snoring that finally led me to where my comrades-in-arms were resting. *"Have you ever spent a rainy autumn night in the thickets of an unknown forest?"* In times like that the darkness is so complete you can't even see your hand, and you lose all faith in your compass arrow. I lay down quietly beside Mietek so I wouldn't wake the others. I didn't want to expose myself to the mockery of my older comrades. In the morning I gave the commander my report. We spent that entire day hiding in the forest, listening to "Goral" talk about the missions that awaited our small team of madmen.

On the following evening, we set off on another march with the indispensable sack and bike once again in my care. I pushed the bicycle across pathless shortcuts, through mud, wilderness, and forest, toward our unknown destination. I wondered why none of those expected had joined our unit. I didn't dare suspect the lieutenant of maliciously sending his youngest partisan to rendezvous with phantoms. After a third sleepless night, having eaten nothing but bread, I was thoroughly exhausted. I was also consumed by curiosity, and I took the first opportunity to peek illicitly into the mysterious bag that hung from the bicycle frame, wanting a glimpse of our ammunition and weapons.

To my surprise I beheld an extra pair of boots, a set of long underwear, a few shirts, socks and towels, shaving supplies, and a raincoat. There were also some boxes of conserves and trinkets that our leader considered essential for his life as a partisan – but no sign of extra arms or ammunition. Whether these had been forgotten or already dispersed I did not know. My pride abandoned me completely. From that moment on I hated the waterproof sack and schemed about how to get rid of it at the first opportunity.

We continued walking north in the direction of the town of Suzany, which lay about forty kilometers from Wilno. Instead of taking a straightforward route, we deliberately covered the distance in a zigzag manner to disguise any traces of our small contingent's passing. Along the way we had to circle the town of Mejszagola, where the German army and the Lithuanian police were stationed. This was harder than it seemed. We accidentally stumbled into its suburbs three times in the dark.

Finally we rapped on the windows of a nearby house and woke the owner, who came out in his underwear and showed us the way. The commander had a machine gun hanging from around his neck and it seemed that the needle of the compass had been turning along with him, leading us in circles. This isn't a criticism of "Goral;" I was happy to know that apparently I wasn't the only one who could blunder in the dark.

I write about these events through the eyes of an eighteen-year-old boy who had rushed off to war with enthusiasm. At the time, I didn't understand our leader's responsibilities and fears. He had been entrusted with the lives and fates of seventeen inexperienced people unused to guns or military discipline. We were always passing through territories controlled by the army and the police. Lithuanian villages were well defended, with machine guns and telephone links to the nearest towns. Numerous Soviet partisan units held sway in the forests. Our commander had been a professional officer in an armored division, and had no experience in leading a volunteer unit equipped only with handguns.

One day before dawn, we hid in a young forest and spent the entire day resting after a grueling journey. Our stomachs were hollow from hunger. Nothing passed our lips, and we could only dream of bread and water. When we asked about provisions our commander told us that we would have to first get out of the danger zone without attracting the enemy's notice. Only when we joined another group near the town of Suzany, would we be a strong enough force to obtain food.

At sunset we again set off to the north, giving all the settlements a wide berth. Despite my thirst and hunger the march seemed somehow light and easy. Only later did I realize with horror that I didn't have the bicycle. Damn it! I had left it in the bushes at our last stop. I ran to the front of the marching column and, strung tight as a wire, told the commandant the bike was lost. I can't repeat what he called me. No printer would publish such a litany. He ordered me to go back for it straightaway, giving me one of his protégés for company. Evidently he didn't trust me to recover the bicycle on my own. But when we got there it was patiently waiting for me where I had left it. Despite it being a valuable commodity in those days, it had not been stolen.

I hovered at the back of the column, afraid of the further consequences of my carelessness. But the storm somehow passed me by. My leader was preoccupied by the seriousness of our situation and for the moment ignored me. The local underground network had brought us word that raids were being organized north of Mejszagola. We were obliged to go into hiding to disguise our tracks and the direction of our march.

That night a resistance member led us to a cave built under a steep riverbank. Thick shrubs concealed its entrance and its thick plank roof was covered with scattered earth. It was an ideal place to rest. All we needed was food. Our co-conspirator had only left us a large loaf of dark bread and a bucket of raw carrots. Our drinking water came from the stream at night. After a few days, our urine was stained red from the carrots. It was, in a way, like the first blood spilled in the fight for our country's freedom. We passed our time by talking and telling stories about the interesting experiences of the organization's members.

The spirit world was the subject that generated the most interest. One of the partisans knew someone who conducted séances to summon and contact dead family members. When we had exhausted every possible topic of conversation we began to compose what would become the hymn of the future Third Brigade of Home Army. It was in this cave that the first words of that famous partisan song were composed.

"The bivouac fire is dying down,
And on the river the mist is rising.
Of the platoon there's no sign and no trace,
Only the sound of the *dziegciar* in the distance. (dziegciar: Russian machine gun)
From somewhere far away I hear,
The moan of the shrapnel as it rises.
The river lies beyond the cliff,
And beyond the river the tomb and the cross.

Under this cross, under this fallen tree,
The soldiers sleep their last sleep.
This is what it means to be Polish,
You, too, can dream this sweet dream.

As you fall in battle may you see
A Poland free and clean as a tear.
Of the platoon there's no sign and no trace,
Only the sound of the *dziegciar* in the distance."

I have very pleasant memories of the time we spent dawdling on the straw under that canopy, between its thick, unfinished beam walls. Nevertheless the moment came for us to leave. The neighborhood had quieted and we marched out again to join forces with the unit of sub-lieutenant "Dzik" who we were to meet in the Suzany forest.

The march was long. We walked only at night, through untamed wilderness, avoiding all settlements and villages. Our days were spent hiding in the forest. In three weeks we ate a hot meal only once, at a farm where we were also able to wash and sleep in a barn. A few members of our group, disillusioned by these conditions, left their guns and disappeared.

During that time we received a shipment of new Russian Tokarew pistols which pleased us very much. As a result of my constant complaining, the unlucky bicycle with its mysterious load was taken away from me. I was assigned to carry provisions instead. Wilnian bread, which I had to tote, was baked in huge ovens and often weighed nearly sixteen lbs. It was usually round and awkward to carry; I even began to miss the detested bicycle. Happily, for me, we didn't always have bread; the company was so starved that it usually consumed all its supplies at the first opportunity.

One night we marched by a Lithuanian village and were required to remain completely silent so we would not reveal our position. Our route led us through a narrow river that had to be crossed using a fallen tree trunk that lay roughly 3 meters over the river. One after the other, we held onto an extended branch, to steady ourselves, and made our way to the opposite side. Whoever conquered the obstacle would then hold out the branch to the next soldier to help him keep his balance.

I was very tired and sleepy. I don't know how it happened, but I carelessly let go of the branch. Unluckily for me, the man then standing in the middle of our provisional bridge, carrying a machine gun and a backpack, was the commander's cousin. In trying to keep his balance, without the use of the branch, he began waving his arms like a windmill in a strong wind, and a piercing bellow of fear issued from his young breast. All this lasted for just a few seconds, and a moment later came a resounding splash as he fell into the water. There turned out to be nothing to fear, since the river was no more than knee high in this spot. The darkness of the night made it difficult to judge the water's depth.

The wretched soldier came out soaked and muddy, leaving his machine gun behind in the water.

Feeling guilty, I jumped into the stream after the abandoned gun. And wonder of wonders, I beheld what I thought was not one but two weapons. On closer examination, I discovered that the gun had broken in half at the catch. Luckily it was too dark for me to see our leader's expression when I handed the lost item to its soaked owner. The commander pushed his face close to mine and whispered that he would have me shot at the first opportunity. I sensed that my career in his unit had been irretrievably ruined and I could no longer hope for any future advancement.

Around Wilno, the month of September already marks the beginning of winter. Rain pours without stopping, leaving a thin layer of ice across the wagon ruts in the sandy roads. When we marched we couldn't always see where we were putting our feet and often fell up to our knees in thick mud. Burdened with a loaf of heavy bread, soaked to the skin, I straggled at the end of the column and cursed Hitler for my unhappy fate. The heavens rained down, my bread grew heavier and heavier, and finally broke in half, covering half my side in a sticky, doughy mess. But there was no question of stopping at night, even for a moment. I had to plod on, orienting myself by listening for the soldier in front of me, and sometimes holding his belt so I wouldn't get lost.

Finally the barking of dogs interrupted the quiet of the night, indicating that we were nearing the estate of civilized people who spent nights, like these, drinking tea in the warm house. The commander called a halt and ordered us to surround the property while he himself went to investigate the darkened estate. We waited, and after a moment lights were seen through the cracks of the closed shutters. Patiently we kept waiting. Half an hour passed, but our leader didn't reappear. Though we had been heated by our march the cold now began to seep into our bones, and it rained cats and dogs, as usual. At a certain point our patience expired. We looked inside through a gap in the shutters. Before our eyes appeared a handsome, elegant salon with a carpeted floor. In the middle of the salon, stood a round table covered with porcelain dishes, and at the table sat the commander, in the company of two ladies, helping himself to cakes from the huge tray.

This was just too much to tolerate. Though we were soaked,

muddy and uninvited, we made our way inside. Panic swept over the householders. They looked with dismay at the muddy footprints we had left on their Persian carpets. Our leader, stunned, tried to eject us from the salon, explaining that this was no way to behave. The two gracious ladies came to our protection. They called for their servants to take our dripping group to the stables and promised us we would enjoy a hot meal.

I wrapped myself in a blanket and dried my wet clothing, mulling over the situation in which we found ourselves. Mietek's violent coughing interrupted my train of thought; he had a severe cold and his temperature was high. Soon the farm servants came back with a kettle of steaming soup and bread covered in butter. It was a feast fit for the gods. After the meal, sleep overpowered everyone. We slept buried in straw and covered in borrowed blankets.

Early the next morning we were joined by a large group of new recruits with whom we were to go on to meet "Dzik's" unit. Neither Mietek nor I had any enthusiasm left for that meeting. We had spent three weeks wandering in Wilno's wilderness and hiding in forests. During that time, we had eaten a hot meal and slept under a roof just twice. The only shot fired had been the commander's accidental discharge as we set out into the field. We were sick of these sorts of partisan adventures.

We knew that we could do much more effective resistance work in the city. But I had neither the desire nor the courage to ask to be excused from the unit. I knew the commander would refuse; he had, after all, promised me that he was only waiting for the chance to have me shot. I didn't want to give him that opportunity by remaining in his small army. That evening Mietek and I left our backpacks in the barn and went outside to relieve ourselves. We never returned. Instead we ran five hundred meters north along the road to Suzany and lay down in a ditch to await the next development.

We didn't have to wait long. An alarm sounded at the farm. We saw the gleam of electric lanterns recede in the direction of Wilno. Just as he had promised, the commander gave the order that the captured deserters would be shot. Luckily the posse didn't find us, and after searching the nearby bushes and the road to town, they turned back to the farm. My friend from school, Janek Piwcewicz, was accused of conspiring in our escape and barely escaped being shot. He had to face a great deal of unpleasantness as a result, and after a few more weeks of such treatment he asked to be dismissed and, subsequently, returned to Wilno. When we met again he told me how furious "Goral" had been at being deprived of two such brave partisans. We waited in the ditch for some time that night and only after our unit had passed by our hiding place, rushed off to Wilno on the double. Without bread, bike or a despotic leader always threatening death, our march was easy. It didn't occur to us that Goral's punishing hand could reach us from afar, especially given that we had taken two of the new Tokarew pistols with us.

Our return to Wilno was uneventful. By dawn we were already in the city. This time we walked straight south, unconcerned about encountering the enemy. That possibility never occurred to us. My parents greeted us with joy. Mietek's adoptive mother was not so welcoming. She complained unremittingly about his torn shoes and clothes. In order to placate his mother, Mietek was forced to sell his gun for twenty five thousand German marks so that he could replace his wardrobe. He had no difficulty finding a buyer; many resistance fighters had no weapons and the demand was great. Only when Mietek returned home in a new outfit, and with a gift for his mother, did the angry woman calm down and leave him in peace.

Mietek and I now found ourselves in a rather unpleasant situation. The police were pursuing us in the city for deserting our work at the German garage. "Goral" raged in the countryside, unable to forgive the loss of two guns and two brave partisans. We didn't give much thought to the latter, unwisely underestimating the extent of his anger.

We were forced to put all of our eggs in one basket. Since we wanted to go back to work at the garage it became necessary for us to go to see Haupmann Plage, the military supervisor of all the garages in Wilno. If we were to be punished for unlawfully deserting our work, let it be on the orders of the highest authority. We presented ourselves to his secretary and explained that before leaving for Germany we had gone to a village to find provisions for the journey. Mietek had become seriously ill and I hadn't wanted to leave him until he regained his health. My friend's thin and emaciated appearance seemed to support our story.

After a moment the door to the richly decorated office opened and the Haupthmann's voice called out "Kom here." Pretending to be afraid, which wasn't far from the truth, we came to stand in front of the German officer's desk. He stared at us for a long time, then finally rose and, shaking his finger in our faces, said: *"Do you know, you young shits, that warrants for your arrest followed you to Berlin? Do you know that even a few days' absence from work could put you in a concentration camp, and you've been gone three weeks? Now get back to garage. I don't ever want to see you here again."* Then he smiled and sat back down. Our youth and our reputation for being good workers had saved us.

Overjoyed with such a positive outcome to our problem, we ran all the way to Trzech Krzyzy Mountain and there, sitting on its slope, gazed out over our beloved city. We laid plans for our future life, dreams of the kind that are possible only when you're very young.

The next morning we stationed ourselves in the garage beside a truck that had stood unfinished since we'd chucked the job. The other workers smiled expectantly at the spectacle of our approaching punishment. The moment soon came for the arrival of the military superintendent, a huge sergeant known to be hostile to Polish workers.

He saw us from afar as we worked on straightening out a damaged bumper. Approaching with a hurried step, he swung his huge paw straight at my head. At that same moment, Mietek managed to blurt out that we had spoken to Haupmann Plage and that our situation had been explained. The hand fell straightaway, but the expression on his face was frightening. He left for his office without saying a word.

Engineer Sznajder, the director of the garage, was happy to have us back at work and ordered his secretary, Giec, to give us ration cards so that we could buy boots. From the expression on his face it was obvious that he was pleased about the return of two such adventurous and hard working youths. We began work at the garage straightway. This time, though, I was not doing any welding, having complained of an inflammation in my eye caused by excessive light.

Our new job was to fix cars that came in from the Eastern Front. Henryk Trojanowski, Mietek and I were a team specializing in fast repairs of passenger autos. Young and strong, we didn't need to use jacks to lift the cars. Henryk and I would grab the front bumper, and we would raise the vehicle into the air. Mietek would position the trestles underneath and begin to dismantle the front suspension. Meanwhile,

Henryk would run back and forth to the warehouse for spare parts, which I then installed on the side that had already been taken apart. Two hours later we would test the brakes and hand the keys over to the waiting soldier.

The gratified soldier would usually give us some cigarettes and say a few approving words to the management of the garage. After a job like that, we had nothing more to do for the rest of the day and loitered around until our shift was over. Master Libers and Engineer Sznajder sometimes wagged admonishing fingers in our direction, but always with a smile on their lips. They liked such quick, clean work on the part of young men employed in the, "construction of the New Europe," as they called the German push to rule the world.

The older workers, however, were of a different opinion. They were Poles and considered us German flunkies. They didn't realize that the reputation we cultivated helped us in our other, secret work for the good of our subjugated country. We took every opportunity to crawl into cars that had come in from the front on the pretext of inspecting the damage. In the process we conducted a thorough inventory and confiscated any ammunition or other military supplies that had been left behind. By that time we had once again been sworn into a new fighting unit in the city. Henryk Trojanowski assured us that our new leader was a brave and collegial soldier, under whom we could soon expect to go out into the field.

Things seemed to be going fairly well. We completely forgot about "Goral," who, in November 1943, changed his code name to "Szczerbiec" and had become the leader of a large partisan group operating south of Wilno. One day, I returned home from work to find my mother waiting for me in the doorway. Frightened, she told me that someone wanted to speak to me. Our guest rose when I walked in. He told me that he was a messenger from "Szczerbiec," who had issued an order for me to be court-martialed and executed. It seems that "Szczerbiec" had not forgotten his promise to shoot me. I was to present myself on the designated day, right before curfew, beside the Orthodox Church on the bank of the Wilenka River, where I would meet two partisans who would carry out my sentence. The messenger added that I should bring both of the pilfered guns with me to the rendezvous.

I went, pondering about having to die so young for stupidly stealing two guns. In my opinion this was all nonsense, and I was only puzzled as to why no one had paid a similar visit to Mietek. I recognized the partisans' execution team waiting for me by the newspapers protruding from their coat pockets. I gave the password, introduced myself as "Sosna," and added that I had come to be sentenced. They read out a short sentence in the light of a dim flashlight, and asked if I had anything to say in my own defense. That is when I dredged up everything that had happened to me in the unit and explained about my underground work at "Farba" and later about making grenades at the garage. I also declared that "Szczerbiec" was prejudiced against me because someone had told him I had looked into his bag.

After hearing this deposition the two executioners said that my sentence would be suspended until my statements could be verified. For now they only demanded the return of the weapons we had taken from the unit. I was forced to lie and to say that partisan "Jodla" (Mietek) had lost his gun while fleeing from the farm. I asked them to let me retain my Tokarew pistol to be used in acquiring another gun. They agreed, giving us two weeks to find a replacement. It all seemed very simple. All we had to do was thump a soldier or a policeman on the head and take his gun. To do this job we made a truncheon from a rubber tube filled with sand, it had a steel tip hammered on one end, and a wooden stopper on the other. It was a formidable weapon, and when I tested it I found that a vigorous blow was capable of breaking a thick plank of wood.

Mietek and I met in Orzeszkowa square after twilight. We were ready for action. What we didn't have was a plan. We wandered through the darkened city streets looking for an armed victim. The object of our attack had to be a German carrying a handgun and preferably one who found himself on a deserted side street. Such stringent requirements would be hard to meet. The soldiers avoided those places and stuck to the main streets, with their cinemas and cafes. They usually walked around in groups of twos or threes. Curfew started at ten p.m. and we would have to get home before then to avoid arrest.

Mietek lived on Bufalowa Gora Street, in a building that had once been a school where his father had been the superintendent. Now it housed a German officer's club. I lived in a single-family home on Zwirowa Gora Street. Because we lived about four kilometers apart we had to stop hunting around nine p.m. in order to have time to get home. Half an hour before curfew, Gendarmes and Lithuanian policemen would start patrolling the city. We had very little time. Disappointed by our unsuccessful hunt we told ourselves we would have better luck tomorrow and went our separate ways home.

The following evening was no different than the first. When we tired we stepped into a café on Wilenska Street for a cup of the black swill they called coffee. We sat down at a table already occupied by a German soldier, who was romancing a girl and drinking beer from a bottle. To relieve the pressure on his swollen stomach he had removed his gun belt and left it on a shelf under the table. We recognized our opportunity right away. Mietek began inching the belt closer to him, blowing on his coffee all the while. I had my gun in my coat pocket and began spastically squeezing its butt, ready to provide cover. The tension in our faces made the German suspicious. He reached under the table and pulled his gun toward him, putting an end to our attempt to acquire a weapon that evening. Our nerves, stretched to the breaking point, prevented us from continuing.

Discouraged by our failure, the next evening we sped off to the narrow streets beside the newly formed ghetto. These streets were patrolled by the Lithuanian police. We hid in an entranceway and waited in the darkness for someone to pass. Soon, we heard a single set of approaching footsteps. We let the guard walk past our hiding place and then began to follow him. But when we came nearer, truncheon poised and ready to strike, we found ourselves within a circle of light from a flashlight. The policeman had sensed the approaching danger of two armed people and illuminated us, blinding us completely. We slowly stepped down from the sidewalk and onto the road, circling the unmoving Lithuanian. The only thing we could see was the barrel of the rifle he aimed in our direction. We walked a certain distance in complete silence, and the flashlight was extinguished. It had been a cease-fire, dictated by mutual fear and good sense.

Our situation no longer seemed so hopeful. Time was passing, and only now did we grasp the enormity of our task. There was no question of stopping our attempts to find a weapon. Our thoughtless appropriation of the pistols was a serious crime in wartime, and the moment when we would have to face the consequences was fast approaching. I no longer made light of "Szczerbiec's" promise to do away with me at the first opportunity. Mietek was showing increasing signs of great strain. He had terrible arguments with his parents about going out in the evenings. His father insisted he needed help in heating the officer's club with coal from the boiler room. My situation was different. My parents knew what we had done and didn't try to keep me from going on our nightly excursions. My mother only cried, waiting uneasily every night for my return. There was no solution but to implement a riskier method. We had to keep our promise to return the weapon within two weeks.

Beside the "Casino" cinema on Niemiecka Street stood a late-night café where soldiers often came for a beer after the movies. While draining their glasses of foaming liquid, they usually hung their gun belts on the back of their chairs. Our plan was simple. One of us would stand by the doors leading out to the darkened street and the other would walk by an occupied table, grab a weapon, and run through the opened doors. The darkness and the slamming of the doors in our pursuers' faces would buy us the few seconds we needed to disappear.

This time it was Mietek's turn. I took my place by the entrance, waiting for the right moment. When I saw that he had reached the carpet by the bar and had the target in his sights, I swung open the doors. And at that very moment three soldiers came in from the street and walked through my opened doors. They said "Danke shoen" to me and went inside with a smile. Mietek froze, evidently not wanting to fall into the arms of three thirsty soldiers. The next day, finally in desperation, we decided to use our gun. Up to this point we hadn't wanted to take anyone's life. War had its own law and when the enemy shot, you returned the favor. But we did not think that it was ethical to shoot anyone, even the enemy, without warning or provocation. Nevertheless, our situation and fear of losing our own lives forced us to consider such a step. A death sentence still hung over our heads.

A small guard post stood beside a railway bridge near the Rossa cemetery. The sentry was responsible for keeping the bridge from being destroyed. The rail line between Wilno and Minsk was an important transportation link for the German army and heavily guarded. One night, as we walked a girl back from a party, we happened to notice a soldier with an automatic rifle sitting inside the hut. It was located in an isolated spot far from any other houses and abutted a high embankment on which the tracks ran. The terrain was ideal for both attack and retreat once done. Now, in our time of need, we remembered it again.

We walked along the sidewalk and talked loudly so as not to raise anyone's suspicions. We had learned from that memorable experience with the Lithuanian policeman. As we passed by the wooden hut, I turned around at lightning speed, ready to fire a few shots inside. But there was no one there. The hut was empty and the guard had wandered off, maybe to relieve himself in the bushes or stretch his legs after sitting so long. We didn't try to figure out where he'd gone or wait around for his return. Fear gave our legs wings. We ran as fast as we could along the pavements of the darkened streets and only stopped, gasping, a few blocks away. Mietek handed me the luckless truncheon and went home. There was nothing for me to do but follow his example.

The next day at work we discussed our tragic situation. Mietek couldn't leave the house anymore under any circumstances; he had to shift coal for his father from the courtyard to the boiler room. After leaving the garage we went to his house and, shovels in hand, moved several tons of coal. By the end we were exhausted. I helped him out of friendship, and because we both wanted to calm his unpleasant domestic atmosphere. It was also a much-needed chance to release nervous energy.

A week went by. As was our routine, on Saturday we went to a private dance, after which we needed only a couple hours sleep to regain our strength. Sunday mass reconciled us with God, and we were now ready to face the coming week with all its attendant fears and dangers. The Sunday prayers had a calming influence on the psyche of two depressed youths.

An army truck was brought into the garage from the Eastern Front for general repairs. The soldier filled out the necessary paperwork, took his things and disappeared, leaving the car in the yard of the garage. We, two young experts, immediately went to work checking what had to be done to repair this vehicle. We began to inspect the cab. When we lifted the seat we discovered a Soviet machine gun in excellent condition. The driver had evidently taken it from a battlefield as a souvenir. When we dug further through some scattered rags we found an ammunition bag, the kind Soviet soldiers used to hold bullets for machine guns and

"Tokarew" pistols. Our excitement knew no bounds; we almost peed ourselves with joy.

We immediately devised a plan for removing our treasure from the garage at the end of our shift that evening. As the taller one, I would carry out the machine gun while Mietek would take the bag with the ammunition. This would be neither easy nor safe. We had to pass through a guard at the gate who carried out random inspections of workers as they left. Mietek shut the car doors, grabbed a piece of cloth and started whipping me around the head with it. Laughing and yelling, I ran away toward the gate, where I tripped and fell in front of the guard. With an expression of pain, I grabbed my knee supposedly hurt by the fall. Mietek helped me get up and I limped back to the garage with my arm around his shoulder.

All that day I walked around limping on my right leg and grimacing with pseudo pain. The Germans proposed taking me to the doctor but I bravely refused, thanking them for their kind offer. We worked without stopping until the evening. After we had punched out we went to the courtyard and, hidden in the darkness, took our treasures out of the truck. I tied the automatic to my leg underneath my overalls, Mietek tucked the ammunition bag around his waist, and we started out. As we passed the guard we didn't forget to say "Aufwidersen." He waved at us in a friendly fashion and watched me limp out onto the street on Mietek's arm.

At home we counted the contents of the bag. There were around six hundred pieces of ammunition, an unbelievable treasure worth much more than just one pistol. It would more than compensate for the lost weapon. We decided to give the automatic to Henryk Trojanowski, who would pass it on to our new cell.

I went to the meeting at the end of that week with a light heart. The same people were waiting for me in the same place as before. I handed over my pistol and asked if they would accept ammunition in exchange for my friend's lost gun. They replied that it was a completely satisfactory replacement. Units operating in the field sorely needed this type of ammunition. I was also informed that my resistance work had been confirmed, and that my sentence had been repealed. The compatriots wished me luck in my new unit, and disappeared into the night.

A great weight had been lifted from my heart. I would no longer have to risk my life sneaking through the city streets at night. Our methods of trying to obtain the gun had not been entirely to my liking. I had not wanted to wound or kill anyone just to save our own skins. Only the threat of execution had made us seriously consider the idea.

The "master of life and death" was quickly forgotten. Youth has its own laws and all our attention was now concentrated on our work and the Saturday dances we attended at private homes. All gatherings of young people were forbidden and parties had to be arranged in secret. We polished the floors all night long to the sounds of the phonograph, taking our first awkward steps in the dance. Naturally none of this happened without a bit of moonshine to give us courage and help us whirl our partners around. Sometimes an ingenious policeman, hearing the sounds of music trickling out through the layers of coats hung over the windows, came in to see what was happening. Then, surrounded by girls who wouldn't let him get a word out edgewise, and glasses of vodka pressed into his hand, the man wouldn't know what to do. Seeing that we were all only young people he would usually just tell us to lower the music. He would chase down his vodka with a sandwich, and disappear into the night, not wanting to make trouble for himself. To arrest such a crowd and deliver it to the station was beyond what a single man could accomplish. He could not tell us to go home because it was past curfew, and no one was supposed to leave the house. So he chose the most rational solution and vanished, pretending to have seen and heard nothing.

Our job at the garage wasn't very exciting, and this sometimes led to pranks and games among the young and energetic. A large, five-ton Soviet "Yaz" truck was handed over for repairs. A few men got ready to push it into the place where it would stand during repairs. Taking advantage of a moment when they were resting I climbed into the back, propping my shoulders against the wall and my legs against the trunk. Now the stubborn vehicle didn't want to roll all the way up to the wall. Though the others pushed with all their strength, looked underneath to see if something was blocking the wheels, and checked the hand brake and gearbox, they couldn't figure out what was causing the problem. They started calling others for help.

In the meantime, suspended in the air and wanting to change my position, I bent my knees slightly. To my dismay, the truck began to move. I could no longer hold back the immense mass of vehicle that had been put in motion. That I am alive today is entirely due to the builder of the garage, who had installed a window right by the spot where I was leaning. I quickly twisted my body and went flying out into the forge along with the window frame and the broken glass. This time the truck rolled all the way up to the wall. I was taken to the doctor, white with pain and bent in two, but luckily nothing was broken. For a long time afterward I had bruises and scratches on my back and buttocks. I explained away my presence at the back of the truck by saying I had wanted to help and had also been looking for the source of the blockage.

Winter was showing its full force. The month of November in Wilno was always frosty, with snow covering the streets and ice on the rivers. This year we waited for Christmas and New Year's Eve with particular impatience. We already knew that in the next few months we would once again have to abandon our homes and our jobs at the garage. Henryk, our friend and superior in the underground organization, had informed us that we would be going out into the field as part of a new forest unit commanded by Lieutenant Czeslaw Grombczewski, code name "Jurand." This time we hoped things would be different; according to Henryk, our new commander was a brave man, different from "Szczerbiec" in every respect. Sergeant Jan Czerechowicz, who had organizational ties with this group, gave us both some guns, old Russian revolvers with six bullets. It was a nice gesture on his part, made in remembrance of how we had worked together in the past.

Time begin to drag on unbearably. Now that we had our own guns we wanted to test both our shooting skills and the functionality of the old revolvers. The one suitable place for such maneuvers was the boiler room in what had been an old school and was now the German officer's club. The sound of shots in the boiler room was indistinguishable from the constant noise of coal being shoveled into the huge central heating ovens. Mietek made quite an accurate shot at the piece of paper we had suspended, hitting it in the corner. I didn't do as well; my gun simply wouldn't fire. After inspecting it, I determined that the firing pin end had broken off and didn't reach the detonator. This had to be repaired. Since I knew how to weld, I added in a small piece that made the gun cock useable once more. We were lucky that we had been so impatient to test our guns. It would have gone badly for us if my gun had malfunctioned while facing our enemy in the field.

# A Long and Wandering Road
(Teresa)

One frozen November day in 1941, a rented sleigh hitched to a shaggy Siberian pony moved along a snow-covered road. This sleigh, packed with Bajorskis and Maseleks, was on its way to a train station far away. They were leaving the camp where they had spent the last few years as slave laborers cutting down trees. They were now free, emancipated by the 1941 amnesty of Poles deported to Siberia. Their situation had undergone a complete change; no longer wretched as they had been two years ago, they traveled south in search of a rising Polish Army, and a much-needed change of climate. Little did these hapless people realize what still awaited them on their long journey! Their enthusiasm and hope of returning to their native land partly erased the suffering of their forced trek to Siberia.

After a few days, they reached a small, impoverished station. The driver unloaded their things and set off on his way back. On the railway tracks, empty cattle cars stood ready to traverse the vast stretches of the Soviet Union. The station, besieged by a human swarm, was a horrifying spectacle. Amassed everywhere were wraith-like figures of what had once been healthy Polish citizens. They sat bootless on the snow in the torn remains of their military uniforms, bare legs purple with cold. Cheekbones protruded sharply from their emaciated faces, swollen gums filled their toothless mouths, and reddened eyes peered out in search of a miracle. They were waiting for a chance to board a train without having to pay for a ticket. There was no room for them in the station house, which was filled to the rafters with travelers wanting to go south. Although the Poles had regained their freedom, they were still treated with suspicion, and these ex-prisoners had been denied all human rights.

A few families from the same camp, including the Maseleks and the Bajorskis, decided to buy out an entire car, so that they would have as much space as possible during the long journey south. The car needed to have a small iron stove installed in the middle, and bunks built along the sides for people to sit or sleep on during the long cold nights. After a few days labor, on the part of some well-compensated railway workers, the car was ready to be occupied. It would be connected to a series of trains heading away from Siberia.

After taking their place inside, the refugees looked with horror at the human skeletons waiting for their opportunity to escape icy Siberia. These wretched souls had neither food nor money. Released from prison camps as a result of the amnesty, they were on their way to rejoin the newly re-forming army. Only now did the Maseleks realize that they had been treated much better than the other prisoners. They had at least received some food and even a paltry payment for their labors. The pitiful horde outside consisted mostly of prisoners of war, and political prisoners, who had served sentences for crimes they had never committed. Now free, they had to find a way to get to the distant army enlistment point on their own. They had no recourse but to beg for a piece of bread and a corner in an overcrowded car. The Bajorskis, Maseleks and others could not find it in their hearts to refuse their desperate countrymen who were in such dire straits.

The train car, now completely crammed, waited seemingly endlessly to be attached to a transport. Trains traveling east to west usually carried soldiers, while those going in the opposite direction brought wounded from the front. After a few days, with a huge shudder of buffers, the car was connected to the tail end of a train heading toward Sverdlovsk. Passengers were overjoyed to be moving once again. It felt good to hear the stutter of wheels, feel the cold air whistle inside, and leave behind the memory of two years in the bedbug-ridden camp barracks.

Not one of the weary passengers in that overcrowded train car could possibly imagine what their trip had in store. The motion of the train was short lived. After a very brief time, the locomotive let out a long whistle and slowed, shuddering with brakes screeching, then stopped, and started again, this time in reverse. Finally it halted in the middle of an open field. The conductor explained that this train had to make way for an approaching military transport going west. This stopover enabled the passengers to disembark. They were able to stretch their cramped legs, wash their hands and faces in the snow, and relieve themselves in the open air. This time no soldiers stood guard over them. They were pleased to be able to move freely along the long chain of occupied cars. After a few hours, the piercing whistle sounded again and the train set off once more. During the day, travel in the packed car had become dreadful, but at night it was macabre.

The insects nesting in the planks revived and began attacking the sleeping passengers incessantly. In addition, the unfortunates taken into the train car were covered with huge lice and fleas, which quickly spread over every food surface. The sheer number of bugs hidden in the ragged clothes covering their emaciated skeletons was indescribable. The eggs they laid formed a thick layer in places closest to the skin. Impatient people waited for a longer stop, near a settlement, where they might be able to visit a bathhouse and rid themselves of at least some of the bugs.

The Soviet Union was famous for its so-called "Waszabojek" (de-lousing points). These bathhouses were made from round timber logs and had a roof usually covered in earth. In the middle of the room was a large fireplace loosely scattered with stones. Three of the walls had berths built in, one near the ground, another halfway up, and a third near the ceiling. A barrel of cold water and a few bundles of woven birch stood near the door.

A dozen or so people entered the bath together - men, women, and children. They stripped off all their clothes and left their lice-infested underwear on the highest berth. Water from the barrel was poured over the stove, whose large stones had previously been heated to a high temperature. The resulting steam rose to the ceiling and killed the bugs and their eggs. People occupied berths according to how much heat they could stand; the bottom for weaker souls, and the middle for those who could endure higher temperatures. Bathers beat their naked buttocks and backs with birch whisks to stimulate circulation. From time to time, they doused themselves with cold water to cool down and rinse off the ash that rose into the air whenever water was poured on the fire. This procedure gave them a few days respite before another insect attack.

Baths like these were built beside every village, settlement and smaller train station, and sometimes even in an open field. Train passengers could take advantage of them during longer stops. Unfortunately, the wilderness through which they traveled meant hundreds of kilometers between villages and stations, and the helpless travelers were forced to wait impatiently for a chance to bathe. One day, as their train stood on a siding beside a village, Aunt Jozefa, and a few other women, disembarked to use this wonderful Russian invention. How pleasant it was to scald themselves in the hot steam and massage themselves with birch wreaths! But their pleasure was brief; the locomotive's whistle announced the trains departure. The women jumped to their feet in panic. They snatched up their clothes and, completely naked, chased after the moving train. Aunt Jozefa dashed through the snow in her bare feet and managed to quickly wrap a pink towel around her waist. Her mother, Katarzyna, anxious about the train's sudden departure and worried that her daughter could be abandoned, stuck her head out of the car. Her eyes searched intently among the running women. Finally she recognized the galloping Jozefa and her pink towel. "Wrap your towel around your neck," she shouted, "You know how easy you catch a sore throat! Don't you worry about your rear end, no one will recognize you by it anyway!" At this time, Jozefa managed to grab onto one of the car doors and jumped inside. Some of the other women did not reach the train in time, and had to remain behind to wait for another train, and hope that they would eventually be reunited with their families. Thousands of people were left adrift, to wander this huge country in search of their loved ones, often leaving their bones behind in the frozen Siberian earth.

Christmas arrived approximately halfway through that journey. The celebration feast was meager. Instead of consecrated wafers, the travelers shared hard, dry bread and offered each other wishes with tears in their eyes: "That you return to our country as fast as possible," or "That you survive this terrible journey and not break down on the brink of freedom." The carols people sang brimmed with sadness, even though they no longer feared arrest, and felt free, despite still finding themselves in this land of terror and hardship. Nevertheless, all families lived in perpetual anxiety, not knowing how much longer they would have to suffer on the train, which sometimes moved forward and sometimes backward. The passengers were at the mercy of stationmasters, who were always looking for bribes from people, even though they had lost all their possessions and had nothing left to give to ruthless railway officials.

They didn't have the slightest idea when the train would set off again or in which direction it would go. The railroad workers attached the car to the first available transport in order to dispense with its constantly complaining passengers. At the larger stations passengers would beg the stationmaster to get them on their way as soon as possible so they could keep moving south, even if it meant a roundabout route. During the trip, when the train stood on the sidings, the deportees ran to the houses they saw from afar to exchange their remaining clothing for food. The few pieces of bread they brought back had to be shared with those who had nothing but their lice-ridden rags.

Such excursions always involved the risk that the transport might leave early. On one such occasion, Aunt Jozefa exited the awaiting train in order to search for food. She misjudged the time of departure, and was again left frantically running toward the train as it departed. Her family's car slowly pulled ahead of her, but Jozefa was able to scramble aboard one of the last cars. Her family had no idea whether she was aboard the train or stranded behind. After three torturous days, Jozefa was miraculously reunited with her family when the train pulled into a small town many kilometers away.

The situation in the train grew horrific, and as time went by, more and more passengers died of exhaustion and starvation. Their bodies had to be tossed out into the snow. Slowly covering hundreds of kilometers of roundabout road, the train neared the city of Chelyabinsk. From here, they would have to travel in a more westerly direction toward Ufa and then on to Kuybyshev or Saratov. It was expected that representatives of the Polish administration would be there to accept volunteers into the Polish Army. The journey grew increasingly difficult due to the constant arrival of an endless stream of emaciated people newly released from jails and labor camps. A terrible hunger spread through the train cars. Everyone shared the meager remains of dry, rock-hard bread. The journey had been endured for over two months with no end in sight. In Chelyabinsk, the travelers caught sight of the first Polish uniform. What happiness it was to see one of their soldiers after so many years!

Chelyabinsk was also where the Bajorski's received the first bread rations as a military family and learned that the army administration had moved to Kazakhstan and Uzbekistan. The direction of their journey changed. Now the train would have to cover thousands of kilometers across the deserts of the Soviet Union's poorest republics. The first large city they entered was Orenburg, where the Bajorski's reported to a Polish information office and registered as a military family. Mother and children received bread ration cards that would be shared with Aunt Jozefa, Grandmother and Grandfather. The rations were small, but would have to be enough to sustain them. Older people, and those who did not belong to military families, received no food assistance. From Orenburg, the train was directed to Tashkent, which lay beyond the borders of Kazakhstan.

Finally, after a long trip of almost one thousand miles, the train stopped at a station in Tashkent, the temporary end of the journey. The wagon sat detached from the train. The family was at a loss as to what to do next. Ice that had formed on the roof and gathered in thick layers inside on the walls. Bunks started to dissolve. After three months of frost and snow, the heat they longed for began to penetrate their clothes and warm exhausted bodies. The family could once again start exchanging winter clothes for food, which was always scarce.

Grandmother Katarzyna was an activist. She trudged into town to gather information about their situation. She returned depressed, bringing the dispiriting news that this was where their road ended and that the city was overrun with exiles and army volunteers. Soviet authorities were almost forcibly transporting people to nearby kolkhozes (collective farms) to pick cotton without pay. In the kolkhozes the unpaid laborers had to live in dirty kibitkas (mud-huts) and cowsheds. A typhus epidemic was raging and people were dying by the hundreds, leaving their orphaned children at the mercy of hostile Uzbeks.

It became necessary, at whatever cost, to find a place in the city to live, where the family would have access to both the Polish authorities and medical care at the local military hospital. Mother Emilia and

Grandmother went to town to look for help. God took pity on them. A passing soldier, a former sergeant in the Polish Army who had, before the war, served in the same regiment as Mrs. Bajorski's husband, recognized her on the street. They greeted each other joyously; a surprise encounter with someone from the old days was always sweet. This soldier's fate had been equally tragic. After the disaster of September, 1939, he had not managed to cross the border into Hungary. He was captured by Ukrainian bandits and handed over to the NKVD (Soviet Military Police). Deported, he was in a prisoner-of-war camp until the amnesty, when he became one of the first military men to volunteer in the new Polish Army. After listening to the woeful tale of the Bajorski family, he promised to help them find jobs.

On the following day, the soldier informed the Bajorskis that there was work for them at the army laundry in the nearby town of Chirchik. He even managed to find them transportation in a two-wheeled wagon, pulled by a slow mule. Grandmother once again demonstrated the ingenuity of a woman undaunted by tough circumstances. She chose a few pieces of clothing no longer needed in the warm climate and went directly to the nearest Uzbek village to look for a place to live. While going from kibitka to kibitka (mud-hut) trying to sell her clothes, she met a Russian widower who owned two clay houses. He agreed to rent one to her. Satisfied with this turn of events, Grandmother Katarzyna returned for her family and led them to their new home. It was a modest house, with clay walls and floors and a straw roof, but it was a place where they could lay their travel-weary bodies at night.

Mother Bajorski and Aunt Jozefa began working at the laundry. It was a disgusting job. After washing and steaming uniforms and linens with a hot iron, they used a knife to scrape away the layers of dead lice and eggs that had baked into the clothing's recesses and seams. The women spent the entire day toiling so they could earn a food ration to share with their elderly parents. Days and weeks passed in the desert climate, with its constant lack of water, cold nights and hot sunny days.

One day Mama Bajorski could not get out of bed. She tossed on the blanket-covered floor with a high fever, unable to recognize any of her family. "Who's the stray?" she shouted, pointing at her daughter Teresa. Aunt Jozefa walked into town, found an army doctor, and asked him to help her sick sister. He refused to drive out to the bedside of an infectious woman. He declared she had typhus and there ended his medical diagnosis. Brave Aunt Jozefa did not falter. She kept searching. Finally she met a doctor willing to visit the hovel where her sister lay. This army physician – a Captain Kocun, whose name they remember to this day, turned out to be a doctor truly worthy of the title.

Captain Kocun gave Mama Bajorski a thorough examination and advised that she be taken immediately to a hospital. He arranged for soldiers to come by with a stretcher and transport the sick woman by wagon to Tashkent. Teresa was terribly distraught, holding on to the moving vehicle, and refusing to be separated from her sick mother. Grandmother forcibly dragged the despairing child away from the departing wagon.

A time of terrible hunger and poverty followed. Aunt Jozefa's ration was not enough to feed two children and three adults. They traded the last of their clothing for food so they might survive until they could leave that godforsaken place. Three weeks later Emilia's devastating sickness reached its crisis point, but the steel-willed woman continued to struggle. Her concern for the small children, who had been left under her parents' care, anchored her to life. Emilia returned home weakened by illness, completely unable to work, but alive and full of hope. The children had become emaciated, until all that remained of them was skin and bones. Their lives had to be saved at any cost. Though the decision was difficult, under the circumstances, an orphanage was the only solution.

The unhappiness of mother and children at the moment of parting was indescribable. Teresa was six years old and already understood the tragedy of the situation. She found herself among strangers and sick, frail children who lay on blankets on the floor. There were no longer any loving arms to cuddle the delicate, cosseted child. The only familiar person was her ten-year old brother, Edek. Teresa found it hard to adjust to the rigors of the orphanage school. No one spoke a word of comfort. All the children had to dress themselves, put away their own bedding, wash, and sit down to a modest meal.

Then the children were given lessons, with sand instead of notebooks on which to make their first scribbling attempts at the alphabet. Studies were followed by a short period of rest, a freedom only a child can fully appreciate. Then came supper, after which they had to wash their own soup mugs, and once they had said their prayers, in thanks for the gifts they had received, it was time to prepare for bed. They slept in a windrow on a clay floor scattered with blankets, with another blanket to cover every two children. The children were malnourished and suffered from dysentery. Mortality rates were very high.

One night, Teresa turned onto her side and put her arm around the girl who was sleeping beside her. The girl was cold and did not budge. Teresa lay beside her until morning, too frightened to move. The girl never awakened. Her blue corpse was taken away in the morning and buried in a local cemetery. For a long time afterwards Teresa could not sleep. Her only contentment lay in her aunt's visits. Sometimes Jozefa would secretly hand Teresa a delicious homemade treat through the wire fence, or maybe a sweet that she had begged from a soldier.

In the summer of 1942, the Polish outpost in Chirchik announced that they would begin registering military families for departure to Iran. In order to leave, all adults were required to prove that they were related to a Polish soldier serving in the West or to someone who had newly volunteered in the USSR. They also had to be healthy enough to report to the registration point in person. The old and the sick would remain behind until the army personnel and their families had left. Only then would it be their turn. This was very depressing and terrible news for Emilia and her sister, Jozefa. They would have to leave their aged parents behind in the Soviet Union to fend for themselves. There was no other option.

Unfortunately, during the registration period, Mother Bajorski once more fell seriously ill with dysentery. She had severe stomach pains and could not get out of bed. Aunt Jozefa went to register alone. The department head read out the names of the eligible in alphabetical order, and when he came to "Emilia Bajorski" Aunt Jozefa cried out, "Here I am," and raised her hand. By the time the surnames beginning with the letter "M" were called, Aunt Jozefa had managed to find a new place to stand, somewhat removed from the first. She took her scarf off her head and when she heard her name, "Jozefa Maselek," she again shouted, "Present!" Thanks to her ingenuity, their registrations were completed without difficulty. The ship was set to sail at the end of September. It would be the last to leave the unfriendly shores of the USSR.

The Soviet authorities were reluctant to allow their free labor force out of the country, and went to great lengths to limit the number of ships crossing the Caspian Sea to Iran. Any latecomers risked being left behind on the shore without a place to live or means of survival. The first train from Chirchik with its load of soldiers and civilians would set off in a few days for a long journey through the deserts of Turkmenistan. The port of Krasnovodsk lay on the Caspian Sea, 1000 miles to the west.

Once again the army doctor came to Mrs. Bajorski's aid. He sent several soldiers with a stretcher to the kibitka at dawn. They carried the sick woman to the already waiting train and slipped her into a car unobserved. Aunt Jozefa had no problem boarding the same car, saying she was there to take care of her seriously ill sister. The good-byes between the children and their grandparents were pained and tearful; only the assurance that the separation was temporary calmed the children a little. The sad, old grandparents stood at the station and watched Edek and Teresa board the orphanage train car, knowing that they were seeing their beloved grandchildren for the last time.

Filling the wagons with the waiting crowds took a long time. The famous Polish bureaucracy once again lived up to its reputation for being inept. Finally, they somehow managed to cope with all the provisions, soldiers and civilians. The transport shuddered, let out a long whistle, and started out on the last stage of the journey toward freedom. This voyage was very different from any of those preceding it. Instead of snow or biting cold, the train cars grew impossibly hot. The open doors provided no relief. They only let in more blazing, sun-baked air. Outside, as far as the eye could see, stretched the unpopulated steppes, at first mountainous and then level, covered in sand and rock. No buildings or living souls were seen. The stops in towns along the way grew longer and longer due to the large number of new passengers. The lack of water began to make itself felt. Water was not available anywhere except at the larger stations, and there it was distributed in only small portions.

The thirsty travelers prayed to God to send a little rain to these parched regions. Somehow Heaven didn't sense their thirst and ignored their pleas. Hunger can be withstood for some time, but a lack of water is unendurable. Their desiccated lips cracked into bloody wounds, and their tongues moved sluggishly in their mouths. Some tried sucking on small rocks to stimulate saliva, but this was only a momentary relief.

The train drove through Samarkand and finally arrived in Ashkhabad, a slightly larger town, where the families stepped into narrow streets teeming with locals. They traded the last of the warm clothing for food and water at the bazaar. Oh, how delicious it was to drink cold, sour milk and enjoy a delicacy bought at a market stall!

At night they fell asleep listening to the voices from the minarets calling out Islam's evening prayers. For whatever reason, this was a particularly long stop. The authorities were increasingly reluctant to let trains full of Poles leave their Soviet paradise. They ignored the agreement they had signed with the Polish government and made every step of the journey West, which had now lasted a month, as onerous as possible. Mother Emilia continued to have difficulty seeing her children. She could only visit them from time to time in the orphanage car, which was part of the same train. The orphanage administrators did not want to let the mothers visit their children for fear they would panic when seeing how undernourished they were, despite the rations handed out by the army. As is usually the case in these situations, the food melted away among the orphanage staff before it reached the mouths of the children. No authority figure would listen to any complaints; the administration presented an admirably united front.

Emilia tried to take her children into her train car but this was not allowed, for obvious reasons. The staff did not want to be deprived of caring for such a steady supply of food. Emilia was suffering greatly, both mentally and physically. She understood about the sickness that raged in the orphanage and the high death rates among the youngest. Finally the horrible voyage ended. The train stopped in Krasnovodsk and the passengers disembarked into the open desert adjoining the Caspian Sea. There was no pretty seashore but rather a cesspool of crude oil. Legs sank into sand mixed with sticky, black oily grease. They would have to live and sleep on this bare sand while waiting for a ship on which they could depart for the Iranian port of Pahlavi.

The orphanage was housed in tents erected by soldiers on the shores of the Caspian Sea. The army had its own separate quarters, also on the water's edge, while civilians had the entire desert of Turkmenistan at their disposal. Everyone could occupy as large a stretch of sand (hot during the day, incredibly cold at night) as they wished. To get food they had to make way along a stretch of road that seemed longer and more impossible to traverse each day. There was absolutely nothing to drink; water was an unobtainable luxury. Emilia Bajorski begged the soldiers for a drop of water and sometimes one of them would give her a sip from his canteen. Finally she could bear the thirst no longer and traded her last dress at the bazaar for a bottle of wine, which she immediately drank. Aunt Jozefa searched for Emilia at the market and finally grew so uneasy that she began to ask her friends and neighbors if, by any chance, they had seen her sister. One of the women told her that she had seen a woman lying out in the desert, unmoving and probably dead.

A desperate Aunt Jozefa ran in the indicated direction and found her sister's loudly snoring "corpse." She found it difficult to arouse the physically exhausted woman, who had fallen asleep after consuming an entire bottle of wine. The wine had done nothing to enliven her; she could barely move her legs and the alcohol had left her with a massive headache. The ship was scheduled to leave the following day, and there were miles to walk to reach the port. Emilia was doubtful about her ability to cope. She grew weaker by the moment. To lighten her burden, she discarded most of her worldly goods, lastly stabbing a pair of sewing scissors, given to her by her husband, into the sand. She turned and walked a little distance away, but then, troubled by having discarded a memento of her husband, returned and rescued the cherished scissors.

In the port of Krasnovodsk, an energetic and enthusiastic line of people climbed the gangplank suspended from the ship to the quay, unrecognizable as the exhausted and emaciated crowd of just moments ago. The thought that they were about to leave had given them a new burst of energy. The deportees were ordered to discard all of their belongings, except food. In order to leave, they were required to hand over all of their Russian money to the Soviet authorities. They were not even allowed to retain the few rubles they had earned by the sweat of their brows. Finally, after the Soviet's had checked everyone's papers, the boarding was completed. The ship, overloaded by the mass of passengers, lay dangerously low in the water. With a siren's howl and the monotonous whirring of motors, they pushed off from shore and were on their way.

The ship, a large old freighter accustomed to coursing the Caspian

Sea, was unprepared to carry even a small number of passengers. It had no freshwater tank and only one filthy toilet. Those who suffered from dysentery immediately formed a long line. Once they had taken care of their needs they immediately went back to the end of the line so they would be ready for the next attack. Whoever was too far away from the bathroom would have to access the side of the deck. A compassionate fellow passenger would hold them in place. Extreme suffering was caused by the unendurable thirst. People lay on the open deck dreaming of a drop of liquid, which was completely unobtainable.

Night approached, and all the orphanage children lay out on the deck unsupervised. Aunt Jozefa, worried about her small niece, found the director of the orphanage and called her attention to the fact that a large group of young children was now on a ship without guardrails. When large waves hit, the ship lurched dangerously to one side and a sleeping child could easily roll down into the sea. She was told angrily, "If you don't have anything better to do, then look out for them yourself. I don't have the strength." Aunt spent the entire night taking turns with the other women protecting the dozing children.

After thirty-six hours of travel, the outlines of the port of Pahlavi, Iran came into view. The ship's siren sounded once more, announcing the end of a voyage across a sea that divided two worlds: a world of misery, hunger and degradation, and a land of general prosperity, where it was possible to see smiles on its citizens' faces. Disembarkation took place quickly; everyone was anxious to leave the ship as fast as possible. It was the last reminder of Soviet power.

Moments later the refugees were greeted by representatives of the British army and the municipal government. Everything proceeded at a whirlwind British pace. A sanitary team inspected each head for lice and sent the infected to be shaved. All of the new arrivals were disinfected and bathed to get rid of the layers of dirt they had acquired during their years in Russia. They exited the baths refreshed and, thanks to the Red Cross, wearing new, ill fitting, but lice-free clothes. The old rags were incinerated. Only then were people taken to the tent camp where they were to stay temporarily.

Refugees ate, the food that the army kitchens prepared for them with hearty appetites. They ate quickly, without stopping, ignoring the warning to be cautious at first about overburdening their starved stomachs. Few heeded this wise advice. With the small handouts of money received they bought fruit, sour milk and boiled eggs at the bazaar. They would do anything to prove to themselves that this was the end of hunger and that they no longer had to fight for a piece of dry bread. All of this gorging had a very dramatic effect. Many people became sick, mostly with dysentery. Stomachs, unused to so much food, rebelled. The stay in Pahlavi was an unforgettable and uplifting time. The Bajorski family could not believe their good fortune in finally regaining their freedom. The only sadness lay in the absence of Grandmother and Grandfather, left behind in Uzbekistan, and the continued separation from the children, who were still in the orphanage.

After a few weeks Emilia learned that the orphanage children had been loaded into trucks and taken with an army convoy to Teheran. The drive through the desert in the terrible heat was grinding. The convoy traveled at breakneck speeds over mountain roads. The Iranians drove like maniacs. Trucks leaped over potholes and rocks, and took sharp turns at dizzying speeds. The terrified children clutched each other and crouched on the floor as the truck rushed over steep passes in the Elburz Mountains. The dust stirred up by the tires settled on the windows of the vehicles that followed, completely blinding the drivers. This caused one driver to overshoot an approaching turn. His truck lurched violently and tumbled into a deep ravine, somersaulted in the air, and bounced several times off the side of a cliff, finally coming to rest at the bottom of a canyon. Moments later a huge pillar of fire and smoke completely obscured the view. There was no hope of anyone surviving the horrible accident. Tears of the children, mixed with soot, bid farewell to those poor souls whom fate had not spared and who had died on the brink of freedom.

In Teheran, the orphanage was set up in an abandoned army camp that was near an airport. The tents were taken over by scouts and the children with their caretakers. Preparations were made for a longer stay. The children began going to school, where lessons took place under the rays of the burning sun. Every child was required to bring two bricks on which to sit and patiently absorb the knowledge dispensed by the teachers. The surroundings made it difficult for them to concentrate; it was much more pleasant to watch the planes take off and to fantasize about what fruit to eat next.

More and more children were moved to the sickbay. The camp was stricken by trachoma, a serious eye sickness, as well as by dysentery caused by fatty food. Anemia was a holdover from the hunger suffered in the Soviet paradise. Teresa will never forget the pain of having medicine dropped in her eyes. She yelled frightfully and tore herself out of the hands of the clinic nurse. Teresa kept waiting hopefully for her mother and Aunt Jozefa to come and carry her away with them. When her brother Edek fell ill with dysentery and lay in hospital, Teresa felt lonely and abandoned. At night she cried at being separated from her beloved mother and aunt. When Edek recovered, he began to visit Teresa, cheering her up with pieces of fruit he had picked or sweets he had begged from the American soldiers stationed nearby.

Finally Emilia was able to locate the orphanage in which her children were quartered. She had no shoes and she was unable to traverse the burning sands. Fortunately, a friend offered to go to the orphanage in the hope of having Edek and Teresa released. Edek was successfully rescued and taken to join his family. Due to the trachoma, Teresa was not allowed to leave. She watched in despair as her brother walked away. The orphanage custodian was unable to restrain Teresa. She tore herself from the nurse's arms, scrambled through a hole in the fence, and raced after her brother. No one attempted to follow her, and the family was reunited once again. Now they prepared to face the future.

Emilia had managed to rescue her children from the orphanage just in time. Edek had already been listed to go to New Zealand, while Teresa, being ill, was awaiting her turn to be deported to Mexico. The orphanage authorities were not concerned about blood ties and routinely separated brothers and sisters to facilitate their adoption in other countries. The family remained in Teheran long enough to celebrate Christmas, 1942. This was a great occasion, their first holidays in three years as free people, and no longer hungry or afraid of being arrested for observing religious rites, as they had been in the USSR. Gathered in a large hall, the deportees listened to Wladyslaw Raczkiewicz, a government representative, and General Wladyslaw Sikorski, as they greeted and congratulated them on having successfully escaped from the Soviet Union. To mark the occasion each received a souvenir in the form of a small identity book.

After a few months stay in Teheran, the entire group was once again taken by truck through the desert to Ahvaz, near the Persian Gulf, where they were temporarily lodged in huge, abandoned horse barns. Lessons began again and children waited as usual for the next stage of their journey into the unknown. The temperatures were unbearable; by midday there was no thought of going outside. Once again they hoped for change and a chance to leave behind the sands and the pitiless burning sun.

Time dragged intolerably. It was too hot during the day to play outside on the flaming sand, and the moment the sun went down horrifying scorpions and spiders appeared. The children were afraid to step out of the tent.

Finally the moment came for them to leave Ahvaz for Abadan, a port on the Persian Gulf, from which they would sail to India and then on to Africa. The Bajorski family did not have to wait long for transport. A week later they boarded a ship that set sail east along the Persian Gulf to the Gulf of Oman. It was not guaranteed that they would reach India without interruption. The ship stopped by the gulf delta and boats took them ashore. Tents had been prepared for them and they were required to wait for the arrival of the rest of the convoy bound for India, under the protection of the English Navy.

This was quite a long wait. The dozens of ships that gathered in the delta waiting for their protective warships made an impressive sight. Because German and Japanese submarines lurked in the Indian Ocean, no ship could hope to make the journey independently. Finally, one night the entire temporary camp was taken by boat to the waiting ships and they set sail in complete silence. Passengers were ordered not to speak, light cigarettes, or throw anything into the water. The ships moved stealthily, cutting through the waves powered by the monotonous revolutions of its huge motors. The most dangerous stretch lay between the gulf and the open ocean, since the submarines most often lurked at the mouth of the gulf in search of victims.

At dawn, the desert shores of Iran had disappeared from the horizon and ships were in the open Arabian Sea. Unused to the rocking of the boat, passengers became seasick and vomited over every side. The journey to India was incredibly tiring. Finally, after ten days, passengers glimpsed the outlines of land. Their ship left the convoy and touched land in Pakistan, in the port of Karachi. Once again the family was put ashore in a different country and taken to tents set up at the ocean's edge. Everything took place under the protective eye of the English army. The kitchen was the same and so was most of the food. Only the fruit was different – fragrant, fresh tasting, and delicious after having ripened under a warm, life-giving sun.

Lessons started up anew in the temporarily disrupted school, not in a room, but in the fresh air under a roof covered with huge palm leaves. The lectures seemed boring to the students. Children were no longer accustomed to school discipline, only to constant change and travel. Teachers demanded obedience and attention, and often harshly punished those who failed to comply. There were few parents to reprimand them. The majority of the children were orphans whose parents had died in the depths of the taiga. The pencil did not want to obey six year old Teresa's fingers, and she pressed it against the page of notebook in vain. What came out were scribbles, not the letters of the alphabet being dictated.

Teresa did not care about the exploits of Polish kings. She had left them far behind in a country she no longer remembered. The teacher's voice would bring the young girl back. "Don't fidget, Teresa! Pay attention or you'll be punished." Such threats worked for a short time, but Teresa was evidently too immature for lessons. Teresa had developed very slowly and was still in the thrall of childish games. Her thoughts were always far away. She waited for her aunt and the sweets she would bring, and wondered where Grandmother and Grandfather were. She wanted to go to Mother and fall asleep for a little while, nestled in her arms. Teresa was very lonely at this school with its tedious lessons.

At night, jackals and hyenas circled the camp's wire fence, their long drawn-out howls sometimes preventing sleep. Younger children gathered shells on the beach with which to play, while older children made necklaces to decorate their thin necks. In April, 1943, the families were informed that diplomatic relations between the Soviet Union and the Polish government had been severed. The news saddened mother Emilia and Aunt Jozefa because they were concerned about the lives of their parents in Uzbekistan. The Bajorski family stayed in the camp in Karachi for three months. It was not long before they tired of the fatty lamb meat, which was constantly served to them, and the piping melodies always being played by the Indian orchestra.

Now they waited impatiently for their coming departure for Africa. From the shore, they could already see the ships gathered in wait to join a new convoy that would take them to a new home. Ships continued to arrive. The silhouettes of massive vessels stretched in a row as far as the eye could see. Finally at the end of the summer, passengers boarded a freighter and spent several weeks crossing the Indian Ocean. The ship traveled in a zigzag course in order to confuse any lurking enemy submarines. The passengers were under a state of alert the entire time and prepared to abandon ship if torpedoed. Finally one day the captain announced that the ship was approaching Africa. People flocked onto the deck to catch the first glimpse of this new land where they would linger for years waiting to return home.

Meanwhile in Uzbekistan (the moment diplomatic ties between Poland and Russia were severed) Grandmother Katarzyna and Grandfather Wojciech were left completely without means of survival. The volunteer Polish army under General Anders withdrew from Soviet territory to Iran to join the English Army. The Russians were indifferent to the fate of the deportees, now free but unprotected. The grandparents had to find work or die of hunger. They left their lodgings in Chirchik and embarked by train to Ashkhabad. There after a period of extreme difficulty, Grandmother found a job feeding pigs on an Uzbek kolkhoz (collective farm).

Grandfather was no longer able to work. His health worsened daily, and he lay in helpless agony on the hovel's clay floor. Soon he closed his eyes forever. With an Uzbek's help, grandmother dug a shallow grave and buried her husband, wrapped in an old sheet, in the earth of the steppe not far from the kolkhoz. His body did not remain in the dry earth for long. The jackals dug up the rock-covered grave at night and ate his emaciated body. Grandfather's bones were scattered across the empty steppes. Grandmother, an exceptionally brave woman, was left alone in an unfamiliar land among strangers. She subsisted on the remains of the scraps fed to the pigs and survived until the Poles were released from the Soviet Union in 1946. Katarzyna eventually returned to her own farm in Poland and cultivated it with the help of hired labor. She lived out the rest of her life in her homeland. In later years, Katarzyna was able to come to America to visit her family. She happily reunited with her daughters and grandchildren again after having said goodbye to them so long ago in Uzbekistan.

# The Home Army's 1st "Jurand" Brigade
(Czeslaw)

The year 1944 brought great changes to the Eastern Front. The success of the German invasion ended at the bloody battle of Stalingrad. New Siberian battalions struck swiftly along the entire German line and surrounded the German army of the Ukrainian front.

Stalin's cunning military trap snapped shut. A massive new army made up of Russians and Siberians was secretly trained on Siberian land. Equipped with food and arms shipped from America to the port of Murmansk, on the Barents Sea, it waited patiently for the right moment to attack. Stalin ordered Stalingrad to be defended to the last man. He had sacrificed his entire southern army while inflicting huge losses on the Germans, all part of his perfidious plan to exterminate as many Ukrainians as possible. The Germans had not expected to be attacked by such sheer numbers of well-fed fighters nourished by American rations. General Paulus' divisions, already exhausted by the difficult battles and the cold, were no match for a motorized Soviet army equipped with the latest weapons and American planes.

The Polish government in London ordered the organization of armed resistance in the occupied areas. The moment Russian divisions crossed into Poland, the Home Army had to be ready to take an active role in the struggle against the Germans and reclaim its former republican territories. All this was to take place with the help of the superbly equipped Polish Army led by General Anders, then fighting alongside our allies in the West. Our soldiers, covered in glory during battle abroad, waited impatiently to step foot back onto their native soil. Meanwhile in Poland, more and more new forest-units were being sent out into the field to train recruits in partisan fighting methods.

The time came once again to abandon my home, my family and my native city and set out for the Wilnian forests, which would shelter me until the end of the war. And so, one evening in early January, 1944, I prepared to walk out of my home and embark on a dangerous journey from which I had little chance of returning. My good-byes with my parents were short and painful. Their eyes, bright with tears, have remained in my memory as the last image of the moment of parting.

At the very last minute my worried mother poured some hot tea into my flask. I was leaving home in the winter, sick with a streptococcus infection and suffering from a high fever and a painfully inflamed sore throat. I had been given time off from work because of my illness and was supposed to be lying in bed until I recovered.

To avoid running into the many Lithuanian police and German military patrols, I walked quickly through the darkened city along the streets I knew best. The route I chose led through the Bernardine Park and along the banks of the Wilenka River that flowed at the base of Trzech Krzyzy Mountain to the neighborhood of Antokol. From there, I made my way along the bank of the Wilja toward our assigned meeting place. Moments later the order to "Halt!" issued from among the riverside bushes. I quickly gave the correct password, and soon we were all in one another's arms. Here were my colleagues from school, work, and clubs, the companions of my youth, dear faces of friends. There were quite a few of us: Witold Strzemieczny (code name "Bohunek"), Henryk Trojanowski ("Hena"), Mietek Fijalkowski ("Czarnota"), Witold Ermow ("Doniec"), Henryk Sitkowski ("Skrzetuski"), Edward Ruszecki ("Barabasz") and myself, Czeslaw Plawski, ("Bej").

After our brief hellos, silence once again fell on the riverbank, broken only by the murmur of the fast-flowing current. Soon the lean silhouette of Lieutenant Czeslaw Grabczewski (code name "Jurand") emerged from the darkness. His first words were "Greetings, men!" He introduced himself with a firm handshake and gave each one of us a piercing look, as if evaluating our ability to fight. This was the first time we had met him and we observed him with equal curiosity. Here was the man who would be responsible for us from now on, taking our fathers' place in times of need.

After a short silence, the lieutenant began to speak in a strong, pleasant voice. "Soldiers, I want you to know that I am not only your commander but also your friend. I will lead you into battle against the powerful German army, the Lithuanian police, and the Soviet partisans that hunt throughout this province. Ahead of us lies a difficult and dangerous fight for our country's freedom. We have no weapons; these we will have to capture from the enemy. We have no barracks; the forest will be our home. For the safety of your families, forget your names and use only the code name you have been given. If you are badly wounded or taken prisoner you will be killed. If any one of you has the slightest doubt about your strength and conviction, now is the time to step forward and go home."

Nobody moved. We had been waiting for this moment for years. Our commander continued: "You are the core of what will become the "Jurand" forest battalion. Our mission is to fight and defeat our enemies. Our area of operations is currently in their hands, and at the very beginning we will have to be careful not to encounter any of the enemy units patrolling around Wilno." His short speech pleased us. "Jurand's" very figure radiated courage and inspired confidence. Mietek and I, remembering our previous leader's speech, were greatly relieved.

"Jurand" finished by telling us that if we should unexpectedly meet the enemy we were to wait for his order before shooting. Then we set off in a northwest direction toward the town of Koniuchy, where we would join Lieutenant Wilhelm Tietmajer ("Wilczur") and his platoon. That entire night we foundered up to our knees in snow through fields and forests, avoiding roads and settlements. Sweat poured into our eyes and our shirts glued themselves to our bodies, wet with perspiration despite the cold. Every once in a while we stopped for a fifteen-minute rest. I reached for the tea in the flask at my belt and gulped the icy liquid down greedily, heedless of the pain in my throat. As the march went on, my tea supply was depleted. While I walked, I scooped up and swallowed fistfuls of snow to cool my heated body and chase away the fatigue that increasingly threatened to overwhelm me.

We had to reach our hiding place before dawn. Finally we stopped in front of a hut at the edge of a small village. No one gave even a passing thought to food. We wanted sleep, only sleep! We collapsed on the straw-covered floor and were unconscious in minutes. Twelve hours of forced march through the wilderness had exhausted the strength of even our young bodies. Our commander's voice roused us from our deep slumber: "Up! Get ready to march! We move in an hour!" Tentatively, I tried to swallow. To my surprise my throat was no longer sore. The snow and the icy tea must have shrunken my swollen tonsils.

That day, walking through a large forest, we encountered the Home Army brigade "Blyskawica," which had been operating in the area for some time. Their weapons and knowledge of the forest impressed us. During the march we imitated their way of moving through the terrain. After we had joined "Wilczur's" unit, we spent the first weeks of our existence as a unit marching endlessly at night. We also learned how to fight and how to use our weapons.

On January 21, 1944, in the village of Bujwidze, our forest unit officially became the Home Army's 1st "Jurand" Brigade. We waited impatiently for some kind of military action. We had grown tired of exercises and theories: We had not left home for theory. Finally, during a noon roll call, our commander ordered, "Every third man, step out!" I stepped out. Again, "Every third man, step out!" I stepped forward once more, and then again. The lucky chosen – enough for two teams, because that was all the weapons we had – were being sent out to destroy a gang of seventy communists who had been stealing cattle and other property from local villagers.

The gangs of Soviet partisans roaming the area consisted of criminals released from jails and death-row convicts from Siberian prison camps. Their task was to suppress Polish resistance and cut German transport lines to the Eastern Front. For this, when the war was over, they would regain their freedom and civil rights under a general amnesty. They were well equipped with weapons dropped from Soviet planes, and hid in underground shelters in the swampy, forested areas north of Wilno beside Lake Narocz. They moved at night, terrorizing villages and carrying out sneak attacks on the Home Army. The local Home Army network had brought us word that one such gang had forcibly occupied someone's house and was now hiding nearby among the vast forests near the village of Majeranka.

Our two teams, led by "Wilczur," marched through the night to join the "Blyskawica" Brigade, which would also take part in the attack. After a sleepless night, we set off on March 1, 1944 with a guide who was familiar with the area. The attack, which was to start at a set hour, was to come from four sides at once, to make it impossible for the gang to escape to the forest surrounding the farm.

Our team blundered through the deep snow, drawing close to its goal. We were about a kilometer away when we heard shots coming from direction of the positions occupied by the 5th "Lupaszki" Brigade, which was also participating in the ambush. Alarmed that the battle had already begun, we ran quickly through the young pines to the foot of a small hill freshly covered in snow. Sweaty and breathless, we stopped to wait for some kind of command from Lieutenant "Wilczur." At that very moment a large group of retreating Soviet partisans armed with machine guns appeared at the top of the hill. Both sides froze, astounded at this unexpected encounter. No more than thirty meters lay between us.

After a short pause the flabbergasted "Wilczur" waved his hand and shouted, "*Wanka dawaj siuda*" *("Wanka, come here").* The Soviets, shocked and obviously only just awakened, could not stand the tension and despite their much greater firepower turned right around and ran back toward the farm. For a moment our lives had hung in the balance because, at such close range, we would not have had the slightest chance against their machine guns. All we had for weapons were antiquated Russian revolvers, some fowling pieces and a few army rifles. Without thinking, we ran to the top of the hill and started shooting at our retreating enemy. The exchange of gunfire shook awake the sleeping neighborhood, which was situated just a stone's throw away.

Those bandits we killed or wounded were shot mainly in the head or the upper thighs since we just did not have the time to set our gun sights for the right distance. Maybe it is not quite appropriate to shoot the enemy in the back, but it did not occur to us to yell for them to turn around and face us. I was so caught up in the fight that I didn't notice a Soviet bandit taking aim straight at me. Kneeling on top of the snow-covered hill, I made an excellent target. Suddenly I heard "Hena" shout – "Bej, get down!" – which saved my life. Machine gun bullets buzzed over my head like a swarm of bees. Several Soviet partisans turned back and tried to break through our lines to reach the forest. They failed. Wounded by our bullets, they blew themselves up with a grenade while attempting to throw in our direction.

Most of the gang managed to escape and disappear into the forest along with their leader, "Brodacz." Of those who remained on the field of battle, twelve were dead and a few wounded. The "Lupaszki" unit took the wounded into custody. Their fate was preordained; they would be tried and shot. In those days the Home Army did not take prisoners, considering them a superfluous burden. Our casualties were minimal.

Only one soldier, "Czolg," was seriously wounded with a bullet just below the stomach. It had been a bloody christening for our newly formed 1st Brigade. We were proud of our victory and happy with our few casualties and the weapons we obtained. When we gathered together at evening prayers, we thanked Our Lady of Ostrobrama for her protection.

Life in the Home Army became reasonably comfortable. Our ranks increased with volunteers from nearby villages as well as refugees from the city who were facing arrest or forced labor in Germany. The brigade grew quickly. It soon became much too large for provisioning or safety. In its own way it also became a kind of old folk's home for those who had exhausted the possibilities in their own organization. We disliked this crew of idlers who could no longer keep up with us younger soldiers. Instead they took up space in our greatly expanding column of transport and supply wagons. When we brought this to "Jurand's" attention he said it could not be helped; they were all higher ranking and we would just have to put up with them. The main task of all the brigades was to gather and train soldiers in preparation for open battle with the enemy. For the moment, we would have to concern ourselves with collecting food and weapons for future use.

On March 20th I received a great surprise. That morning my brother, Tadek, walked into the house where I had spent the night. We fell into each other's arms, overjoyed at this unexpected meeting. I asked why he had left his printing job, and he gave me a quick summary of what had been happening in Wilno.

For a few months after I had joined "Jurand" the nerve-wracking work at the printing house had continued as before. Then, one day at the beginning of March, word came that one of the editors of the

*Independence,* code name "Baryk," had been arrested. He had the singularly bad piece of luck to be at a restaurant on Arsenalska Street when the Gestapo came charging in, searching for illegal gold traders. During the document check the Germans found his notes for the newspaper as well as fake personal papers with Tadek's photograph. That evening, my brother received a warning from a member of the underground organization who urged him to immediately go into hiding.

"That night," Tadek recalled, "We got a visit from the Gestapo. They raided the house and carried out a thorough search. They scrutinized every nook and cranny, from attic to basement, but did not find what they were looking for. Tadek was already at our aunt's place, locked inside her grocery store. Finally, they showed our mother his picture and asked where he was. Mama had sufficient presence of mind to say that he was working in Germany, and showed them one of his letters from the factory in Kassel. They looked at the stamp, took a photograph of him from the sideboard, and wordlessly left the house. The city was now too hot for him; he had to get out as soon as possible. He heard through the underground network that a patrol from the 1st Brigade was in Wilno and would soon be heading out into the countryside with new volunteers. He got in touch with them immediately. On meeting the leader, he was overjoyed to see that it was none other than a dear friend of mine, Henryk Trojanowski ("Hena"). The patrol marched throughout the night without incident and reached camp at dawn. My brother immediately set off to find me, which he did. We had no end of stories to tell one another. Tadek wanted to know all about life in the brigade, and I was curious about the fate of my friends and acquaintances in Wilno.

At the evening roll call the commander greeted the newly arrived "recruits." Tadek was assigned to the 2nd Platoon and given the code name "Rakoczy." Sergeant "Puljan," formerly (Franciszek Stankiewicz), was a man with the uninteresting personality and attitudes typical of a former career soldier in the Polish Army. He and I had recently experienced a slight disagreement. The sergeant had been given the task of conducting military drills in the camp. During one such simulated attack he ordered us to topple to the ground just as I found myself on the edge of a muddy puddle. Being a seasoned soldier, I managed to avoid the mud and land to the side on the grass. The sergeant, newly arrived in the unit, was very annoyed by this maneuver. He ordered me to get up and take a fall into the mud. Instead, I walked up to him and whispered quietly that I would gladly do it if he took the fall also. I also told him I had seen bigger snobs than him in my life and did not obey stupid commands. "Puljan" reported me to the commander, who in turn warned him not to antagonize the storm platoon, which formed the core of the brigade. From then on the sergeant became much friendlier with the boys, the commander's "pupils."

That night we marched out during a blizzard, buffeted by strong winds that blinded our eyes with snow. The storm lasted the entire night. We waded through the snow, pulling our tired legs out of the deep drifts with difficulty. My brother, unused to such marches, had come to the unit dressed in a short jacket, without a sweater or warm underwear. By the time we reached the town of Sorok, Tadek was freezing. When I noticed this I went to the supply wagons and brought him a Soviet flight suit, an aviator's cap, and a Soviet gun with four bullets in the chamber. I was on friendly terms with the leaders of the transport and supply columns, and had no difficulty in getting the gear. The warm clothes raised my brother's spirits. Dressed in this manner he looked like a Soviet foundling adopted by the Polish legions out of compassion.

We stopped in a village a few kilometers from Starych Swiecian, where General Plechavicius' Lithuanian volunteer battalions were stationed. The Home Army's network brought word that a few more Lithuanian army battalions were heading in our direction from Wilno. Not wanting to be ambushed, "Jurand" immediately gave the order to march toward the Rudnicki Forest. He then handed leadership of the brigade over to "Wilczur" and set out for Wilno, where he was to meet with the Home Army command and receive his orders. Our unit was nearly at the edge of the forest, when we heard shots coming from the direction of the village of Skorbuciany. The mounted reconnaissance that had gone on ahead had found Soviet partisans hiding in a hut in a nearby part of the woods. A short battle ensued, during which Corporal "Chrabaszcz" (Jerzy Turski) was shot and killed. The Soviets escaped into the forest. At the last moment "Sep" (Jan Podworski) managed to hit one of them. "Chrabaszcz" was buried in the village cemetery in Skorbuciany, having given his life for his country's freedom.

A few days later we learned from the local network that a large supply of weapons and ammunition was being stored in a train bunker in the village of Rykonty. "Jurand's" deputy, evidently wanting to impress his commander, sent my storm platoon to attack the fortified bunker without prior preparation or sufficient weapons. Newly enlisted soldier "Rakoczy" was also to take part in the action. Thinking that there was no need for two brothers to go out on the same dangerous mission, I asked that he be exempted from the action. My request was granted.

On April 1, 1944, during a bright, moonlit night, our platoon walked into the village of Rykonty in search of our target. The barking of the dogs rent the crisp night, waking the whole neighborhood. The platoon leader, Sergeant "Czarny," knocked on the window of a small house and asked for the location of the bunker. The frightened villager pointed toward a building just fifty meters away. There was no time to think things over; we just bounded as quickly as we could across the snow-covered fields in the indicated direction. We did not get far. Machine gun fire pinned us to the ground, making us even more visible against the snow's white background. The Lithuanians were shooting us like fish in a barrel. The barking dogs and the knock on the window had warned them of our attack. The entire action had been carried out without a plan or prior scouting of the terrain – it was inexcusably stupid. Our platoon did not even have an RKM machine gun.

After firing off a few shots, I felt a sharp twinge near my left elbow. I knew I had been shot but didn't feel any pain. The spot under my uniform grew warm and wet. Grenades exploded and bullets rained down all around me. Mud mixed with snow spattered our faces. There was no sense in lying there, waiting for an undignified death. We were ordered to retreat. We bolted from the exposed field to the shelter of the nearby buildings and from there into the forest. Three of us were wounded, none seriously. Moments later one more soldier came running across the field. It was "Czarnota," shot in both legs. He reached the edge of the forest and fell into the waiting arms of the nurses.

He explained to us how he had been wounded. He had been standing behind the outhouse when he was shot. He had not heard the command to retreat and only when silence fell did he decide, despite the pain, to make a run for it and find his unit. Unfortunately, another one of our soldiers, the "Condor," was not so lucky. He was knocked unconscious by a grenade explosion and lay unnoticed in a nearby ditch. Captured by the Lithuanians, he was taken to Wilno bound in barbed wire, and handed over to the Gestapo. He survived his brutal interrogation in prison, and after the city was liberated from German occupation in July 1944, he volunteered to the Polish People's Army.

After this defeat, our platoon retreated to the brigade's camp. Unfortunately we had no way of hearing how "Jurand" greeted his deputy after his senseless and ill-advised attack. The fact that there were four wounded and one dead soldier in an action undertaken without thought or planning was a bitter blow. The brigade did not have proper medical care and the wounded would have to be immediately sent to secret hospitals in the city.

Our nurses were only able to dress our wounds temporarily. Despite my protests, the girls wrapped me like a mummy, securing my whole arm to my side until I couldn't move at all. In my opinion my wound was not serious because there was no damage to the bone, but this did not occur to my young nurses, "Jedyna" and "Paczek" who were completely engrossed in their medical role. They packed us into wagons, and we set off to the city under "Hena's and "Pistolet's" armed escort.

Also along on the transport was a captain carrying secret documents for district commander "Wilk." For security reasons the old captain sat with me in the first wagon at the front of the convoy. "Hena" was right behind us with the wounded "Czarnota" and "Tatarczuk" in a wagon covered with straw, while "Pistolet" followed in a third wagon with "Smagly," who had been shot in the hand. We were taking a roundabout route to avoid a joint German military and Lithuanian police blockade on the Trock highway. Our intention was to sneak through between the military airport at Porubank and the estate of the same name where a Wehrmacht unit was stationed.

Everything seemed to be going according to plan until we reached the end of the village, when two Germans came running out from behind a hut. They yelled for us to halt and approached us with their weapons raised, demanding identification. The captain showed his documents and explained that his son had a broken arm and we were going to the hospital in Wilno. After checking our papers, the German told us to move on and approached the next wagon, which was some thirty meters behind us. A moment later the German again yelled for us to stop. The captain, thinking the German wanted to inspect our wagon, told me to toss my Tokarew pistol into the ditch, which I did.

One of the soldiers pointed his automatic at us to make us turn around, then told us to stand against the barn wall where the other already had his gun trained on "Hena" and "Pistolet." While checking the contents of the wagons, the Germans had found our wounded, hidden under the straw. One of the soldiers, evidently a Silesian (region in south of Poland) spoke a bit of Polish, which made it impossible for us to communicate among ourselves. He was very hostile toward Poles and kept shouting, "Shoot them, they're Polish bandits," whereas his colleague insisted that we should be taken to the command post. The situation was rapidly deteriorating. "Pistolet," knowing I had been carrying a revolver, began signaling me to start shooting.

I was standing slightly off to the side and the Germans were not paying that much attention to me because of my bandaged arm. Unfortunately I had nothing to shoot with; my weapon was lying in a nearby ditch. Seeing me shake my head no, "Pistolet" began speaking, saying that this was just a misunderstanding, and explaining that we were railway workers who had been ambushed by Soviet partisans and were now on our way to the hospital in Wilno. He added that we had proof of this hidden in the first wagon.

One of the Germans told him fetch the evidence, and this was their undoing. As "Pistolet" walked past the soldiers, he took advantage of their momentary inattention to pull his FN out of his pocket and unload the entire clip in their direction. He alternated between firing at their heads and their backs. One of the soldiers, mortally wounded, managed to get off a shot and fell screaming into the mud; the other did not even have time to shout. One of "Pistolet's" bullets passed right through him and hit the captain in the shin.

Panic ensued. The horses, frightened by the shooting, reared on their hind legs and turned in circles. "Pistolet" and the injured "Smagly" took a shortcut through the fields to the nearby forest. "Czarnota," wounded in both legs, rose from his hiding place in the straw, grabbed the reigns, and urged his horse down the road. I managed to grab my pistol out of the ditch and jump into an empty wagon. Unfortunately,

as I vaulted in, one arm completely immobilized, I did not notice my
gun fall right back out of my pocket onto the ground. "Hena" caught
up with me moments later, having briefly stopped beside the captain
and taken the incriminating documents. With five hundred Wehrmacht
soldiers stationed at the adjacent estate, there was no way we could take
the injured man along.

We rode at a gallop into a nearby forest where a group of Jews was
cutting down trees under German guard. The guards apparently did
not want to interfere in other people's business, and despite having
heard the shooting, pretended not to see us. Our galloping horses and
wagons passed by unhindered and disappeared around the corner. We
rode through the forest and reached the outskirts of Wilno. There we
separated, not wanting to be conspicuous in a large group. "Czarnota"
and "Tatarczuk" took the wagon and pressed on unarmed. "Hena" gave
me one of his grenades and we walked on foot through the now-familiar
neighborhood to the first of the organization's safe houses.

After a wash and a brief rest, we headed across to the other side of
the city. As we walked through the streets, our suntanned bodies and
long, uncut hair caught everyone's eye. Despite the fact that we had
obviously just come from the forest, no soldier or policeman stopped
us. We had a certain reputation, and nobody was foolish enough to
bother us.

All the wounded reached the safe houses without difficulty.
"Czarnota" led the wagon up to "Hena's" house and there, unable to
get out on his own, stood helplessly waiting for someone to come along.
Luckily Hena's older brother saw them and carried both wounded
inside. The captain, who had been left lying on the ground, told the
Germans who had come running shortly thereafter, that he had been
attacked by Soviet bandits while speaking to the soldiers. The bullet in
his shin served as useful proof of his story. He was taken to a military
hospital and given free treatment. After he recovered he returned to
work in the underground organization. A search of the neighborhood
yielded no results, and no one was arrested.

My time in the city was not one of my most pleasant. I spent a large
part of the day locked in someone's house while they went to work.
I had become used to an unconfined life out in the field. The hours
dragged on unbearably. The inactivity got to me. After a week, I fled

the organization's protection to spend a few days with friends. My injury healed splendidly and a few weeks later I was healthy enough to return to my brigade. A promotion to corporal was waiting for me, and I was admitted to the newly established officers' school.

The captain sent news that some boy in the village had picked up my Tokarew pistol. I asked the commander for a short leave so I could recover my weapon obtained in my first encounter against the Soviets. A short investigation in the village told me where many of the young men lived. After taking some of them aside, and asking a few questions, I was able to repossess my gun, but only after I threatened death to the young man who appropriated my army weapon.

Life in the forest battalions was not always so unpleasant. My fellow soldiers and I spent some unforgettable nights together beside a roaring fire. We were united by our common determination to free our country from enemy hands. To have survived battles and other dangers bound us in a friendship stronger than even family ties. Time passed quickly, as we reminisced about the families, friendships, and loved ones we left behind in the city. We interrupted our talk to sing songs composed by our fellow partisan, "Doniec." They sweetened the moments we spent by the fire as much as the burning slabs of wood. We could forget our exhaustion and hunger, the insects, the cold, and the war. Everything faded away as we dreamed about new and better lives in a liberated Poland, once we had fulfilled our responsibilities as citizens and soldiers.

> "The world sleeps peacefully
> And doesn't know
> That war is nothing like
> A soldier's song."

The words of this song dissolved into the darkness and took flight across the forest, to the loved ones we left behind, and whose absence we so keenly felt. We longed for our families and our mother's cherished cooking. Often we went to bed hungry on the forest floor, waiting for what the following day would bring. Grief for our fallen comrades and longing for the girls of our dreams kept us awake long into the night. Our lullaby was the constant buzz of mosquitoes thirsting for our strong, young blood, but the fleas were the worst. Just one flea crawling into your pants through the gap near the top of your boots was enough to chase away all sleep and romantic dreams. Catching the little black creature jumping in the dark was quite an art. Generally it was best to pretend you did not feel its shenanigans, and just let it gorge itself on your blood.

In the winter, we mostly slept on clay floors in one-room village huts. A huge clay-and-brick oven commonly stood in one corner of the room, taking up one-third of the entire space. Such ovens were used for cooking and baking. Most importantly, however, they served as the heat source.

Around all that warmth, there was a horde of children. Under the oven was a space for chickens, to protect them from the cold. At poorer farms the far side of the room also housed the family cow. A thick layer of straw was thrown on the floor to serve as a bed for us tired boys. The combination of boots, sweat-soaked socks, flatulence from the pea soup we had eaten, and the smell of cow dung produced a very special kind of oppressive atmosphere.

By morning, even the flies could not flap their wings to take off. Sometimes the lack of oxygen would make our heads hurt, but we would forget all that once we had done our exercises in the fresh outdoors and washed our faces in icy water. In Byelorussian areas, the lady of the house would make us a breakfast of soup or giant blinis (potato pancakes) with curds or sour milk. The blinis gave us no trouble; we would simply roll them up and dip them in the communal dish. The soup, which was served in one bowl, presented a bigger problem. It stood in the middle of the table and had to be eaten with huge wooden spoons unfamiliar to our city hands and mouths. The soup would vanish from the bowl in moments, most of it spilled on the table during our hurried eating. Only the bread we clutched in our fists kept us from going hungry after these contests of skill.

In future encounters with the enemy, the metal spoons we found were considered valuable spoils of war and carefully stored in our boots. Meat was a luxury, and only available after raids on German or Lithuanian farms. Those were days of indulgence, washed down with an excellent liqueur we made from moonshine, eggs and sugar. Afterwards we would rest, glancing covetously at the barefoot girls wandering through the neighboring gardens.

One of our soldiers, "Gil," liked to show off by using flowery language. He would approach a girl and declare that she had classical legs. Blushing, the uncomprehending Byelorussian would glance covertly at her manure-covered feet and complain, *"Czort wazmi kakije u mienia hlazycznyje nohy."("What the devil does he mean, I have classical legs?")* She did not understand what the little soldier had in mind; his unsuccessful wooing was incomprehensible to her. Sometimes while quartered in a village like this, we would find a musician to play us a lively polka on the harmonica. Our barefoot maidens would dance with us, careless of our hobnailed boots. They paid no attention to their bloodied toes – they were insignificant compared with the joy of dancing with Polish soldiers!

Real war is different from that described in stories by authors who have never been near a battlefield. Descriptions of long and bloody battles are always fascinating to read about, but unfortunately far from the truth. Their heroes never panic and run away, and the girls they meet by chance are always beautiful. We did not eat grilled pheasant and hunter's stew with meat. Our girls had cracked and bleeding soles from working in pigsties and usually smelled of fresh milk. Happily I was too young for dalliances that would have stayed with me to the end of my days.

Our preferred method of fighting was a surprise attack at night and an even faster retreat. The goal was to obtain supplies, weapons and ammunition while losing as few of our men as possible. On Easter day, the 1st Brigade left Skorbuciany for the Oszmiana highway, where they were to rendezvous with our commander, "Jurand." At the head of the column marched the second platoon led by platoon officer "Kulwiec." My brother, "Rakoczy," was given the task of securing the column's left wing. It was tiring work – the scout had to bolt like a rabbit every time the column turned a right corner. I knew what it required because I had done the same kind of work many times myself. The platoon officer always chose boys who could run fast and had a lot of endurance. So "Rakoczy" got a good workout from the very beginning of his service in the unit.

In the evening, the brigade was supposed to cross the Lida highway near the village of Czarnobyl. When they were already near the highway and walking through a small forest they heard cars coming from the direction of Lida. Those at the head of the platoon ran to take up shooting positions on the hill and in the ditch by the road. Three trucks full of soldiers appeared on the road headed by an armed "Adler" car. "Gil" (Henryk Paszkiewicz) ran out onto the road, aimed his machine gun at one of the trucks, and shouted: *"Halt! Hande hoch!"* In response a Wehrmacht major jumped out of the car and shot off a round from his "szmajser" (machine gun) wounding "Gil" in the backside.

The Germans leapt out of their cars into the other ditch and opened fire on our boys. Sergeant "Czarny" (Jan Piatek) saw what was happening and shifted part of the platoon to the opposite side of the highway, attacking the Germans along the flank. Fighting bravely in this group was "Trok," (Jan Kukuc), who had deserted from the German army and was now shouting in German for them to surrender.

The battle was short-lived. Once they lost their leader, the soldiers raised their arms and surrendered. Among the German dead were the major and a couple of soldiers. Quite a few wounded German lay in a ditch. All the wounded were packed into trucks and sent back with the other disarmed soldiers to the city from which they had come. A few of the Ukrainian soldiers who had been fighting for the Germans wanted to join the brigade, but "Wilczur" refused them. Our side had three wounded. "Gil" had been shot in the buttocks, "Kozak" had a hole in his cheek and lost a few teeth, and "Wilczur" had a bullet to the stomach; a metal army buckle having saved his life.

On April 24, upon his return from Wilno, "Jurand" disguised himself as a local and went to scout the terrain around the town of Bezdany. Home Army intelligence indicated that the Germans were planning to kill a large number of Soviet soldiers imprisoned in the concentration camp. They had been working in the peat fields. One night the brigade set out to stop the execution. Heading for the sandy road that led through the forest and into the peat bog, we marched in complete silence. The advance scouts tied scraps of white fabric to their backs so those behind them could see them in the dark. At four a.m. the brigade took up position along the forest path. The prisoners were to be executed by a unit made up jointly of German and Wlasow soldiers.

Gen. Wlasow was the leader of Ukrainian Division that was fighting on the German side.

After we had waited a few hours "Hadza" came galloping up on a horse and signaled that the convoy was approaching the forest. "Rakoczy," lying with his colleagues along the right wing of the ambush, was the first to see the German scouts walking ahead, gazing watchfully at the edges of the forest on both sides of the road. Behind the scouts came a convoy of horse-drawn wagons filled with soldiers. Suddenly a shot rang out. Bullets blanketed the convoy along the entire line of the ambush. Unfortunately, by this time only a few wagons had driven into the forest, and the rest were able to turn around and escape. The Wlasow soldiers and a few Germans jumped out of the besieged wagons into the ditch on the other side of the road. The skirmish was short lived. The enemy soldiers did not want to die, and soon put their hands in the air and surrendered, shouting: "Don't shoot!" The Germans followed the example of their Ukrainian friends and gave up the fight. Our booty included one machine gun, a few automatic pistols, about thirty rifles, a few teams of horses and thirty-five badly needed pairs of boots. We had not lost any men and contentedly retired to Majkuny. The village of Majkuny stood on a hill behind a river that ran through a deep ravine.

After taking possession of the cottages near the river, Hena's platoon spread out in teams to rest after the action at Bezdany. Soldier "Siodemka" (Wladyslaw Markowski) took up guard duty on top of the hill, surveying the surrounding area. The rest of the brigade was scattered throughout the neighboring cabins. We were relaxing swapping stories about our wartime experiences. Suddenly we heard rifle shots and machine gun fire from the direction of the river. Grabbing our weapons, we ran out and hid behind the coal heap. Our troop leader, not knowing what was happening nearby, ordered us to immediately retreat toward the village. We reached the top of the hill and took up defensive positions. It turned out that a large German unit on its way back from a gathering point, had noticed "Lada" (Zbigniew Wolodzko) sitting on the edge of the forest. As he sat drowsing against a tree, happy with life, the poor man was shot in the head and killed.

At the sound of the shot "Tankietka" (Andrzej Szafranowicz), who had been on duty beside his machine gun, fired a few rounds at the

German soldiers. The Germans retaliated with a firestorm of bullets, forcing "Tankietka" to retreat. He threw his RKM on his back and ran up the hill. A German bullet hit the barrel of his gun and propelled him to the ground. The Germans also fired heavily at the Home Army soldiers on the hill, forcing them to abandon their positions. Yet they did not have the courage or the will to press on toward Bezdany. Instead they began to turn back, encouraged in part by "Walter" (Jozef Krawczuk), who dogged them with round after round from his RKM. Our interrupted rest had ended with the death of one comrade, the loss of a great deal of ammunition, and the wounding of "Orzel"(Albin Wyszomirski) and "Czarnota" (Mietek Fijalkowski), now injured for the second time.

Sometimes the brigade had to take on the duties of the police and protect the locals from the Soviet gangs. On May 1ˢᵗ a peasant came to the village of Kozaki, where we were staying, and complained that he was being robbed and harassed by a gang living in a nearby forest. That night the 1ˢᵗ Platoon set out on a raid with two troops from the 2ⁿᵈ Platoon. Our guide was a local who had made the complaint and who more or less knew where the gang was hiding. The action, led by Lieutenant "Korab," would involve about seventy soldiers, who would be needed to completely surround the thick wood in which the gang had built its underground bunkers.

Our guide led us to the edge of the forest, indicated the general direction with his hand, and hurried back to his farm. "Korab" divided the group in half and ordered three teams to surround the forest and spread out to meet the rest of the raiding party. We crossed the old forest and came out into a thicket of young spruce trees. In time we saw movement among the saplings. We were ready to shoot until we recognized the familiar faces of our comrades coming toward us. The entire group stood around, uncertain of what to do next. It was then that "Siodemka" noticed a pair of socks drying on a branch. In a flash we surrounded the underground bunkers behind the socks and the bandits who slept within.

The raid began. "Siodemka" fired his rifle into a bunker. "Troczek" jumped on top of the fortification. "Czyz" and I stood near the entrance and shouted, "Come out with your hands up." In response a hand grenade flew out and landed at our feet. We instinctively threw ourselves to the side. Just then a couple of Soviets jumped out and fled into the bushes. The grenade did not detonate. As I lay on the ground, I managed to fire off a few shots at the escaping bandits. At that same moment one of our boys gave the bandits inside a taste of our own grenade. The earth around the dugout shook, and then there was silence; from the entrance came only smoke and the smell of ash.

The sole sound after the explosion was the distant crackling of branches in the thick growth surrounding the bunker as our boys searched for the escaped bandits. "Rakoczy" circled to the other side of the earthen dugout, reasoning that there had to be another way out. His instincts were correct. A minute later the bushes rustled, and a bandit came out in his bare feet. He stood there amazed, seeing a man in a Soviet flight suit, and thought he had been saved. He was even more amazed when this man pointed a Russian revolver at him and told him to drop to the ground. "Rakoczy" fired off a shot into the air to indicate that something was happening and a minute later "Czyz" (Zygmunt Nowak) came running to help search the captive. The bandit was taken prisoner and handed over to our leaders.

On May 8, 1944, Jurand's 1st Brigade and Szczerbiec's 3rd Brigade met in the town of Kamionka, near the city of Turgiele. The meeting had a great deal of propaganda value. Many of the Home Army's high command had come from Wilno to admire the parade of our units, marching proudly as the now well armed Polish Home Army. Presiding over the parade was Captain "Szerbiec" in the company of our commander "Jurand." Marching in the first row of my storm platoon, I was able to see the silhouettes of both of my leaders. One had wanted to have me shot; the other liked and valued the young "Bej."

When the parade was over, we sat around bonfires and listened to our officer's talk about the formation of the forest battalions. When "Szerbiec" started to go on about his heroic early exploits I quietly corrected his version under my breath. My entire team burst into suppressed laughter until "Korab," who knew that I was telling the truth, hushed us and pointed out how unpleasant it would be for me if "Szerbiec" recognized his former comrade. I shut my mouth, just in case. At night the brigades parted and went to their separate quarters.

The parade had been organized to celebrate our great victory over General Plechavicius' troops at the town of Murowana Oszmianka. Four of our brigades had attacked and disarmed a garrison of seven hundred Lithuanian and one hundred fifty Wehrmacht soldiers. Around this time "Rakoczy's" military career came to an end. On the day following the parade he was called in to see "Jurand," who had received orders from General "Wilk" that Tadek Plawski was to be transferred from the brigade to the Bureau of Information and Propaganda in Wilno. "Czarnota," who was being sent for treatment of the wound he had sustained at Majkuny, would accompany him. In one day, I lost the company of the two people closest to my heart, my brother and my best friend.

The front was rapidly nearing Poland's old borders. The Home Army began to prepare for the approaching war by stockpiling as much ammunition and weaponry as they could. A raid was planned on a fortified bunker on the Komorowszczyzna estate. The bunker was a multi-story brick building currently occupied by the Lithuanian police, which controlled the entire surrounding area including the town of the same name. The estate on which the bunker stood was twenty minutes by road from a German Wehrmacht base. Its heightened security meant a night attack was out of the question. Instead, the attack would take place in the early morning of June 18, just before breakfast, when guards were the least alert. The entire action could not last longer than the time it would take for reinforcements to arrive.

My platoon approached the building unobserved, cutting the telephone lines along the way. We were no more than fifty meters from the guard post when a policeman saw us. He leapt up and ran shouting into the bunker, but did not have time to shut the heavy doors behind him. The first team ran after him into a dark, windowless corridor. On either side of the corridor were doors leading to the bedrooms. We rushed inside two by two, looking for policemen who were no longer there. The windows in each bedroom had been reinforced with iron bars to protect the garrison from external attack. It also made a clever trap for intruders. A moment later a grenade fell through the openings in the cement roof and landed in the middle of the room. There was no time to lose; we jumped out along with the force of the explosion and back into the long corridor. At the end of the corridor lay stairs leading up to the first floor, and there we were once again met with fire from the machine gun stationed at the top.

The machine-gun fire and the smoke and dust of the explosions kept us pinned against the side of the wall. "Hena" shouted, "Retreat! Get out, two at a time!" He didn't need to repeat himself, and soon it was "Doniec's"and my turn. After taking a few long steps we no longer had to rely on our legs. An exploding grenade swept us outside like a broom. We looked a little comical, sitting side-by-side on the sand by the bunker unharmed, but for the moment, completely deaf. There was nothing much we could do, so we fired a couple of rounds at the windows on the first floor. Someone proposed setting the building on fire; there was plenty of straw in the nearby barn. Our commander spoke out against it, saying that we were soldiers and not murderers. It was not the custom in our brigade to torture or kill prisoners of war. Soldiers who surrendered were usually disarmed and set free.

We retreated to a nearby village, where we were met with an enthusiastic welcome from the locals. They shouted, "Long live Polish soldiers," and offered us food and water. It was a wonderful reward for an unsuccessful attack. I will not describe all our battles, the enemy's spilled blood or our own. We had to fight in order to survive. We were hunted like animals, and we had to defend ourselves. Graves of those who believed in their nation's freedom and right to exist were scattered all round Wilno. We fought for disputed lands once occupied by our ancestors, who had lived in a unified Poland and Lithuania. Mixed Lithuanian and Polish couples once worked the farms that yielded their life-giving crops. Today we can only visit the graves of innocent people, victims of uncompromising battles on land occupied by their common foes. They died because they found themselves at the wrong place at the wrong time.

After our failed attack on the police garrison, the brigade relocated to the Olszewo estate for a short rest. Through the local intelligence network we learned that a Latvian unit would shortly be crossing the estate with no intention of fighting the Home Army. Having first set up a machine gun on a hill beside the road, our soldiers spread out across the farm. Our orders were clear – don't make any threatening moves. The boys took advantage of the beautiful June day and undressed to lie in the grass in the orchard. Some tried to pluck the lice and fleas from their pants and shirts. I sat at the edge of the orchard and cleaned my gun.

At a certain moment we heard the rumble of approaching cars and three Volkswagens carrying a troop of twelve German high-ranking officers armed with machine guns drove into the courtyard. They were coming straight from the Eastern Front to Wilno, obviously on an important mission. At the sight of our unknown army, bivouacking on the lands through which their road led, they stopped in astonishment. "Zmija" (Adam Bobrowski), who was just then crossing the courtyard, approached the first car, saluted, and then just stood there, speechless. He was completely shocked at the sight of German uniforms and at the questions he was being asked in a language he did not understand. After a moment, he turned on his heel and called Commandant "Jurand" out of the building. To this day I remember how our leader came out unarmed, his shirt unbuttoned, and walked up to the Germans and saluted the highest-ranking officer. They asked him whose army this was, he replied that we were Polish Home Army, and there the conversation ended.

Wheels screeched in the sand and the cars disappeared around the corner in a cloud of dust. All the while we continued to sit quietly, obeying our orders. Luckily no joker started a shootout. That would have ended with the massacre of our entire unit. "Jurand" continued to stand rooted to the spot for a long time, unable to grasp what had just occurred. Soon after, a large unit of the Latvian army passed us on the road. We stood and gazed greedily at their equipment, wondering uneasily if the truce would hold. At that point, we were ready for anything.

At the beginning of July, we already knew that the front was rapidly approaching in our direction. Retreating German troops began to appear on the roads. Wanting to obtain more arms and supplies, we arranged an ambush on the bridge across the Zejmiana River. We positioned machine guns on a hill and then hid in the bushes beside the road, waiting for a transport to come along. In the distance, we heard mines being detonated under the railroad tracks. The explosions came closer and closer. We could already see the smoke and the outline of German sappers on the tracks. A long column of wagons was moving beside the tracks. A moment later, the first German wagons drove onto the bridge in our direction.

Lieutenant "Ptasznik" (Boleslaw Sztark) walked out onto the road and stopped the column with an upraised hand. The machine gunners, seeing the Germans reach for their guns, let off a round in their direction, killing the horses pulling the first wagon. That was enough. The soldiers immediately raised their hands into the air and surrendered. In a flash our boys hijacked the rest of the wagons. It had been a lightning raid that gave the enemy no time to organize a counterattack. Nevertheless, moments later a thick spray of bullets flew at our backs from the other side, but we managed to quickly distance ourselves. Our booty was impressive; the wagons were filled with weapons and other kinds of army equipment. I perched on one of them and savored a tin of French jellied frog legs. The weather was beautiful, my stomach was full – life could not get much better. I had a rifle, a gun, and a few grenades. A few kilometers later we freed our prisoners and told them to rejoin their army at the bridge.

On July 6, 1944, the Home Army's 1st Storm Platoon, which had been sent on a reconnaissance patrol near the village of Fabianiszki, encountered a Soviet army patrol for the very first time. The Soviets emerged from the bushes and stood astonished at this unexpected meeting with soldiers wearing the uniforms of various nationalities. After a moment's silence, the Soviet sergeant asked us *"A wy kakiej soldaty?"* (What soldiers are you?) After we had explained who we were and informed him that our brigade was quartered nearby, he agreed to come and speak with our leaders. A higher-level meeting followed, and as a result our brigade was attached to the 277th Infantry Division of General Gladyszew-Bielkin. Around this time we were given temporary Polish identity cards. Mine stated that Corporal "Bej" (Czeslaw Plawski) was a soldier in the Polish Home Army and registered in the district of Wilno.

A few days later, our storm platoon, led by Lieutenant "Korab," and the 173rd Infantry Platoon, led by Colonel Morozow, took up defensive positions near the village of Ozierajki. In expectation of an onslaught of German tanks we were given bottles filled with gasoline and extra ammunition. Our positions lay on an open hill. We were hidden in trenches we had dug, waiting for the enemy to attack. A bottle is a rather dubious weapon against a huge "Tiger" tank, but there was no one who would listen to our compaints and we resigned ourselves to our fate.

At noon three low flying Messerschmidts appeared against the blue of the sky. A moment later they dove and opened fire on our positions. We lay flat in our trenches with our hands over our heads, who knows why, since they certainly could not protect us against large caliber bullets. The planes returned three times, showering us with earth uprooted by the barrage of machine gun fire. It was a miracle that none of us was hit. The only casualty was a Soviet soldier who died when he jumped out of his hiding place to catch a frightened horse. We were lucky the expected tanks never materialized, or there would be no one to write this story.

By evening our platoon was pulled from the lines and we marched through the night to the region of Zielone Jeziora, where we were to rejoin the brigade. On the following day our patrols came across refugees from the city who told them the Lithuanian authorities were immediately abandoning Wilno, preferring not to wait for the coming of the Soviet and Polish armies.

Days of hard fighting at Mejszagola and around the Zielone Jeziora region followed. The 277th Soviet infantry division led by General Gladyszew and the Home Army's 2nd Division fought the panzer division of Hauptmann von Werther. We chased the Germans for a while, then the Germans chased us; it was a game of hide-and-seek played out in open fields and under cover of the green forests. A somewhat bloody game, filled with corpses, in which no one knew who was winning. It made for an uninspiring spectacle; war is more palatable when it is viewed on the movie screen, accompanied by soft seats and delicious candy.

After the Germans retreated from Mejszagola, "Jurand" decided to send a patrol into the city to assess the exact situation. On July 10, 1944, at about five a. m. Corporal "Skrzetuski" (Henryk Sitkowski), Corporal "Bej" (Czeslaw Plawski) and (Senior Rifleman) "Doniec" (Witold Ermow) set off toward Wilno, which had now been partly liberated. Our assignment was to identify the German defensive positions in the surrounded city. We quickly covered the twenty kilometers on our bikes and entered the suburbs of Losiowka, which had been spared the destruction that had leveled the neighborhood of Antokol on the other side of the Wilja River.

The Germans still occupied the entire city center between the Wilja and Wilenka rivers. From an old Dominican "cloister-turned-bunker" on top of the hill, they controlled the whole eastern part of Wilno. The city lay within easy reach of their artillery, which had an excellent observation point in the bunker. Another point of resistance was Bufalowa Mountain, which was used to secure the road, along which all the German troops defending Wilno, were to retreat west. An armored train guarded the railroad tracks leading from Nowa Wilejka and blocked the train station and the road west of Grodno. The neighborhoods of Kalwaryska, Losiowka and Antokola were already in Soviet hands. "Szerbiec's" 3rd Brigade attacked the Germans from the direction of Nowa Wilejka and Kolonia Kolejowa. The attack was repelled by the arrival of another armored train from the west. The unit lost a lot of men and had to retreat from the field of battle.

Our patrol crossed the river by boat and landed in Antokol, where we found a large number of discarded weapons in the forest near Borowa Mountain. We took an anti-aircraft gun with us and returned to Antokol. Today it is difficult to convey the enthusiasm and joy of the people we met along the way. Every face we saw was covered with tears and smiles. "It's our boys!" they cried. They kissed and embraced us, tearing us out of one another's arms. We were the first Polish soldiers they had seen since 1939.

Our assignment had been partly fulfilled; it was time to return to the brigade. "Doniec" and I spent the night with a friend, Danusia Wilusz, in Losiowka. On the morning of July 11th, "Skrzetuski" went back to the unit with our newfound weapons while the two of us set off in search of our families. As I pedaled through Bialy Zaulek, not far from my house, a shot was fired in my direction. That same moment I saw a Soviet tank standing around the corner. Its entire crew soon caught me, they shouted "*Ot Germanska swolocz*," (German pig) and in seconds stripped me of my weapons and watch, and tore the top part off of my German uniform. They shoved me against the fence, completely ignoring my red-and-white armband and the documents I showed them that had been issued by Home Army. They walked a few steps away, guns raised and were ready to fire. In that moment my entire life flashed before my eyes. I was certain the end had come. For the Soviets, my German uniform was sufficient cause for immediate execution. Many members of the Home Army, myself included, wore confiscated German uniforms. Now, I feared that this jacket, which I had pilfered, was going to seal my destiny.

I was not fated to die young against a fence. At the very last moment, I saw a civilian riding a bike toward us. I yelled out, and the man pedaled up and asked what was going on. I showed him my identification and asked him to explain that I was not a German but a Polish soldier fighting on their side. Luckily he spoke Russian well and was able to stop my execution. Nevertheless, even though he translated my documents for them, the Russians did not believe him straightaway. Finally I told them that my family had lived on the next street, and they followed me to my house, which we entered through a broken window.

I showed them my family photographs. Only then did they apologize and return my weapons and the other things they had taken. They also told me to discard the uniform that had nearly cost me my life. After this unpleasant episode I set off to look for my family, which had been relocated to another neighborhood. Unfortunately I did not find my father alive. He had been killed during a street battle.

Here I have to recount an interesting incident that took place right before my father died. He had never been a very religious man. He believed in God but did not make a show of it in public. In preparation for the defense of Wilno, the Germans moved the entire population of Zarzecze to the city center. While the street fighting raged, my family was living in Zaulek Skopowka. On the morning of July 10, while I was bicycling toward the city on the reconnaissance patrol, my father had a premonition and feverishly began to pray. He gathered a crowd of people staying in the same building and, kneeling in the courtyard, began to repeat the litany of Our Lady of Ostrobrama. When he finished, my mother astonished at her husband's unprecedented behavior asked him what was going on. "I never thought you had it in you to pray that zealously," she said. My father replied that he was praying for my return from the partisans. "I don't care about anything, not even my own life," he said, "as long as our boy returns safely."

After saying these words, he went out into the street to look for his beloved dog, which had run out the building frightened by an exploding grenade. He never returned, dying on the sidewalk on Zamkowa Street with a fatal wound in his chest. A missile fragment killed him instantly.

It was eight a.m., the very moment that a Soviet soldier took aim at his son, Czeslaw. I believe that my father gave his life for mine. I believe this absolutely, because the Soviet bullet was fired from so close that it missed me only by a miracle.

On the following day, I joined the 1ˢᵗ Brigade's storm platoon, which was on its way to take part in the fight for Wilno. Armed with equipment from the guard tower on Kalwaryjska Street, we reached the Wilja River near the Zielony Bridge, which lay collapsed in the water. We took a boat across to the city center, which was still in German control. Dashing down Wilenska Street, we crossed Mickiewicza and Ludwisarska and approached Mala Pohulanka. The Germans were not putting up much resistance and were retreating west, strafed by Soviet bombers, intending to ford the Wilja around Zakret Forest. Our platoon followed the retreating enemy, occupying the university buildings on Zakretowa Street along the way as well as the field hospital, Feldlazaret, which was bursting with wounded.

Approximately two thousand Germans led by General Stahel succeeded in crossing the Wilja and withdrew west toward the village of Krawczuny. German parachute units waylaid our brigade as it walked at the head of the Home Army on the way to fight for Wilno. In the ensuing bitter battle our leader, Commander "Jurand," was cut down by machine gun fire and killed.

Zakretowa Street presented a horrifying sight. On the sidewalks lay corpses of Wehrmacht soldiers who had tried to take shelter under the trees from the Soviet bombers. Parts of destroyed supply and transport columns lay scattered on the road, mixed with the flesh and blood of men and horses. The air attack had taken the retreating units by surprise. Grasping the opportunity, we filled an entire wagon with weapons and retreated with our spoils to the city center.

A large Soviet partisan unit stopped us on the street and demanded to know where we were going with our load of weapons. Their attitude was very hostile. They ordered us to accompany them to a makeshift Soviet command center to explain ourselves. When the officer in charge there had listened to our assurance that the weapons were intended for use against our common enemy, he told us to leave the city and go to the village of Kataniszki. An Independent Polish Division was being formed there to fight the Germans alongside the Red Army. He added that we should take a roundabout route so we would not block traffic in the war-damaged city. As we drove along, volunteers and resistance fighters joined us as well as soldiers separated from their divisions in the midst of the battle. The long column of new arrivals following our truck into the countryside made an impressive sight.

The next day Lieutenant "Korab" sent me out on reconnaissance patrol. When I returned I reported to him on our dangerous situation. We were surrounded by a great number of Soviet army units, all of them unfriendly. I had seen hidden tanks as well as cavalry and infantry soldiers quartered in nearby villages. Everywhere our patrol went, we were treated as adversaries and not co-combatants.

That day, I asked the lieutenant to release me for a few days so that I could attend my father's funeral. "Jastrzab," the son of Senior Sergeant "Strug," a column leader killed in battle near Krawczuny, put in the same request. Before heading to Wilno I changed into civilian clothes. I asked "Korab" when and where I was to rejoin the brigade, he told me he would leave it entirely up to me. I mentioned that maybe the boys should be allowed to go home, but he just shook his head sadly and said, "Bej, I have to obey our leadership's orders."

On July 17th, when I was already in the city, I heard that the NKVD (Soviet Military Police) had arrested all the Home Army officers assembled near the town of Bogusze. "Korab" was among them. Then on July 18, 1944, the Russians surrounded and disarmed those units of the Home Army gathered near Rudnicki Forest. The prisoners were briefly held in a camp near Miednik, and a few days later were told that whoever wanted to continue fighting against the Germans would have to join the ranks of the Red Army. For a moment the prisoners were undecided. Some began to raise their hands in acceptance of the proposition, but the majority shouted them down with cries of "traitors!" and would not let them choose that option. In hindsight this was the wrong thing to do. In those hopeless circumstances it would have been better to choose to fight beside an ally than be deported to Siberian labor camps. After the war those people, full of patriotism and love of their native land, could have assumed important positions in the army and the government and worked for the interests of their country and its Polish citizens.

Days of doubt and sadness followed. Hiding in the city on false documents and unable to find work, we established contact with some of the others who had managed to evade arrest. The yearning to fight this new enemy gave us no peace. We had to act. On the evening of August 2, 1944, six of us met one last time before heading out on a reconnaissance mission. The goal of this mission was to assess the situation in the field and determine if there was any chance that we could continue to fight the Soviets and survive this new occupation. "Hena," "Sep," "Bohunek" and "Walter" came to see us off. The patrol was made up of soldiers from "Jurand's" 1st Brigade, young in age but old in experience. We carried only small arms, for the time being our first order of business was to recover the weapons that "Pistolet" and "Orzel" had hidden in an abandoned barn.

We spent our first night near Lake Topiol. The next morning we had to cross to the other side of the Wilja. Luckily we saw two boys in a boat, fishing. We yelled to them in Russian, *"Dawaj siuda."*(come closer) They came, and we ordered them to take us to the other side. When we were already on dry ground the boys shouted, "Long live the Polish army!" We asked them how they had guessed and they said, "By the jib of your mugs!" After we had dug out the hidden weapons, we were transformed into a dangerous partisan group, armed to the teeth. "Orzel" and "Pistolet" had German M.P. (machine guns), "Rakoczy" and "Jastrzab" Russian machine pistols, "Czarnota" a ten-shot rifle and I a fast-firing Czechoslowakian M.G. (machine gun). With ammunition belts hanging from around our necks we looked like Mexican bandits not to be challenged.

After a short consultation we decided to walk to the Stocki forests, build an underground bunker, and hide. There we would wait for some development. We continued to naively hope that our Western Allies would come to their senses and cross into Poland with their armies. These were youthful dreams, buoyed by broadcasts from London telling us to not give up and to continue the fight for our country's freedom. At the time we still hoped to form a new partisan unit that would fight the Reds. We took our time on our journey. Nourished with food requisitioned from the kolkhozes (collective farms) already being formed, and blessed with beautiful weather, we spent some pleasant days in the field. We dodged around in the forests, changing where we slept each night and searching for the right spot to build an underground bunker in which to spend the coming winter. On those occasions when we met Soviet soldiers we told them that we were a militia searching for deserters. The machine gun I held in my hands was sufficiently convincing, and for the time being no one was willing to inquire further. Naturally we avoided any of the larger groups of Soviet soldiers that had begun to cross our path with increasing frequency.

One night, seeing the light of an oil lamp shining in the window of a small hut, we gathered round and peered inside to see two Soviet soldiers sitting at a table heaped with food. The temptation was irresistible. We had eaten nothing that day, and our guts were playing the sad march of hunger. "Orzel," "Pistolet" and "Rakoczy" went in and demanded that the gluttons gorging on Polish food produce their leave papers. "Jastrzab" and I stood outside impatiently and peered through the window, mouths watering. "Czarnota" had been given guard duty and circled the building to protect us if a larger group of Soviets came by.

Inside an old man and woman sat on a bench beside a huge, white oven, watching their food disappear. A large cloud of flies hovered above their heads, forming a dark stain against the oven's white background. "Jastrzeb" pointed his automatic at this natural target and said to me, "How many do you think I could kill with one round?" To this day I don't know if he pressed the trigger by accident or not. The noise of the shot and the shattering window threw the small room into chaos. It is hard to explain how five adults could all fit themselves under one small table in seconds. The light went out and everything was silent. After a moment someone cried out fearfully, *Nie strelaj my swaje ludzi!* ("Don't shoot, we're one of you!") But there was nothing to shoot at; the entire swarm of flies had escaped to the ceiling. After assurances that this was all an accident, everyone came out of the house. Unfortunately, there was nothing to eat or drink; everything lay trampled on the clay floor. No longer interested in the Russians' papers, we told them to rejoin their unit, and took off to the next village, hoping to find sustenance there.

A complete change had taken place in the ability of an armed group to operate in the forest. During the German occupation the Wehrmacht had usually avoided forests and small hamlets and kept to the larger towns. The countryside had belonged to us. Now the situation was just the opposite. The Soviets stayed in underground forest bunkers and patrolled the surrounding areas. There was no chance of forming an armed resistance. The local population was divided. Many communist sympathizers collaborated with the new regime.

One day, we were driving three wagons through the forest, when we saw that the road was blocked and a guard was walking back and forth beside the blockade. The forest was full of cars and tanks from a panzer division. There was no way out. The only place to turn back the wagon was in a square that had been cleared of trees, right next to the blockade. Slowly we reversed our horses while the guard stood unmoving, pretending that the armed individuals before him were none of his concern. We backed away without any outward signs of panic, as if we had every right to be on their territory and to be carrying weapons. We broke out in a cold sweat. It was a moment we would not soon forget. Evidently a seasoned veteran of the front knew better than to whip up a storm when he was right in the heart of it.

The militia and the army already knew about the suspicious armed unit roving the forests. Attempts to ambush us became increasingly frequent. We hid in barns and watched through holes in the walls as trucks filled with soldiers circled the neighborhood in search of our little group. Hiding in the open fields and dense forests grew more and more difficult. It was not even possible to move along the village roads at night. Sentinels were stationed at the crossroads and stopped all travelers. On a few occasions a round of machine gun fire in the direction of the voice yelling, "Stop!" was all that prevented a closer encounter with the enemy.

During this time the weather changed for the worse, and the cold and rain became unbearable. We had no clothes suitable for fall weather. To complicate matters, as we were resting in a village one evening drying our uniforms, a small boy came running up shouting, "The Soviets are coming!" We did not have time to grab our clothes and sprinted out with just our weapons in hand. We were met with a storm of gunfire from an approaching infantry unit. We bolted uphill on the wet earth, stopping only when we had reached the thickly wooded peak. A round from my MG discouraged the Soviets from continuing. We spent that night in a forest a few kilometers away, lying on the bare earth clad only in our pants and shirts while the cold autumnal rain poured down on us incessantly.

After three weeks, exhausted and starving, we decided to return to

Wilno. We would have a better chance of surviving between the walls of its familiar streets. We split up into two groups. "Bej," "Rakoczy" and "Czarnota" took one route, and "Orzel," "Pistolet" and "Jastrzab" another. All of us reached the city safely. Unfortunately, our report to the high command was discouraging – there was no possibility of maintaining an army in the field or offering further armed resistance. On our return, my mother confined us for the night in the grocery store she was now running, closing the huge padlock with a key to protect us from any surprise raids on the house.

In those days there were difficulties with the supply of food to the city. Wanting to help my mother stock her store, I set out with my uncle on a shopping trip to the distant Oszmiany. I was not allowed to return home with my father's brother. Our car was stopped by a Soviet patrol at a tollgate and I was asked for papers showing I had been dismissed from the army. It was a military recruitment unit. Men my age were being conscripted into the army in Byelorussia. Provisioned with bread, bacon, and a bottle of honey from my uncle, I went to stand with the other conscripts. We were taken to the local jail, where a sergeant behind a desk checked our documents one more time and amended them to state that the given individual had been drafted into the Soviet Army. Next he ordered me to empty my pockets. A pair of small folding scissors that had once belonged to a German soldier kindled his interest. Noticing how greedily he gazed at this industrial wonder, I told him he could keep it. He thanked me, playing with it like a small child with a toy.

We spent a night in jail, and at dawn all fifty of us gathered in the courtyard and then were hurried toward Molodeczno, not far from the Soviet-Byelorussian border. We walked down the road surrounded by eight Soviet partisans carrying automatic guns, and four armed soldiers with two huge dogs on a leash. After a couple of hours of marching we stopped for a short rest. The guards counted us carefully. They did the same when the rest ended, anxious not to lose anyone. There was not the slightest opportunity to escape; anyone foolish enough to try would have been torn to bits by the dogs in the blink of an eye.

As I walked in line, I saw that the leader of the convoy, the sergeant to whom I had given the scissors, was carrying my wallet, which had my identity card inside. I asked him politely if I could have it back. He gave it to me without a word and walked up to the front of the line. I peeked inside. My papers lay untouched. At that moment I began to think of ways of escaping. I knew that only the first try would succeed.

That evening we were herded into a village compound beside the road. A fence surrounded the entirety, forming a closed square. Guards stood at each corner. The detainees, exhausted by the daylong march, collapsed on the ground to catch their breath before heading off to the barn to sleep.

The sun was already hiding behind the horizon, as an evening hush enveloped the entire village. I sat down close to the guard who stood beside the gate and began to eat. He looked hungrily down at my delicacies. When I had satisfied my hunger, I broke off a large piece of bread and bacon and offered it to him. Then I asked permission to go into the house for a drink of water. This permission was granted. Then I asked if he would guard my bag, filled with the rest of the food, while I was gone. He agreed. I put the bag by his feet. I went into the house and cracked open the window facing the road. The guard was savoring his bread, holding a hunk of it in one hand and a piece of bacon in the other. His gun was slung over his arm.

That was the moment for which I had been waiting. With one jump I was on the road and leaping across the fence to the other side. I crossed the large, brush-filled meadow in the blink of an eye. Behind me I heard the guard yell out and shots being fired. Evidently it took him time to put down his food and take his automatic off of his arm. The bullets whistled far over my head. I suspect that he shot too high on purpose. After all, I had left him an entire sack full of food, and one conscript more or less would not make much difference. I never suspected I had the strength I needed to jump across the bushes and the stream at the end of the meadow. Darkness was falling when I slowed down and turned west toward my home, eighty kilometers away. A long journey lay ahead of me. On the following day I would have to cross the border between Byelorussia and Lithuania.

I jogged along the road, slowing every once in a while. To avoid the city of Oszmiana, I took a small detour, and after crossing the Oszmianka River rejoined the highway leading to Wilno. As I walked through a village, I came across a military truck that was taking passengers into the city. The driver was not interested in taking me along. He asked if I had any moonshine. Unfortunately, I did not, so I would have to continue on foot. After a moment the truck passed me, but the driver was going a little too slowly to compete with my young legs. I caught up and jumped into the back of the truck, which was filled with bags.

The ride was wonderful. I stretched out my legs to rest them after their long journey. Only my stomach complained, grumbling extraordinarily with hunger. My inborn curiosity prompted me to peer inside one of the bags. It held only cheap tobacco, but another bag was more rewarding. It was packed full of tins of American pork. I would have to choose between food and a lift. Hunger won out. I took off my shirt and tied its arms together to make a provisional sack. I packed it full of tins and tobacco, threw it into a ditch, and regretfully jumped out after it.

I lay down in the ditch a little way from the road and used a rock to pry open one of the cans. It made for glorious eating, even without bread, fork or spoon. I walked the rest of the way to Wilno through fields that ran beside the road, avoiding the army patrols and the road police. Then, just as I was passing the city toll and its guardhouse, I heard my mother's voice cry out, "Czeslaw, where did you come from?" She had been waiting for a car to come along so that she could go in search of her son, who had been conscripted into the army in his summer shoes, without any winter clothing. My mother's voice inadvertently brought us to the attention of the Soviet traffic warden directing cars into the city. She came and ordered me to show my documents, having heard my mother mention, while waiting, that I was in the army. Luckily my papers indicated that I had been conscripted into the Red Army in Byelorussia. I told her that I had been dismissed so that I could re-enlist as a Lithuanian citizen. The ruse worked. A pair of valueless scissors had saved this former partisan from serving in the ranks of the despised Soviet army. My mother and I rushed back into the city together, happy not to have missed each other.

Once again came the days of danger and reclusive nights. I was not at loose ends for long. Ryszard, a Polish Army lieutenant who lived near us, came to me and proposed that I take over the leadership of a platoon that specialized in diversionary actions on the railway tracks. To this day I do not know the purpose of that platoon, or what became of it. After I had carried out a few training runs in Byelorussia on Ryszard's orders, I learned that NKVD had arrested him. I never found out the reason for the arrest but knew he did not betray any of us. This marked the end of my military adventures. From that moment on, I began to think of my safety and of my mother, who lived in perpetual fear of my dangerous excursions. I continued to put myself at risk by walking around the city without work papers and with a gun in my belt. But I always believed that a fast pair of legs was a much more effective means of escaping danger than bullets.

Bialy Zaulek was unlucky for me; I nearly died there a second time. Walking on the sidewalk toward my house I saw a Soviet patrol on the other side of the street. They saw me as well, and one of the soldiers began to take his rifle off his arm while the officer gave his orders. Between us, in the tall fence on my side of a street, was a partly closed gate. I unobtrusively hastened my steps and opened the gate, slipping inside the fence. It was lucky for me that the gate had not been locked. I shut it behind me and sped away as quickly as only fear makes possible, vaulting over the high fence on the other side of the courtyard. I heard rifle fire but paid absolutely no attention. I ran through the beet field like a man possessed, not looking behind me. Only after I had trampled through several gardens did I breathe a sigh of relief and take a slower roundabout route to my house in Zwirowa Gora.

One more incident indicated that someone up there was looking out for me. One evening, returning home after meeting my friend Mietek and spending several pleasant hours in the company of a mutual girlfriend, I had to walk past a Lithuanian police post on Polocka Street near my house. I did not notice the policeman standing inside the gate. He stopped me and took me at gunpoint into the police station. He indicated with his hand that I was to sit on the bench, and turned his back to me to remove his gun and hang up his coat. As he did so I rose from the bench and, nodding smilingly to a second policeman sitting behind a desk, walked out calmly into the courtyard. There I was no longer so calm. One leap and I was out of the gate, running like a frightened rabbit in the darkness.

Despite the danger of being arrested, I continued to visit my friends, avoiding streets frequented by the police. Mietek and I usually met at the houses of girls we both knew, in whose company all politics were forgotten. The army, the fighting and the marching seemed very far away. When I returned home at night I was again incarcerated inside the grocery store, which at that time was our only means of support. The huge locks on the doors guaranteed a peaceful night. In the morning my mother would make me a hearty breakfast in the small room adjacent to the store, where I spent most of my days. This was a safe place for me to be sequestered, since the store was owned by and registered to my aunt. She had no sons and, therefore, was in little danger of being visited by police looking for members of illegal organizations.

# The Dark Continent
(Teresa)

The monotonous sound of the ship's propellers and the beat of the waves against the hull were interrupted by a cry: "Land on the horizon!" The deck came alive with passengers. People put their hands up to their foreheads to shield their eyes from the glare of the strong sub-equatorial sun, which sparkled on the waves in moving ribbons of silver and gold. Everyone was impatient to see the land they had crossed the Indian Ocean to reach. What would they find on this new continent? The question preoccupied curious minds. Finally the siren blared, confirming that the ship was nearing the place where they would spend the coming years waiting for the war to end.

The directors of the transport had already informed the emigrants that they would live in Tanzania (Tanganyika) East Africa, near the city of Arusha, in the newly established Polish camp of Tengeru. The camp stood on the boundless steppes that stretched fifty kilometers from the base of Mount Kilimanjaro. Not far from the camp was another mountain covered in virgin forest, fifteen thousand feet high, Mount Meru. Between it and their settlement lay fields of fallow, fertile soil already prepared for the cultivation of vegetable gardens.

On the opposite side, behind a river and a strip of jungle, were villages of reportedly friendly natives. The newcomers were not completely convinced by these assertions. All varieties of fantastic tales circulated among the fearful and ignorant. People were filled with dread at the thought of encountering wild cannibals, carnivorous animals, poisonous snakes and spiders whose bite meant instant death. Passengers waited apprehensively for their moment of arrival on the shores of the green land they glimpsed from the ship. During years of wandering, the nomads had lost faith in any kind of assurances or promises. Distrust had become second nature to them all.

From a distance, they could already see the buildings of the port Dar es Salaam into which the ship was swimming. Soon thick ropes were thrown from the deck and the ship was secured to the quay. To the surprise of all, they were met by an enthusiastic welcome rarely experienced in the Russia they had left behind. Representatives of the city's inhabitants greeted them from the shore. Though incomprehensible, their greetings were visibly very sincere. The overjoyed crowd threw exotic fruits onto the deck. For the first time in their exile, refugees saw smiling faces. They were cheered by the welcoming black faces with teeth as white as pearls. The passengers concluded with relief that they did not look like the teeth of cannibals thirsting for the blood and flesh of the white arrivals from beyond the sea. No one had much baggage, and unloading took place very briskly. A bus took them to a transit camp, where a representative of the British authorities met them. He informed them that for the present time they would be under both British and Polish protection. He also assured them that the newly erected Camp Tengeru already had houses, a medical building and a food supply system in place. The adults would be given work, and the children would attend classes suited to their age and academic levels.

These were encouraging words. Mama Bajorski cried, overjoyed at not having been abandoned to the whims of fate in a foreign land. From then on, everything proceeded with British efficiency. A narrow-gauge train was already waiting at the station, and the cars, which had windows, but no glass, soon absorbed the milling crowd. The children took their seats by the windows, eager to see a country they had only heard about from stories. A short time later the locomotive whistled, shuddered, and set off toward their future home. Sitting comfortably on clean benches, the passengers were able to favorably compare this train to the insect-ridden cattle cars in which they had traveled across the vast reaches of the USSR, when they were filthy and starving.

Outside of the windows passed a world untainted by the white man's step. Various kinds of animals fled at a furious pace, spooked by the iron dragon rattling along the steel rails. Slender antelopes leapt gracefully over stunted shrubs of dried vegetation. Giraffes circled around the acacia trees in the distance, their long-necked heads reaching for the tiny, high-hanging leaves. Every few minutes little Teresa would shout out, "Mama, look at those animals with the long noses marching in a row! And look, there's a herd of large black cows with huge horns eating grass!" Her small finger pointed at the wild African buffalo. The black-and-white coats of grazing herds of zebras enlivened the yellowed, sunburned steppes. They raised their heads to gaze uneasily at the moving train and then went back to their search for food. The families that came to Tengeru would long remember this engrossing trip.

Finally the train stopped at the small station at Arusha, and from there busses took the new arrivals to the camp. As far as the eye could see there were small round huts built of volcanic clay. Their palm-leafed roofs and lime-whitened walls looked quite picturesque among the newly planted acacia trees lining the road. The Bajorski family was assigned housing in sector six, in the farthest corner of the far-flung camp. They, and their belongings, were driven there in cars. The hut had a small glassless window in it, and an earthen floor of dried mud. Inside, three beds stood side by side covered from top to bottom with mosquito nets. The makeshift table and chairs were made from wooden crates. It was a tidy little place and proved to be pleasantly cool, even during the hottest part of tropical days.

The family recognized that in their three years of wandering, this was the first corner they could call their own. Cooking water had to be carried from a well in a square near the hut. After a moment's effort a gush of clean, cold liquid would pour from the neck of the pump. The outhouses were very primitive, no more than holes dug in the earth and covered with wooden planks. Screens of banana leaves shielded the crouching people from view. They were set a considerable distance from the houses, and this made things very inconvenient for small children, especially during times of violent stomach trouble.

A cooking oven to be shared by several families stood in the square right beside their house. It was made of baked clay and had a huge hearth covered by a steel plate.

After all the family members had acquainted themselves with their surroundings, they were gathered together and told when and where to report for provisions. Supplies were brought by car twice a week from a warehouse in the adjoining sector, and distributed among the families in the surrounding homes. Except for women with small children, all healthy adults were assigned jobs on the grounds. Children over the age of six were required to go to schools that were organized by Polish teachers who had come from India on an earlier transport.

Having learned the camp rules, the new settlers now had the opportunity to examine the interior camp sector. From the window of their huts, they could see the towering Mount Kilimanjaro in the distance, with its eternal cap of snow. The snow appeared a different color depending on the time of day. As the sun rose at dawn it took on a silvery blue tint, then whitened, and finally grew yellow-orange at sunset. Against the blue of the sky, it resembled the golden roof of a great church.

Much closer, only a few kilometers away, stood tall, green Mount Meru. The springs that cascaded down its sides became the fast-flowing river of Malala that encircled the camp. Its rapid icy current irrigated the fertile volcanic soil, and created a deep gorge overgrown with buoyant tropical vegetation. Massive trees grew on both sides of this ravine, forming a canopy impenetrable by the sun. From the boughs of the trees hung lianas that herds of monkeys and baboons used to climb across the river. Huge butterflies with beautiful colors and designs, seen only in nature, fluttered in the quiet, searching for nectar in the blooming flowers. The melodious chirping of birds, perched high among the branches, brightened the virgin forest still steeped in the half-light and mist of an early dawn.

All around the settlement lay ploughed fields ready for cultivation. Beyond the fields were the steppes, covered in waving grass and stretching all the way to the foot of those tall mountains that touched the sky. There began the land of the Masai, a tribe that lived by hunting and raising cattle. Right behind the river, a few kilometers from the camp, stood native tribe villages with their small banana and tropical fruit orchards. The inhabitants of those settlements were often employed as laborers on the perimeters of the camp, but not allowed inside.

Life under the new conditions slowly become routine. The Bajorski's new home, though primitive, gave them a feeling of ownership and stability. They knew that they would be staying here for some time, and that the drudgery of constant travel had temporarily passed. At night, when the petroleum lamp had been extinguished and the family lay in beds under the mosquito nets, their thoughts would turn to the terrible times of hunger and deprivation they had endured. They were grateful to the British for giving them the gift of freedom and security, and for allowing them to feel like human beings again instead of homeless wanderers. Sleep slowly overtook them. Moonlight fell through the window and illuminated the chamber, and from afar came the muted calls of the wild animals. The croaking of small frogs and crickets hidden among the leaves of the roof, and the constant bite of huge termites devouring everything in their path, lulled them to sleep.

In the morning after breakfast, Edek and Teresa donned their sun helmets and ran to school. This was quite far away from the house. They spent the next few hours studying, perched on benches under a roof that protected them from the sun's burning rays and unexpected downpours of rain. It was difficult to concentrate on lectures. The students were surrounded by a world as uncomplicated and free as God had created it. Through the open walls they gazed out at the wonders of tropical nature. Gorgeous butterflies and birds fluttered all around them. Insects settled on their noses with a buzz. How, then, could they pay attention to the chalk-covered blackboards?

The bell announcing the end of class breathed new life into the children. From that moment on, they were free. They quickly gathered up their few books, which sometimes had to be shared among four students, and dispersed outside in the blink of an eye, yelling with joy. They rushed for home and the cool of its interior. At noon the heat became unbearable. The sun hung high in the sky, parching the earth and making it impossible to walk outside in bare feet. The air shimmered and the sun rose higher. In the course of a few hours all life died down into silence. After a short rest, the children helped their mother prepare dinner. This was more play than useful help, but Mama was grateful for any interest the children showed in household chores. After dinner Edek and Teresa completed their homework, and then their time was their own. The jungle and the river with its cold running water and fantastic vegetation on its banks, was the terrain of wild childhood games.

Soon after the Polish settlers had arrived at the camp, a group of Africans carrying huge fruit-filled baskets on their heads appeared at the edge of the jungle. They were apprehensive about approaching the camp land. The women of the camp, prompted by curiosity and the sight of the magnificent fruit, gathered their courage and drew near. They were greeted in Swahili: "Abare-Mazuri." (How are you? good?) The women were shocked and exclaimed among themselves: "Oh dear Lord, how do they know we're Mazury?"(Mazury- north section of Poland). The Africans gestured toward the fragrant bananas and rubbed their fingers together to indicate payment. An understanding was established, and on the following morning there was fresh fruit on the doorsteps of the huts, delivered during the night by one of the Africans. The ambitious early supplier turned out to be a very intelligent and industrious man who, pointing at his breast, introduced himself as Kiwandaj. From then on, there was a constant supply of fresh fruit. The bananas were exceptional - small, with a wonderful smell and a tart-sweet taste.

Native visits to the camp did not always end happily. From time to time, camp police patrols would swoop down unexpectedly to catch any trespassers. The black policemen would beat their captives with truncheons until they bled, and then imprison them. Sometimes a fugitive, frightened by the raid, would run into a resident's house and hide under a bed until the authorities left. The occupants sympathized with the victims and always tried to help them. Kiwandaj learned Polish quickly and would walk into the camp in the mornings singing: "The Wisla (river in Poland) is wide, tell me girl what I'm thinking," etc.

He soon became the interpreter for the black workers and their supervisors, who were Polish women. Aunt Jozefa oversaw the group employed in the vegetable gardens. She taught the Africans how to plant and tend vegetables, and prodded the slower, lazier workers with "Kazi-Kazi" (faster, faster). The native mothers often brought along their children – small and thin with swollen stomachs and spindly legs – who would go off to beg while their mothers worked. They would rub their stomachs and call out "Mama-Kula-Kula," which meant "eat, eat."

It was not only the children who were looking for food. Monkeys also stole into the gardens. Tempted by the ripe vegetables, they would tear out carrots by the roots and escape into the nearby trees. The Africans threw rocks and machetes to try to bring down this delicious game. The animals, unscathed, would settle in the trees and laugh loudly and piercingly, taking pleasure in the hunters' failure.

Monkeys understand the meaning of derisive laughter - Teresa had absolute proof of this. One day she saw a monkey awkwardly dragging a bunch of uprooted carrots and started laughing at its efforts. The monkey dropped its find and attacked her, baring its teeth in anger. Teresa, frightened, ran inside the hut, but this did not stop the furious animal. It jumped onto the bed after her, and bit her painfully on the knee. It then returned for the abandoned carrots and disappeared into a thicket.

On a few occasions, the camp had unexpected guests from far away. They ran up to the edge of the houses and stopped. These were Masai warriors, whose custom it was to have one side of their faces painted white. For a moment, they would stand quietly in a row, unmoving, holding their spears and shields. Their only covering was a sheet of fabric that hung from their arms. Then, in complete silence, they would begin to jump rhythmically on straightened legs. The entire row would rise evenly, higher and higher, into the air. It was a curious sight, and ended as unexpectedly as it began. They left the camp at a run, sometimes taking with them a few of the laundered sheets that hung on the washing line, perhaps as a memento or as payment for their performance. They had crossed the wide savanna to see the white arrivals previously unknown in their land.

Time in the tropics changed people's appearance. They tanned brown and the soles of their feet thickened from walking barefoot on the hot sand. The natural hard sole that formed protected them from the stings of prickly plant thorns and the cactus seeds that the wind scattered across the camp. These were always digging into their skin and wounding feet. The refugees were not able to protect themselves from the small fleas that crawled under their fingernails and burrowed into their skin, where they laid their eggs. When the new fleas hatched they caused infections and a terrible itching. The only solution was to remove the egg sacs with a needle before they hatched. Equally nightmarish were the unsightly tropical sores that formed on people's legs. There was no medicine for them; they had to be burned away with a red-hot iron. The remaining scars were permanent and irremovable mementos of the exiles' stay in Africa.

One morning the Bajorski's were alarmed by the screeching cry of a woman. Edek and Teresa quickly ran to find out the cause. Their next door neighbor had neglected to shake out her sweater before putting it on. A poisonous spider hidden in one of the sleeves had bitten her on the arm. Edek and Teresa raced straight to the neighboring sector for an ambulance and rode back in it to pick up the patient, proud of the importance of that mission. Fortunately, at that time of year the spider's venom was not as deadly as it would be at another time. After a few days, the careless victim returned home with a reddened and very swollen arm.

There was no way to completely protect oneself from sickness or disaster in this land of oppressive heat. One day Edek complained of a headache and pain in his joints. As he was lying on his bed, his body began to shake with cold and uncontrollable trembling. He continued to shiver despite being covered by three blankets. The doctor diagnosed malaria and immediately took Edek to the camp hospital. A few days later the chills subsided but his temperature remained high. Cold compresses were applied to his forehead to lower his temperature. The prescribed quinine medicine was unbearably bitter, and the small patient swallowed it with great difficulty. His stay at the hospital lasted a few weeks.

Edek took another malaria drug, atabrine, which caused a yellowing of the eyes. After he had taken a few of those tablets the yellow coloration became quite noticeable. When he returned home he was exhausted and weak, and always threatened with the recurrence of the disease. Malaria was treatable but not completely curable; the only real solution would be a change in climate. A series of attacks may kill a white person in as little as five years. At that time there was no possibility of leaving Africa. The war was still raging and the family had nowhere else to go.

Days, weeks and months passed under the scorching African sun. The children used oranges as substitutes for balls in their games. Teresa dreamed of having a doll. The surrogate for this was a moppet made from a towel and scraps of old clothing. There was always great excitement and happiness when shipments from Red Cross arrived. These gifts from America were highly prized by people who had traded away everything they owned in exchange for Russian bread. The residents chose wisely, trying to get whatever they needed and what suited them best. Teresa managed to obtain a very small pair of high-heeled shoes that did not fit any of the women. She put them secretly aside, and would often play with them, pretending she was a teacher who was all dressed up for her job. The flowers were her students, and she punished the disorderly ones by beheading them with a ruler. These were the simple games of a child growing up during a time of continuous change and constant struggle for survival.

Teresa was already eight years old but still quite immature. She was given to pranks to which their neighbors sometimes became victims. Across the street from the Bajorski's hut lived their nearest neighbor, Mrs. Cock, who shared a house with her grown daughter. Mrs. Cock was an ill-natured woman, with an explosive temper and a tendency to maliciously provoke her neighbors. It was no surprise that she was the constant target of playful pranks. In the evenings, when dusk fell, Teresa and her friends would sneak up underneath Mrs. Cock's window and crow like a cock. The irritated woman would open the door, swearing at the invisible source of the noise and calling them scamps and rascals. As she stood in the doorway, they would douse her with cold water from hoses they fashioned out of pig intestines, usually used for making sausage. With just one hard squeeze, a long fountain of water would fly through the small openings they had made and drench the shouting woman. She was too fearful of the snakes and scorpions that came out at night to leave her hut, and so Theresa and her friends would run back undetected in the dark, overjoyed at the success of attack. Naturally, the blame usually fell on the boys, Edek and his friends.

Mrs. Cock did not refrain from retaliating on her neighbor. Around noon the next day, Emilia was standing by the just lit oven and preparing to bake bread. In walked Mrs. Cock with a pail of water, with which she proceeded to douse Emilia's fire. Poor Mama had to sweep out the wet ashes, re-light the fire, and wait until the oven reheated, all the time standing guard until the baking was finished. The neighborhood war did not end there. Its next casualty was a beautiful white rooster, Edek's pride and joy. The defenseless rooster was scratching in the dirt beside his hut when it was whacked across the back with a stick. The result was tragic; the rooster was gravely wounded and had to be killed. He became the main ingredient in a pot of chicken soup. The children cried bitterly at their loss and swore a bloody vendetta against the murderer of the beloved fowl. Deprived of their handsome suitor, the neighboring hens cried with them. Only the other roosters did not feel the loss of their rival too heavily. The entire affair was broadcast across the camp – "Mrs. Cock has killed a cock."

Edek also had a pair of beautiful pigeons that flew around the house, beating their wings against the eternally blue, cloudless sky. Even they did not have a carefree life. High above them circled huge hawks, waiting for the right moment to strike. They hurtled from the air at lightning speeds and snatched at the defenseless birds. Bloodied feathers fluttered to the earth, bringing tears to the children's eyes. The hungry hawks attacked anything moveable and edible.

The most anxiously anticipated event at the settlement was the arrival of the meat rations. At the sound of the word "meat" all able residents, old and young, ran to the distribution point for their share. Even cats recognized the word and ran meowing ahead of their owners hoping for some of this delicacy. On one of these happy occasions, Teresa, having received her share of meat, was carrying it on the top of a cabbage leaf. She did not get far; the beat of wings and a blast of air alerted her to the fact that her meat had ascended into the air, held between the claws of a huge hawk. That day's portion ended up in a nest as dinner for hungry hatchlings. From then on, Teresa's portion of meat was securely covered with a second cabbage leaf, to conceal it from the hunting birds. It was not only the birds in the air that searched for food, their eyes riveted on the ground. The earth, also, crawled with all varieties of amphibians and other small predators. Sometimes these small, well-organized beings formed a dangerous army that destroyed every living thing in its way.

One morning some of the camp residents noticed a dark, brown belt moving on the ground from the jungle toward the houses. It wound nearer to the camp like a huge, meter-thick snake. Millions of large ants marched in a disciplined step, overwhelming everything that blocked their path. Larger ants patrolled the sides, maintaining order and directing the march. These were the scouts and soldiers in the army of marching ants. There were soldier-ants with strong pincers that attacked victims biting them deeply. They ate other insects and carcasses of dead animals leaving only white clean bones. Nothing but fire and water could halt their movement. These marching ants seemed to be heading toward Bajorski's hut, which was located on the perimeter of the camp. The family hastily escaped from their home, taking chickens and pigeons with them so that they would not fall prey to the devouring insects. The rows of marchers reached the walls, submerged them under a mass of small brown bodies, and crawled past the windows onto the leafy roof. The hut changed color, going from white to brown-red and vibrating with a moving layer. The invasion was short but all encompassing. An hour later all that remained was the acidic smell of ants. The inside of the hut had been cleaned of all other insects more thoroughly than possible with the best vacuum cleaner. Even the invisible termites and their eggs had disappeared. Here and there lay the skeletons of small, devoured creatures. The marauding horde continued its devastation until it was sated, and then marched back into the jungle, to return at a later time.

Another unprecedented experience for the campers was the arrival of a swarm of locusts. The murmur of a million wings announced that something unusual was happening. A moment later a cloud appeared from the direction of the grassy savanna and completely blocked out the sun. The Africans quickly lit large fires onto which they threw fresh leaves. The smoke was to scare away the insects and prevent them from descending on their gardens and orchards. Nevertheless some of the locusts settled on the ground. The Africans went after them with branches, scaring and killing the ravenous insects. Every once in a while, one would bend down to grab a living locust and eat it. From the appreciative crunching it appeared that the natives savored this delicacy. This time the refugees were fortunate; the largest part of the cloud passed their camp and disappeared over the horizon. If the locusts had landed in that area, they would have stripped the earth of every plant and left behind only bare stems and branches.

Every minute of the Bajorski family's stay in Africa was saddened by the knowledge that their grandmother and grandfather were somewhere far away in dry, waterless Uzbekistan. The two old people had been left to their fate without protection or means of survival. They were alone, without family, among hostile, primitive Uzbeks, in the USSR's poorest republic. Mama and her sister, Jozefa, were very distressed at this separation, and cried when they remembered their shared years of exile.

In those difficult times there were also flashes of happiness. An unexpected letter arrived from England. Emilia's husband Jozef had located his family, with the help of the Red Cross, and they began to correspond. He was stationed in Scotland, serving in the Polish Army under British command, in the tank division under General Maczek. Soon he began sending packages of candy to camp. He had received the candy as part of his army rations. The children waited anxiously and impatiently for a notice from the post office that a shipment had arrived. For the children it was a moment full of excitement and happiness. It gave them the opportunity to take the bus to Arusha. After picking up the package they would walk around and admire the window displays. Teresa gazed at the beautiful Eskimo doll on the store shelf with wonder and excitement. She did not dare ask Mama to buy it for her; she knew her mother was saving money so they could leave Africa for yet another unknown country. Teresa quickly forgot about the doll and gloried in the ice cream her mother had bought them as a treat. To lick the cold ice cream under the searing African sun was an indescribable pleasure. They all returned to camp with the delicious taste still lingering on their lips.

The joy of the anticipation of reestablishing contact with their father and husband, Jozef, was short lived. In January of 1945, they received word from Jozef's brother, in France, informing them that Jozef had been gravely wounded. He had taken a bullet to the head, and was in a military hospital in Germany. This was a great blow to his Emilia. She had found her husband and the father of her children, after all these years, only to have him struck down by a merciless bullet in the last days of the war. The family anxiously awaited the next letter, dreading the news. Their worst fears were confirmed. Jozef had died. Emilia's despair was overwhelming. She was left without her husband and with two young children in a strange and exotic country, far from her family and friends.

In spite of the family's sorrow, life continued. They had to reconcile themselves to tragedy and hope that this time God would not abandon a poor widow and her small children. There was no reason for them to return to communist Poland. Ukrainian gangs had plundered their farm and their family was scattered across the globe. Here, under the protection of the British authorities, the family was assured a living and a roof over its head for the next three years. Of great spiritual help in those difficult moments was Msgr. Jan Sliwowski. This brave curate – a great organizer and an energetic human being – was able to maintain his parishioners' faith and trust in God. He had come to Tengeru from the United States to aid his countrymen in recovering the human dignity they had partly lost during their exile and enslavement. During his beautiful Sunday sermons he reaffirmed their Creator's love for them and encouraged them to raise and educate the growing generation with faith. Thanks to him people began to regain their self-esteem and their confidence in the future. Mama realized that she had to be strong and focused and continue with the same kind of persistence she had shown in the past.

Finally, in the summer of 1945, the radio announced that the German Army had surrendered. The camp went crazy with joy. Once again the exiles began to hope that they might return to their homeland and reunite with their scattered families. People danced and sang patriotic songs, excited by the news. They kissed and congratulated one another on surviving and not succumbing to the evil fate that had hurtled them into years of wandering through foreign lands. They promised each other that they would return to their familiar towns and farms in their beloved country. In their imagination they could already smell the flower-covered meadows and the ripening wheat.

Unfortunately, the political situation dampened the enthusiasm elicited by the end of the fighting. The Yalta agreement once again handed Poland into the hands of the despised USSR. Most people did not have the slightest wish to place themselves again under the yoke of the Soviet system. Life became troubled. The camp was to be shut down after five years for health reasons. A longer stay in the African climate would be unhealthy for Caucasians. No one knew where they would be taken this time. A few months later a letter from England brought a great surprise. Once it had been translated from English to Polish, Mama learned that as the widow of a sub-lieutenant in the British Army she would be receiving a monthly pension. Soon she received a check for a respectable sum. It was a great relief in their situation. A modest regular income was now assured.

Around this time the family's health began to suffer. Edek fell ill more and more frequently with increasingly stronger attacks of malaria.

Mama and Teresa followed suit. The number of malaria victims grew, and the small hospital was always full of patients. The camp slowly became depleted. Some people had tired of wandering, and decided to return to Poland. A number of the older girls married Indians who owned plantations in Eastern Africa. The majority of the Polish deportees, however, elected to travel to England. They put their faith and trust in the British, appreciating the care they had always shown the Polish people. Mama expecting hard times to come, was always prepared. She dried pieces of bread and melted lard to pour over sausages that she had packed into meat tins for the long journey to the unknown. She was not the only one doing such things. All of the campers remembered the poverty and deprivation they had experienced in the past, and tried to prepare themselves against any eventual hunger.

By the end of the summer of 1948, the camp population was greatly diminished. People liquidated the small gardens they had planted around their homes. They killed the chickens and pigeons they had raised with such care. The household dogs and cats were given away to African friends, who promised to take good care of them. The families packed whatever was most essential for a long sea voyage and gazed one last time with tears in their eyes at the place where they had spent the last five years of their lives. It was very sad to see Kiwandaj crying and telling them that he would die when they departed, he expressed his grief in fluent Polish.

Despite hunger, thirst, sickness, the lack of basic necessities and the absence of comforts for small children, they had experienced some unforgettable moments. These refugees had visited many continents and witnessed natural wonders the average person would never see. The magnitude of these memories has lingered to this day. They survived terrible times enveloped in tight and indestructible family bonds, full of love and sacrifice.

Now the Bajorski family had to prepare for another separation and another long journey. This time to rainy England, where they expected to stay until Poland was free from communism. Once again came the terrible moment of parting. This time it was a separation from Aunt Jozefa, who had to remain behind in Africa. Only the most immediate family of a soldier was eligible to depart to England. Emilia, Edek and

Teresa cried uncontrollably at the thought of leaving Aunt Jozefa. They had spent eight years together wandering across the world.

Teresa refused to leave her aunt's arms, and had to be forcibly removed. Jozefa was left all alone, and no one knew if they would ever see her again. It was another chapter in the tragedy that had befallen their family. Fear and uncertainty overwhelmed Emilia once again. How would she manage in a foreign country with two young children, not speaking the language and having no profession?

Emilia took the bus to Arusha to take all her savings out of the bank. She placed the check that she received in a small bag and hung it from around her neck in the safest place possible, between her brassiere and her breasts. She packed what little food and clothing they had and readied it to be loaded onto the ship.

At the very last moment Mother made a sign of the cross over the hut where they had spent the last five years of their lives, and then boarded the bus. Everyone cried at leaving a place so strongly associated with memories of close friendships, childhood experiences, freedom, and the beauty of exotic nature. As they set off for the train station in Arusha they prayed together to the Virgin Mother for her continued protection. Once again refugees passed the wild steppes teeming with animals and rushed through the wide, uninhabited savanna toward Mombassa, which lay on the shore of the ocean. The Bajorski family stayed there for several days waiting for their turn to board ship, the huge "Winchester Castle." The time in the transit camp was happily spent visiting the city and its surroundings. The houses in which they were staying stood among tall palm trees on a fascinating beach. Kids gazed with curiosity at the coral reefs that spread across the waters of the bay, spending hours daydreaming about the fabulous shapes.

Finally it was time to depart, and the family walked across a bridge and boarded the colossal ship that would take them on a journey across the Indian Ocean, the Suez Canal, the Mediterranean Sea and the Atlantic Ocean to distant England. They marveled at the inside of the ship, which was a veritable labyrinth of floors, steps, corridors and cabins. After being given a key to their new quarters, and led there by the ship's steward, they had the chance to collapse on the clean, freshly made beds and close their eyes in momentary rest. However curiosity did not let them waste time on sleep. Minutes later Edek and Teresa were already on the top deck, admiring the sight that spread before their eyes. Mombassa in all its glory lay before them. The bay, with its jagged coral edges and blue water, reached up to the shore, on which they could see the city's white buildings interlaced with the green of growing trees.

After their modest baggage was brought to their cabins they changed their sweaty underwear and donned their best clean outfits. In the midst of doing this Mama glanced into the sack that hung around her neck. The check inside was a pitiful sight. The amount that had been printed on it was completely unreadable. Sweat borne of excitement and the heat of the noonday sun, combined with dye from the fabric, had completely obscured the figure. Despair intruded once again and marred the pleasant beginning of new voyage. The crying woman could not be calmed. She thought that she had lost her entire, painfully hoarded savings.

The ship unmoored from the pier and with a blare of sirens swam out into the vast ocean. Emilia, Edek and Teresa spent day after day on deck, watching the prow of the giant ship cleave the frothing waves. Walks were interrupted by meals served in beautiful dining rooms, by waiters who gracefully maneuvered delicious dishes between the tables. At night they sat on benches listening to the first-class orchestra playing in the ballroom. For the first time in their lives, the family felt like royalty and not destitute tramps.

A few days passed. The ship reached the mouth of the Suez Canal, where it was anchored and waited its turn to enter the busy waters of the canal. Small boats bearing all sorts of goods approached the ship. Shouting Arab merchants showed off their beautiful carpets, fruits, sweets and various creations made of colorful fabrics, praising their quality and price. If the negotiations were successful, the goods were hoisted onto the deck by rope, and the payment sent down to the merchant in the same manner.

After a long wait, the ship floated into the waters of the canal, which stretched for miles through yellowish sandy desert. Next they sailed into the Mediterranean, where the travelers were cooled by the first small gusts of a brisk wind. One week later the huge Rock of Gibraltar appeared on the horizon. As they approached the famous rock, the captain asked for a moment of silence, in remembrance of the fallen soldiers of the Second World War. With a salvo of cannons from the fort situated on the Rock of Gibraltar the ship entered the Atlantic Ocean.

A few days later the passengers saw the outlines of England in the distance. The canal of La Manche greeted them with stormy waves and mist, and in its embrace the ship reached the English port of Southampton. Another chapter of their lives had passed and a new one was about to begin.

# On the Road to a Free Poland
(Czeslaw)

During the fall of 1944, Wilno was no longer a bustling city filled with life, happiness and youthful students strolling through Mickiewicza Street. The sounds of guitars and the lyrics of happy songs, which had been heard on the green of Orzeszkowej Square, were silent. Due to the disarmament of the Home Army (A.K) units by the Soviet army, and soldiers being deported to Siberian work camps, clouds of uncertainty and sadness hung over the city. Because of this sad reality, people wondered if their situation was worth all the hope and enthusiasm they had demonstrated. They thought about all the lives sacrificed in the fight for the liberation of Wilno from the hands of Germans, and hoped this loss was not in vain.

News of the "Warsaw Uprising," which erupted on August 1, and the sixty-three days of bloody battle that followed, added to the powerful feeling of depression. Again, history was repeating itself. The Red Plague flooded the beloved city, robbing it of its most precious treasures – happiness and pride, along with a belief and hope for the future.

Wilno, together with its surrounding areas, had been given to Lithuania, which again found itself a Soviet possession. The city, at that time, was not a safe place for Polish youth. Units of the NKVD (Soviet Military Police) and the Lithuanian police frequently apprehended young people throughout the streets of the city. Those arrested were taken in for questioning. As a result, they would often find themselves in jail or in the ranks of the Red Army. My brother, Tadek was a victim of this circumstance and was sent to do forced labor in a Soviet concentration camp.

Lithuanians had the goal of ridding their reclaimed land of young blood – the youth of Polish descent. The Soviets also aimed to be free of enemy elements capable of raising an inner-armed resistance. A few of us remaining officers of the former Home Army had been able to avoid arrest or being sent into the depths of the USSR. It was not easy to hide being unemployed or without a permanent address. Constantly having to hide, we waited for some way by which to leave the area, which was constantly under the surveillance of Soviet agents.

After many decisive battles, Poland's eastern front was defined as ending on the banks of the Wisla River. Lithuania and Byelorussia recovered their doubtful independence in the Republic of Russia. The eastern part of Poland remained liberated. This was the area that my friends and I hoped to reach, so that we could escape from Lithuania.

During this time, it would have been impossible to cross the new border, which extended from Lithuania to Romania. The border, all along the length of the river Bug, had been surrounded by the Polish communist People's Army, Units of the Border Protection, and the Soviet Army. Their task was to capture and liquidate former survivors of the Home Army who attempted to make their way to the Polish side. On August 1, 1944, the Polish Home Army made the decision to liberate Warsaw, the capital city, from German occupation. The city, battling against the Germans, called out for help to those experienced in battles, and for supplies of weapons and ammunition. The Soviets, meanwhile, intentionally held back their offensive on the eastern border of the Wisla River, waiting for the defeat of civil volunteer's and the Home Army.

Stalin strived to destroy the patriotism of the Home Army dependent upon the commands of the Polish government quartered in London. Airplanes flying from Italy, carrying supplies of arms, medicine and food did not receive permission to land and refuel on the eastern side of the Wisla River, which had already been taken over by the Soviet army. Units of the communist Polish People's Army had a very clear and specific order to stop at the banks of the river and wait for further developments. Only a few platoons of brave soldiers spontaneously disobeyed these orders in order to help those fighting in Warsaw. The commander of the People's Army, General Berling, was removed from his post for disobeying the orders given by the all-powerful Stalin.

The German army was prepared for the uprising. It was not a surprise to them. They sat waiting in bunkers built at key posts, with perfect vision of the gunfire on adjacent streets. The Uprising was suppressed after sixty-three days of heroic battle, which claimed the lives of approximately two hundred fifty thousand Poles. Warsaw was leveled to the ground. What remained of it was only piles of rubble and protruding individual chimney stumps of burned tenement buildings. The German army, after this costly and disgraceful victory, had a loss of approximately twenty thousand select soldiers and, with trepidation, anxiously awaited the coming spring's Soviet offensive. Battles on the German-Soviet front subsided for a while. The bitter cold winter of 1945 restrained both armies from further fierce struggles. The Soviet Army prepared itself for a final attack upon Polish territory occupied by Germany and a further attack on Berlin. After the stifling of the Warsaw uprising, the German Army was preparing itself for a strong resistance in defending the Reich border. The threat of Soviet soldiers entering German territory hung irreversibly in the air.

For me, the autumn days passed in a constant fear of arrest by the NKVD patrols, which collaborated with the Lithuanian secret police, prowling the streets of Wilno. Winter came in full force with the bitter cold of January. Throughout the city of Wilno, signs were hung everywhere, indicating that recruitment for the communist Polish People's Army had begun. This army had been organized in Russia under communist command. At last, there came the opportunity to leave the seized Soviet territory of the province of Wilno.

A large mass of young people reported to register at the open draft office on Wielka Pohulanka Street. Crowds of people filled the hall, stairways and corridors of the large building, waiting their turn to sign-up. Personal identification documents were taken from the volunteers as they were being put on the general recruiting list. Because the recruits would be arrested if they went onto the city streets without their documents, they had to remain in the office for several nights. They were awaiting the organization of a rail transport, which would take them beyond the Lithuanian border into the already free Polish city of Bialystok.

My friends Mietek, Leon and I went to the draft office to familiarize ourselves with what type of documents were needed to sign up for the communist People's Army. This was our one and only chance to leave Wilno. A young girl was collecting identification documents from the incoming volunteers, adding their names to an overall draft list. She held back the personal identification documents, putting them aside into official briefcases. Registered individuals received a scrap of paper on which was a small stamp of the People's Army. This stamp proclaimed that the given citizen was enlisted into the ranks of the infantry unit. This procedure was very precarious for us. We possessed false documents issued in assumed last names, given us through an organizational network during the time of our affiliation with the Home Army (A.K.). We could not, therefore, leave them in the hands of communist officials.

By chance, the young girl who was in charge of the documents, was a friend of mine. I had met her while attending studies at the Technical School from 1939-1942. I reminisced with her about those times, entertaining her with conversation during moments free from work. I flirted with her, apologizing that this current meeting came at such an unfortunate time, approaching our departure from Wilno. At the conclusion of her work day, I walked the young woman home and assured her that tomorrow we would return, and register. Before we parted, I admitted to her that we were hiding from the police as former soldiers of the Home Army (A.K.) and that we currently did not possess actual identification documents. At our parting, I stole a kiss from her, hoping that this would encourage her to be more sympathetic to our cause.

The next day, we went to the draft office once again, and gave the young woman our papers. The pleasant young lady gave us a certificate of registration into the army, adding our names into the collective list of volunteers. However, she was required to keep our counterfeit documents. In thanks for the favor, I tore out the photos from the documents, giving them to the kind office worker as a remembrance of our friendship. We were thankful that the papers without the photographs were the ones required by the army officers.

The next morning we were herded, by rank, to temporary quarters in an abandoned building where coal was stored. Conditions were terrible. The cold in the unheated warehouse was almost unbearable. This was the beginning of January and it was frigid. After attendance was taken, those present received a modest portion of provisions consisting of a piece of bread, canned fish and a few cigarettes. A guard, the sergeant of the communist People's Army, announced that on the following day we would be loaded onto a train that was headed for Poland. To spend overnight in these deplorable conditions was unthinkable. Most of the recruits had already spent several nights on the stairs of the draft office, sitting on their backpacks. Now we were expected to spend another night on wet, mud covered ground in a freezing storage facility. My friends and I did not take kindly to this, especially since we were in our own city where we had many friends.

We slipped away, unnoticed, from the warehouse, and headed for the home of our friend, Stanley Mieczaniec, who lived just a few streets away. Our friend's wife cooked a modest supper for us and prepared bedding in the guestroom. We spent our last moments in Wilno very pleasantly with them. In the morning, after having washed and shaved, we returned to our temporary barracks, easily assimilating into the crowd of newly gathered soldiers. It was a pitiful sight to view people smeared from head to toe with coal dust and mud. There was no water. The tired, sleepless individuals washed their faces with snow, which they gathered from the street. Unshaven, the soldiers came and stood for the morning assembly. The sergeant read out the collected names from a list, to which those assembled replied "Here I am" when their name was called. Luckily, we were just in time for our roll call so that we could attest to our presence.

Next, the large group of men walked out in groups of four, in the direction of the train station. Divine providence continued to keep watch over us. Along the way, my mother caught up to us, carrying a small bundle of fried hamburgers. She had found out where we were quartered and came to bid goodbye to her son possibly forever. Crying, she ran alongside the rows of marching men. I saw her making the sign of the cross in the air. My last vision of her was standing alone in the abandoned street.

Unit by unit, we approached to the holy place. We had to go through the gated entrance to the chapel in which hung a picture of the Blessed Mother Ostrobramska (Our Lady of the Gate of Dawn). This is a prominent painting of the Blessed Virgin Mary, Mother of Mercy, and is venerated by the faithful who pass through this chapel. The original painting is one hundred sixty-three by two hundred centimeters, and was painted by an unknown artist on eight oak planks around the year 1630. In 1671, the effigy was covered with silver and gold facing, and on July 2, 1927, it was crowned with a double crown and entitled the Blessed Virgin Mary, Mother of Mercy.

The "Gate of Dawn" was built between 1503 and 1522, as a part of defensive fortifications for the city of Wilno (Vilnius). The namesake for the gate was the borough of *Ostry Koniec (Sharp End)* to which the gate initially led. It has also been known as the *Medininkai Gate* as it leads to the village of Medininkai (Polish: Miedniki), south of Wilno. Of the nine original gates, The Gate of Dawn is the only one remaining. The others were destroyed by the order of the government at the end of the 18th century. During the 16th century, city gates often contained religious artifacts intended to guard the city from attacks as well as to bless travelers. The Chapel in the Gate of Dawn contains a renowned miraculous icon of the Blessed Virgin Mary, Mother of Mercy. For centuries, the picture has been one of the symbols of the city and an object of praise for both Roman Catholic and Orthodox inhabitants.

As though on command, our entire unit fell to their knees, paying our last tribute to the caregiver of our nation. The sound of quiet pleas for blessings carried high into the hills. They were pleas for care and protection over this young generation, now leaving the place of their birth and upbringing. We were youth going into the unknown future, into battle with the enemy, holding within their yoke, the entire country. A country of people who were leaving their families, their farms and their surroundings. People who were to fight alongside another enemy, Russia, whose goal was to destroy their patriotism and belief in God.

After arriving at the corner by the chapel, our row of soldiers was not far from the Wilno rail station. There on the byroad stood the long commodity train with its cattle cars, waiting to absorb these young army volunteers. There was not a glimmer of enthusiasm evident in this group of former Home Army (A.K.) soldiers who were now fleeing from the Soviet-Lithuanian yoke.

The recruits rapidly boarded the train, each one hoping to acquire some small, private spot. All of us were exhausted and wanted a place to rest our weary bodies. As the transport was about to leave, two young, attractive girls appeared at the station, desperately searching for room on this already overcrowded train. They peered into the crowded cars, hoping that someone would take pity on them and allow them inside. The girls lamented that they needed to go to their parents who lived in the city of Lida. They had been separated from their parents by battles on the front, and had not seen them for a very long time. Having arrived in Wilno during the spring of that year to visit close relatives, they did not have any way of returning home.

After having spent many sleepless nights and menacing days waiting to leave, the soldiers being loaded into the train cars were unfeeling to their many pleas and charms. Our situation was different. We were quite rested after having spent the night at our friend's house. In addition to that, a few fried hamburgers provided by my mother invigorated us, so we had no objection to the pleasant female companionship. We pulled them into the car despite the reluctance and resistance we got from those already on board. After all, there were three of us, so the opposition was not all that impressive.

In a short while we set out on our way. Despite the fact that it was bitterly cold outside and there was a strong wind resulting from the speeding vehicle, we did not feel cold with the girls sitting on our laps. We spent the entire day's drive to Lida in this very friendly atmosphere. Toward evening, with the screeching of brakes, our train ride stopped at a station in Lida. The sergeant shouted orders to immediately vacate the cars. We reluctantly detrained onto the deserted, littered platform, not finding solace in the rough tone of voice used by the soldier in command.

Our young ladies were already at the point of their destination. Grateful for the pleasant trip, they gave us their address as they were leaving, inviting us to come over for supper sometime when we had the chance. Our Army commander informed our unit that we would have to wait until morning for the next train. We graciously asked our leader if he could give us a more definitive time of departure. His reply was very tactless, the kind that can not be repeated among civil people. We, therefore, did not see any purpose in waiting for the promised transport. We took our backpacks and quietly left the station. Some helpful pedestrians pointed us in the direction of the address given us by the girls.

The girls' parents cordially welcomed us; thankful for the help we had shown their daughters during the trip. We were invited to their table which was filled plentifully with various dishes – a lavish supper for war times. After consuming these gifts from God, the parents suggested that we spend the night in their home rather than the cold railway station. We did not have the heart to refuse this welcoming proposition.

We fell into a deep sleep and morning arrived quickly. We were not anxious to leave these hospitable surroundings. We dawdled in our grooming process, and then readily partook of the delicious breakfast we were offered by our gracious hosts. Thanking them warmly, we finally left their friendly doorstep, marching quickly toward the railway station to join our unit. We recognized the station when we arrived, however, we could not find the people who had been there. Asking the stationmaster about this, he looked at us and with a wry smile, replied that the soldiers had left on the night transport. This was, from our point of view, unforgivable. The commanding officer had told the unit that we would not be heading farther into our trip until morning. They had left us poor waifs in the cold weather, at a deserted, quiet station, without the care of our boisterous sergeant. We had nothing else to do but wait for whatever train would come next heading in the direction of the border. There was some possibility we could catch up with the rest of our army unit now escaping us.

After several hours of waiting, a long line of train cars rolled into the station, loaded with large metal pontoons used for building temporary bridges. A red star on the locomotive announced that this was a Soviet war equipment transport. Unnoticed, we jumped into one of the last cars, hiding ourselves under a huge boat. The ride itself was quite smooth, with the exception of the extreme cold permeating our clothing. Despite the fact that we wore winter boots, our feet were not moving much and became numb from the frigid temperatures. Huddled together, we were forced to remain silent as we shook from the cold of the strong wind blowing as the train sped along.

We rode west in pursuit of our volunteer army. The train often stopped at side roads, letting other war transports by. During such stopovers, we had to lie still so that the convoys would not hear the uninvited passengers being carried aboard. If the train was standing, the Soviet soldiers, who constituted the transport's crew, entered into a devious kind of trade with the people they met near the railway. One of them would sell, or trade, army shoes for food supplies or vodka. After completing such a deal, he would vanish, and in his place came two different individuals accusing the innocent village people of illegally trading army equipment. Afraid of risking arrest, these poor people returned the purchased shoes and disappeared in the blink of an eye. A crew of four individuals was at every stop, taking part in these dishonest deals selling the same shoes repeatedly. We did not want to confront the continuously drunken soldiers. Therefore, we sat quietly so as to avoid any meeting with them, fearing that our backpacks, filled with food and extra clothing, would be confiscated.

That was the first day of our trip. When evening came, we hid under the steel pontoon, huddled together, and fell into an unsettled sleep. In the darkness of night, we were awakened by the light of a lantern held by a soldier in the army convoy. "What are you doing here?" he asked. "It's very cold." We replied that we were trying to catch up to our army unit. He expressed his sympathies and invited us to a car he occupied with three of his friends. "It'll be warmer for you there and we'll treat you to some bread with pork fat," he announced. Without much enthusiasm, we followed him, hiding our backpacks under one boat. The soldiers kept their solid promise and offered us food and a slug of moonshine from a bottle. We sat around a burning iron stove, talking with the soldiers and awaiting the coming of day. We were suspicious of the fact that one of them would often leave, as though to check on the status of the transport.

In the morning, after thanking them for their hospitality, we returned to the abandoned car. When we looked under the boat, we found nothing. Our backpacks were no longer there. Our extra clothing, underwear, and that little bit of food had disappeared without a trace. We were left with only one briefcase, which I carried with me the entire time. We knew the perpetrator of this robbery. It was not without reason that one of the soldiers kept exiting so often from the comfortable and warm car. Immediately, we returned to the car, accusing the soldiers of the theft of our supplies. Their reply was not a very kind one. We saw the barrels of automatic guns being aimed in our direction, as well as the wagon door being moved aside with a grinding sound.

"Jump out because we're going to shoot!" The threat seemed very meaningful; and we had no reason to doubt it. One by one, we left the rushing wagon, jumping onto the fleeing railway embankment covered with snow. The rush of the train, along with the wind, momentarily twisted my body. I did not have the slightest control over my movements. I felt myself tumbling through the air, and within a split second, whiteness completely surrounded me. I was bouncing upon the frozen snow, and rolling in the depths of it like a rubber ball. I collapsed, motionless, with a snow filled mouth.

For some time, I did not have the courage to try moving my arms and legs for fear of pain from possibly broken limbs. Actually, we all were very fortunate. None of us had broken our neck. Apparently the snow had softened the blow of our fall. We picked ourselves up, covered with snow, and with only small scratches on our faces and the palms of our hands. We had to spend quite a bit of time looking for our hats and for my briefcase.

Steel tracks stretched before us, over which escaped the friendly Soviets and our backpacks. Step by step, counting the railway ties, our threesome marched toward the west. We were on the lookout for some kind of housing settlement or station in which we could warm up and get something to eat. Lucky for us, I still had my briefcase, which contained a small amount of Soviet rubles, extra underwear and a razor for shaving, plus a piece of soap.

We could see no buildings ahead of us. The tracks continued to pass into the distance, while on both sides grew the impenetrable pine forests of Podlasie. Winter was at its peak. It was only the quickness of our steps that maintained a modicum of warmth for our bodies during that freezing January day. We continued walking in the direction of the border with the hope that somehow we would make our way to the other side, and that by the time the war ended, we would catch up to our lost army members.

After an entire day of walking, we began to see the end of the forest. The buildings of a small railway station appeared before us on the horizon. Next to it, on a side road, stood a long train, the kind which from a distance was unrecognizable. Fortunately, we soon determined that it was not the one with the pontoons. On the locomotive and wagons was painted the large symbol of the International Red Cross. This was an army war hospital. Surrounding this train were several bonfires being enjoyed by people in Soviet dress. We first approached some young Russian girls, who were sawing wood to be used as fuel in their wagons. We walked up to them and offered our help in this difficult task they were performing. We told them that we were very cold and wanted to warm up a little by sawing. They gave their saws to us without much hesitation.

Among the Soviets, not many courtesies are known to be shown to the female gender. The equal right to work rule is about all that is equal in their society. Every woman must do each activity the same as men. While sawing, we started a conversation with them, telling them about our tragic loss of the army transport, which we are currently trying to overtake. The girls in turn told us that they were going to the city of Bialystok where the head office of the International Red Cross was located. We took the sawed and chopped wood to their standing wagon, establishing a friendly atmosphere between those Soviet nurses and three young Polish Army volunteers.

In reciprocation for the favor we had done for them, they offered us a piece of bread with some hot grain coffee. While we ate, we asked them whether there was any possibility we could go with them to Bialystok. The pleasant girls replied that they would be very eager to have us along, however, the major, commanding chief of the hospital, would have to give his approval. "It is definitely forbidden for us to bring men into our wagon," they said, "but," they added with a smile, "the door to the wagon will be left slightly open and if someone should jump in while running, the responsibility will fall upon him." After consuming the modest meal, we, weary from our long trip, relaxed and warmed our feet by the burning fire.

After the sun had set, the freezing air had become even colder. Our weary eyes were closing. Tired bodies demanded sleep. It was fortunate that there was more than enough wood for heating. A strong fire warmed us from one side. Within a short while, we started another fire. Sitting between the two fires, we dozed from time-to-time, being awakened every now and then by the need to change positions due to our frozen feet. In this way, we awaited sunrise.

Activity all around the wagons began with daybreak. The sleepy staff of the train crawled out from within it, gathering around the fire and cooking coffee in pots. Again, the girls brought us a portion of bread and a pot of coffee. The hot liquid tasted splendid despite the fact that it was without milk and sugar. Lena, one of the girls, casually mentioned that the vehicle will soon be on its way.

"Be ready; the door will be slightly ajar," she said. We extinguished the burning fire and slowly walked to the head of the train so that we would be ready to jump into the passing wagon. We had no problem vaulting into the inside of the wagon. At first, it was difficult to orient ourselves as to where we were. We fell from the brightness of day into the semi-darkness of closed quarters.

The inside of the wagon was surrounded with bunks on three sides. There were two tiers of bunks that were occupied by the twenty-seven girls who provided hospital medical services. In the middle of the wagon stood an iron stove, creating pleasant warmth. We found ourselves in the midst of a most homey, family-type atmosphere. It was just too bad that there were too many girls, twenty-four too many. They introduced themselves to us, one by one, giving us their first names. They asked us about our background and life in Poland. Those were such pleasant and friendly moments spent among that group of young hospital nurses.

For a snack at noon, they offered us some millet porridge and tea with a small piece of sugar. Toward evening, when the train stood on a byroad in Wolkowysk, awaiting the arrival of an army transport traveling in the direction of the war front, the commanding Major of the hospital came to the wagon. When he saw us he demanded to see our documents. After checking all the army recruitment certifications, and hearing about our unlucky delay, he allowed us to travel farther with them. Alas, we would have to leave the friendly wagon at night and spend the night outside.

The following day, the transport reached the border. The wagon doors opened and a sharp order reverberated "Leave!" commanded the Russian sergeant of the border patrol. With weapons aimed, they hurried us toward nearby guards, demanding we show our documents, which permitted our crossing over the international line. They did not pay any great attention to our draft certificates. One after the other, they searched everyone individually. After they had inspected us for weapons they took note of my briefcase. In a moment, they found within it, a bundle of czerwoncow (at that time, these were Russian monetary banknotes, highly valued and red in color) which stood for the sizeable value of six thousand rubles. At the sight of this amount of money, their eyes bulged! My friend, Leon, knowing the Russian language and psyche of its people, immediately took advantage of the soldiers' stupefying moment.

"We're going to fight the Germans and maybe never have the opportunity to use this money," he told them. "If you give us a receipt stating that this money will remain held until the war ends, and then returned to us, that would be the safest way for us to invest it." The soldier quickly tore a piece from a newspaper. On this scrap of paper he acknowledged that he had in his possession six thousand rubles belonging to three Polish army volunteers who were crossing the border. This money was to be secured and returned to the owners at the end of the war. The sergeant scrawled an indecipherable signature on the bottom, and handed us the folded document. We three friends looked in each other's eyes, thinking the identical thought - that is the last we will ever see of our six thousand rubles. This transaction proved to be worthwhile because from then on no one ever questioned our version of losing our unit. Miraculously, one of the soldiers suddenly remembered that just the other day some kind of transport had left this area. It became apparent that they wanted to get rid of us as quickly as possible, so that they could start enjoying our confiscated money.

Guards pushed us out the door and advised that we run quickly to the train, which was leaving immediately. We did not need a lot of encouragement. We knew that in just a short while, we would forever bid farewell to this Bolshevik country of terror. Happily, we discovered that the door to the hospitable wagon was again partially open. We jumped inside and were warmly greeted by the hospital nurses. It was apparent by the girls' faces, that they had taken a liking to the Polish boys and their gallant flirtations and friendly overtures toward the young girls. These girls had been exposed to something unknown in their country, common courtesy and respect.

In a short while, the traffic signal turned green, which meant that the train was free to cross. Slowly, the locomotive crossed over the border, pulling behind it many wagons of the Soviet hospital. Secured in one of these wagons were three young boys who had endured a hard and dangerous journey. We were leaving behind us a part of our lives filled with youthful adventures. We felt a great longing for our families and that enchanting land to which we thought we would never return. With great sadness we had bidden farewell to our homeland. It was difficult for us to hold back tears of remembrance. Thanks to those girls, and the cheerful songs they were humming, we were torn away from our pensive thoughts, and began to look forward to the future.

The snowy fields of Poland now stretched before our eyes. This land, freed from German invasion, now awaited cultivation by Polish hands. What it was not expecting, however, was that it would soon be groaning under the wheels of the state's farming tractors, only to have its crops hauled away into the depths of the USSR. After a few more hours of traveling, we were able to see in the distance, the tall chimneys of Bialystok's factories. Bialystok was a city that had been famous for its textile products before the war. We had not planned on concluding our trip at the main railroad station where Russian, as well as Polish, military policemen were roaming about. It would be difficult to explain to them our tardiness in reuniting with the forces from which we had become separated.

We three vagabonds bid a sad goodbye to our charming custodians. We told them we were planning to visit relatives whom we had not seen for a very long time prior to our going into the army. We hopped off the train, and ran to the nearest fields. By way of the fields we skirted past many buildings and arrived near the center of the city. It was there, with alarm, that we saw streets filled with army patrols, checking the young people who entered. We tried to avoid a confrontation by going in and out of various buildings and stores.

We came upon an open market, and after gathering together our small change, I succeeded in buying a piece of smoked salt pork and a loaf of rye bread. That satisfied us to some extent, and we were now ready to search for an exit out of this city. Night was nearing. We knew we were in a precarious situation. We no longer had the certificates issued through the recruitment office. They had been issued in assumed names, and we had not considered them important. We were tired of the war and the army. We now considered ourselves civilians and as such wanted to remain within our homeland. We decided to go south toward Lublin.

We traveled along the side streets, to avoid being stopped by the army patrols. Upon rounding a corner, I recognized a familiar silhouette. It was my good friend, Lieutenant "Zetka" – Zygmunt Kondratowicz. During my time in the Home Army I had helped him get from Wilno to the "Jurand Brigade." He had been threatened with arrest and needed security within the partisan unit. "Zetka," accompanied by two young men, was approaching us. He recognized me immediately. "Bej, what are you doing here?" he shouted.

Our greeting was joyous, interwoven with a hodgepodge of storytelling about what had been happening with each of us since we had last met. Understanding our tenuous situation, he proposed that we stay with him for the night. He was renting an attic room in a small one-family house. We were very happy to accept his invitation, and soon after, found ourselves sitting by a table eating soup. There seemed to be no end to our recollections that of the times survived in the brigade and of the sad losses our group had endured.

Miraculously "Zetka" had also been able to escape arrest. He had crossed over the border together with his former subordinates. Presently, he was hiding in the city without having decided where to go or what to do next. He asked about our plans for the future. Our plans were definite and clear. We wanted no more war adventures. We intended to follow the front lines west. Our aim was to get to Krakow, and remain there. "Zetka" did not talk much about his plans. I felt that he hoped to convince us to do further army service. With these reflections the evening passed. Tired, we finally settled down on a floor covered with hay, and immediately fell asleep.

We awoke to the thudding sounds of rifle butts hitting the door of the house. Through the window, in the moonlight, we were able to see military forms surrounding the building. Someone evidently had delivered information to the authorities about the suspicious individuals who were staying here. The housekeeper opened the door, allowing the soldiers in. We heard the army personnel bustling about the first floor, and after a while, the heavy footsteps of soldiers reverberated on the stairs which led to the attic.

"Zetka" sprang from his bed, pulled out a roll of banknotes from his pant's pocket, and stood next to the closed door. There was a period of dead silence. We waited. With a pressure upon the doorknob, the door slowly opened. There stood the powerful form of a Polish soldier from the communist People's Army. He stared at us, stunned by the presence of the six young people. We heard Zetka's quiet words, "Mister – we want to live," and saw his hand surreptitiously pass over the roll of money to the newcomer. There was a moment's hesitation, our visitor turned, and subsequently we heard his descending steps. We remained still, for what seemed to us like an eternity. Shortly we heard his Russian-speaking voice traveling toward us: "No one is there," the voice was saying. With relief, we heard the soldiers leave the house. No one spoke, and we returned to our resting places. There was very little peaceful sleep in store, since our jangled nerves kept us wide-eyed throughout the night.

Fortunately, "Zetka" had not given away all of his money. When daybreak came, he offered to lend us enough to sustain us for a while. We said our thanks and good-byes to the housekeeper who had befriended us, and set off in the direction of Lublin. I never heard about "Zetka's" fate; he disappeared without a trace. The weather cooperated with us beautifully. The dry, freezing air, with snow crunching beneath our feet, enticed us to march along vigorously. A signpost with the writing of *Bielsk Podlaski,* directed us toward the south. We were in no hurry. The war still continued. Krakow still belonged to the Germans. There was no point in heading closer to where the battles were taking place. We happily ambled through the countryside, enjoying our feeling of freedom. We chose ruined railway stations in which to spend our nights. Lying on the cement floor we would drift into a sleep that was frequently disrupted by the cold.

Entering into villages along the way, we would seek out the local authority figure and plead with him for assistance. Often he would be happy to help, and recommend us to someone who would give us lodging for the night. For our meals we stopped at church parishes that we passed. Knocking upon the door of the priests' quarters, we announced to the terrified housekeeper that we had come for breakfast. At that time, the sight of three young, unknown men was enough to engender a modicum of fear. Although we were always polite and composed, we were also forceful and determined. We were governed by the one unassailable fact that we were hungry, and we felt we deserved an honest meal.

We passed Bielsk Podlaski, heading in the direction of Czeremchy. Further on, the road carried us toward Siedlce, Lukow, Deblin and through Naleczow to Lublin. After marching for two weeks, we stepped into the city of Lublin. Disappointment met us there – a situation perhaps worse than the one we had encountered in Bialystok. The streets were filled with both Russian and Polish army personnel. The situation near the front was that at every step there were military police patrols checking the documents of young people. There was no possibility we could wander in this city for even a little while. We headed straight for the city's administration office, hoping to receive some kind of certification stating that we were looking for our families rumored to be living in Krakow.

We rambled through the corridors. Our aim was to find an office overseen by what appeared to be a youngish single woman. We knew from past experience that this sort of person was most prone to flattery from kind, well-mannered young men. Our intuition did not disappoint us. The young woman we chose was not able to deny our requests. We asked that she certify one fact – that we were immigrant citizens from Wilno and we were searching for our families. A seal with the communist People's Army eagle found itself upon a scrap of paper, which was now in our possession. To add more weight to the importance of this document, Leon stopped a Soviet Army sergeant on the stairs of the office bureau. "Friend," he said, first offering him a cigarette. "Can you do a small favor for us and certify this document which was given us, adding in Russian the fact and goal of our trip?" The sergeant, without a moment's hesitation, fulfilled Leon's request, signing the document in a sprawling handwriting.

Now we were in control of the situation, being able to converse in Russian and in the possession of such an important document. We could rest assured and go to Krakow. We left the overcrowded Lublin, this time heading southwest to a city that was still German occupied. Slowly we dragged ourselves along, following the front lines by a road to Tarnobrzeg. There we waited for further successes of the Soviet Army so that we could proceed. We did not have to wait much longer. The city of Mielec, and then Tarnow, became freed from the hands of the enemy.

On the way to Wieliczka we saw the devastation caused by the Soviet air attack waged on the highly regarded German Army. The destroyed army transport was a horrific sight to see. The flesh of people and horses hung on telephone wires. Pants with legs in them swung in the blowing wind. The road's asphalt was covered with hardened human blood, over which our shoes slid. Such a gruesome sight is never forgotten. The horrors of war cannot be fully comprehended unless experienced, and they awakened feelings of compassion even for the defeated enemy.

Finally from afar, we were able to see the city outlines. With relief, we discovered that the uncompassionate turmoil of war had bypassed Krakow. Krakow was almost untouched. Only a few buildings had submitted to destruction. Here we were. What would we do next? How would we manage here with no friends or family? Where should we turn for help and advice?

After crossing the bridge over the Wisla River, on a street which led to the city's center, we came up with a plan. We first had to find a place to stay. With this in mind, we started ringing doorbells at tenement houses. When the caretaker answered, we, in a friendly manner, told him briefly about our losses since being displaced from Wilno. We added that since we knew the Russian language well, we hoped to establish trade relations with Soviet soldiers. We needed someone who would sell these goods on the local market. Did he know anyone who would be interested?

At such a proposition, the eyes of the brick tenement building's caretaker began to shine. Momentarily, he agreed to cooperate with us. However, the matter became complicated the very moment we announced that we had nowhere to stay. We repeated the same story in each successive house we came upon, also without results. All the apartments were full. We walked the length of Starowislna Street until we almost reached its end. On its corner with Kazimierza Street, house number 63 proved to be lucky. After hearing our story, the caretaker of the tall brick building became enthused at the prospect of this future business and led us to the fourth floor. The creaking which resulted from the opening of the lock was like music to our ears. No one needed to invite us to go inside. Open before us stood a furnished room along with a kitchen. The caretaker declared that the Germans had abandoned the apartment. Wishing us well he returned downstairs.

We felt this was a success beyond this world! Within just one day, we had been assured of a roof over our heads in overcrowded Krakow. Some wood was stored in the kitchen. A lit fire had begun to warm the abandoned apartment. Further searching around the apartment resulted in our being rewarded with the discovery of a bag of frozen potatoes, a tiny bit of salt and a jar of ground pepper. After a while, we had boiling potatoes gurgling on the stove. My friend, Mietek, made a sauce out of the pepper, which he poured onto the newly cooked potatoes. This was his last feat in the preparation of meals. We had to drink an incredible amount of water after having eaten that supper! The three of us spent the night huddled together on one bed - we slept directly on the bed's springs, as there was no mattress.

The next morning, feeling hungry, we set out into the city in search of some kind of provisions. Around noontime, we happened upon the hospitable door of a greasy spoon type place where nuns were giving out soup to the homeless. The barley soup, along with a piece of bread and margarine, tasted wonderful! Warmed by the hot dish and finding ourselves, therefore, in a much better mood, we explored the beautiful city, not paying much attention to the historical monuments and architecture.

Finally, in some abandoned barracks, we found pallets filled with hay. We needed these pallets desperately because we had hope that the next night would be spent upon some soft bedding. However, hope is the mother of fools. During the night we were attacked by thousands of fleas. There was no escaping from the black jumping pack. The pallet then got tossed down the stairs, onto the street, and one match turned it into a huge burning torch. This was a mass murder committed on bothersome insects, in the winter of 1945, on Starowislna Street.

The next day, as we walked about we came upon a marketplace that was located not too far from where we were staying. With the rest of our remaining money we purchased what we considered to be the most necessary of food supplies. We now had to think about some sort of steady income, which would assure us a standard of living. Work could not be found. Krakow was filled with native people, as well as additional displaced persons from Warsaw. Therefore, trade would have to be the temporary source of our income.

Leon, an expert in the Russian language, was going to establish contacts with soldiers returning from the front. They brought all kinds of old clothing and items robbed from the Germans. Mietek's assignment was to sell the recently acquired items at the nearby market. My job was to take care of stocking and maintaining necessary supplies for the apartment as well as preparing our meals. Our established business began to give us sufficient funds with which to support ourselves as well as pay taxes. Our building caretaker sold gasoline that was brought by the Soviet soldiers in barrels, sharing his income with us. He walked around proudly and very satisfied with his young tenants.

Spring came. In Krakow's parks early tulips bloomed. Soon after them, fragrant lilacs appeared. Swarms of people walked along the streets, intoxicated by the beautiful sights of nature, forgetting about the ongoing battles.

Finally, in May of 1945, the bells of many churches rang, announcing the greatly awaited moment of surrender by the German Army. The city went wild with excitement. It was finally the end, and finally life would return to normal. People cried from happiness and fell into each other's arms. We also took advantage of this occasion, choosing young female students as the object of our happiness.

Old Krakow appealed to us, with its historical monuments and academic youth that filled its winding streets. We got the feeling of wanting to stay in it forever, to return to a peaceful way of life, after years of trying to survive in danger. We saw fewer and fewer Soviet soldiers in the Krakow marketplace. There began to be a shortage of goods to exchange, so we decided to go in search of the alcohol deprived Red Army. We hoped to exchange moonshine for clothing and food. I went off with Mietek to Gliwice, which was in the direction of Slask. It was not easy finding a place in the overcrowded train wagon that was heading west. However, for the young, there were never any obstacles. After some hesitation, we found ourselves on the roof of the train's wagon. I sat comfortably on the top of a brake shed, content with the view and the fresh air.

We were merrily breezing along when I thought I heard a shout, perhaps a cry of warning. I paid no heed until, suddenly, I was whacked across the chin and mouth. My head snapped back and my body followed. Mietek grabbed me by my legs, and kept me from falling between the speeding wagons. A low hanging telephone line had interrupted what had promised to be a pleasant trip to Gliwice.

We slid off the roof at the first station, and had to find our way back eight kilometers to Krakow. Mietek could not stop laughing at the sight of my swollen and bloody face. I tried to retain some semblance of seriousness since every smile caused my mouth pain, and I really had little to smile about. In the city, people stared at my bloody face. I went to two different dentists and was turned away by both. They did not want to treat such a serious injury, and said that I should go to the hospital. I did just that.

After examining the damage to my mouth, the hospital surgeon told me that I was missing two teeth and six teeth were broken within my jaw. All he could do was to sew the tear on the side of my mouth. He added that this would hurt a little as he did not have anything with which to numb the area. I kept fidgeting my legs around while the three stitches were being inserted, but other than that I remained quiet. The mere sight of the needle was enough reason to start anyone squirming.

After the surgery, I returned to the apartment wondering what had happened to my two teeth. I thought maybe they had remained on that telephone wire, answering some kind of crazy telephone call! For a month, I only drank condensed milk because I could not open my pained mouth completely. I must admit that my friends treated me well. They tried hard not to make me laugh because that was so painful.

After my mouth healed, I went to see a professor at the Dental Institute at the Jagiellonski University, for a consultation. I promised him any sum of money imaginable if he could save my teeth, and restore my face so that I would look normal. He fitted me with braces, and removed the torn nerves from my black and dead teeth. The results were outstanding, and my teeth were no longer black! To this day, I can bite and chew hard apples with no problems. Dentists in the United States are always amazed when they hear the story of my teeth.

That was my first and last unforgettable trip on the rooftop of a train wagon! This was not, however, to be my last accident in this beautiful city. Coming home late one night from a date, as I was approaching my apartment, I was stopped by a Russian soldier dressed in his army uniform. He demanded that I show him my identification documents. While I was taking out the documents, he grabbed me by the wrist. "Give me your watch," he demanded. I pulled my arm out of his grip, but as I stood in the light of his flashlight, I saw the butt of an automatic pistol aimed in my direction. He ordered me to go forward and walk toward the marketplace on Kazimierz Street. My situation was not healthy. We turned into a side street and he told me to stop.

"Give me your watch!" he repeated. I tried to plead with him. The answer to this attempt was very clear – a short series of shots fired above my head. *I'm still alive,* I thought. *But what will happen further?* "Stupaj," (Go) said the soldier, pointing me in the direction of the Wisla River, and we marched some distance to its banks. He stopped again by the very edge of the water.

"For the last time," the soldier said, "I'm telling you – give me your watch!" I could hear in the tone of his voice that this soldier was not joking. Again, I began pleading with him, telling him that I had a large amount of money and that he could take it if he wanted to. But I begged that he not deprive me of this remembrance from my deceased mother. I was playing the last card possible, knowing that even the most hardened character possesses some recollections about a person dear to his heart.

For a moment I was in doubt, and then I saw a hand extending for the promised money. With trembling hands, I gathered together all the money I had and gave it to the soldier. He took the money, saying, "You're lucky that you speak Russian. Otherwise, I'd leave you here – dead." After saying those words, the soldier disappeared into the darkness of the night, probably looking for a new victim. I returned to my friends, poorer and wiser, and sad that I had to lie about my mother's demise.

"Why are you so pale?" they asked. It was not until the following morning that I told them about my unpleasant adventure. It was a new lesson – not to trudge about the streets of the city at night, alone. Until this day, I still think how crazy it was to test my luck to such limits. Was that watch really worth endangering my life?

Our existence was forever uncertain. Mietek and I always lived under fake last names and with forged documents. We were pleased to read the announcement that a commission had been established to liquidate the Home Army. That would give us the opportunity to return to our real last names, and a chance to enjoy a normal life. We would again be legal citizens of our own country. It was not without fear that we stood before the Communist Liquidation Committee. After the committee had examined all the evidence of our affiliation with the illegal army, we received advancement to the position of sergeants, medals of the Peoples Army and crosses of bravery for wounds acquired in fighting the enemy. Our obligations had now been completed. We shook hands all around and walked out into the street. The enormity and repercussions of this event had not yet impacted us.

Shortly after having taken care of that matter, we received letters from Wilno informing us that our families would soon be arriving in Poland. We felt that we had to find places for them to stay. It was impossible to think about their settling in Krakow, as it was already extremely overcrowded. The next day we boarded a train and headed for the war-torn area of Gliwice. On the station's platform, as well as in the railway station hall in Gliwice, lay piles of rubble, which remained from the heavy Soviet artillery bombings. By the exit, we were stopped by a Soviet soldier. He pointed to shovels, which were lying there, and commanded us to each take up a shovel and begin cleaning. He intended that we join the German workers already working there. After a moment he was face to face with Leon. In his most assertive Russian Leon said: "You fool. You better tell us where we can find the city war chief." This was enough said – the Soviet soldier saluted us and stepped out of our way, permitting us to leave. A perfect Russian accent was, during those times, the best pass.

The main street, which led from the railway station to the center of the city was in part, demolished and burned. Other districts of the city had survived. Houses stood empty – their owners had fled to Germany. We found the Red Cross office and were assured of a place to stay for the first night along with some dinner. The clerk there informed us that there would be no problem obtaining jobs, and as far as apartments, there was an abundance of them. After spending the night in an actual bed, covered with huge quilts, we felt well rested. A modest breakfast satisfied our hunger.

We needed to set out in search of a place to live for ourselves as well as our families, who were due to arrive shortly. This was no problem. By the end of the day, we had found furnished apartments for everyone. Just to be on the safe side, Leon wrote notes and hung them on the entrance doors to these apartments. In Russian, these notes informed and warned intruders that the authorities in power in the city already reserved these quarters. Hopefully, this would keep the apartments safe until we had officially filed an application for the lease of these units with the city's administration. That next night we shopped for food, and had a pleasant evening on the town.

A few days later, we managed to get jobs at the garage of Slask Technical University. They were awaiting an allotment of trucks from "Unra." Leon began working at City Hall, and had already purchased a "Tempo" car. This was a small vehicle with one wheel in the front and two in back. It ran, which was at that time the most important thing. Our salaries were less than minimum wage, but for us this was not a major obstacle. Since we had keys to the garage, we also had access to the vehicles within that garage. This allowed us to deliver goods we had purchased from the local soldiers up to Krakow, one hundred-ten kilometers away. When we returned the truck to the garage we settled up for whatever gasoline had been used. The Russians were very happy to exchange fuel for Polish moonshine. And so, with our weekly earnings, plus what we gained with our trading, are incomes were more than adequate.

Good news arrived by mail during the summer. Mietek's parents were on their way, while my mother was packed and waiting for her turn to leave Wilno. After a few weeks, we had a heartwarming reunion with my friend's parents. After such a long and tragic separation it seemed unbelievable that we were together again. Soon after that, my mother arrived. In spite of the many difficulties she had endured, she looked very well. Her oldest son, my brother Tadek, was thought to be somewhere in Russia, where he had been forcefully taken to join the work crew.

For many years, my mother had had no news whatsoever about me, either. After the death of my father, and with no news of her two sons, she had been sentenced to a very lonely life. After we found each other she could not let me go. Crying, she spoke only my name, over, and over, unable to find other words. She almost could not believe that she was seeing me again, after so many years of not knowing whether I was dead or alive. We had so much to talk about, and for weeks my mother kept asking me to tell her every small detail about my escape from Lithuania.

Soon, we received more very happy news. My brother, Tadek, had been released from the Russian work camp, and he was now in Wilno. He was already registered on a list of expatriates and he hoped to join us soon. After a few months time, Tadek arrived in Gliwice and we had a joyful reunion. With elation we fell into each other's arms. Our family was now almost complete. Only our father remained apart from us. He was buried in the Bernardinian Cemetery in Wilno, not far from the home where he worked so fearlessly for the Polish cause.

Shortly after our family had been reunited, Tadek began to tell us about his adventures and misfortunes. These started with his arrest in Wilno in the fall of 1944. He said that one day he had gone into town with a female friend. She had to take care of a property matter at the town office, and Tadek was strolling along the sidewalk across the street waiting for her return. An office window opened from above and an office worker in a Russian uniform beckoned for him to come inside. He waved his hand, inviting my brother in. Innocently, Tadek went inside. An older soldier standing guard, and speaking under his breath, said: "Don't go inside." Tadek paid no heed.

He was soon met by an officer who asked why Tadek had been roaming the streets. Tadek explained his situation and was then invited into the soldier's office. "Sit here," he indicated with his hand to a chair, which stood by his desk. He looked at Tadek for a while, and then he asked him three short questions.

"Do you know any navy blue policemen?" he asked. "If you do, give me their names and addresses." (Prior to the war, the Polish police wore navy blue uniforms.)

"Do you see upon the streets of the city any former officers of the Polish Army? Do you know any of the Home Army partisans?" In answer to the last question, Tadek responded that he knew several of them. "Where do they live?" To this question, the answer "in Siberia" carelessly slipped from Tadek's lips. The officer sprang from his chair and threatened him with a fist waving up against his nose, shouting: "You will now die in jail!"

After this most unpleasant conversation, the officer led my brother to the guardroom and gave him to the care of the sergeant on duty. Several detained men of varying ages were already sitting there. Every once in a while a new delinquent was brought in and none of them knew why they were arrested. Conversation was strictly prohibited. Around 2:00 a.m., a group of guards came on duty. Immediately, one officer took a pistol from his holster and put ammunition into the barrel. He warned them that if anyone even made one move toward attempting to escape, he would fire and kill without warning.

Thirty of those detained were then stripped of their belts, and buttons were torn from their clothes. They were led out onto the street, holding up their pants with their hands. Tadek was among those thirty. They were led through the streets to the NKVD (Soviet Military Police) office, which was on Ofiarna Street. There, in a windowless room, lit only by candles, the prisoners were examined by investigative officers. All of the officers were Asian. Questions were asked about the army, service in the A.K. and other political organizations. Examinations were carried out very efficiently without torture or force.

Later the prisoners spent a sleepless night in the basement of this building. Early the next morning, all the arrested were led out onto the street, forming rows that immediately were surrounded by officials of the Investigative Office. The group again was quickly herded in the direction of the Lukisk jails. They were told to kneel in the snow, right in front of the entrance gate, and in this position they were to wait for the gate to open. This lasted for more than an hour. The prisoners' feet were becoming numb from the cold snowy ground, and from the fact that they were not allowed to move. Their nerves were stretched to the limit, for they did not know what the next hour would bring.

Finally, the double doors of the jail opened. The entire group was let inside. Immediately they were rushed into the bathhouse, where they were ordered to undress completely. Their clothing and underwear were taken away to be disinfected in huge ovens. The clothes were then returned, hot, but not to their rightful owners. The jail staff seized better items, while the prisoners were given torn and shrunken clothing. It was explained to them that the heat had destroyed their clothing. The now clean prisoners were quartered in jail cells. Twenty to thirty prisoners were crammed into the smaller cells while seventy to eighty people were loaded into the larger ones. At night the prisoners would lie down on bare flooring and use their arms for pillows. In the morning they were each given a cup of brown liquid that looked like coffee. For dinner there was some kind of canned soup or other canned food items. The liquid looked atrocious. It came in smelly boxes that had not been washed for a very long time, and was mixed with leftovers from the previous day's supper.

Tadek and the others had to endure terrible thirst. After being given salty dishes to eat, the men were never given enough water to drink. Prisoners had to secretly drink musty, rust-colored water from small holes that had been made in the radiators by previous residents of these cells. Prisoners were often moved from room to room. This was done to make them harder to find. Packages from family members were usually taken by the staff members because, supposedly, the prisoners could not be located. Food and clothing seldom reached the intended recipient.

More and more people were being arrested and brought to the prison, thereby creating a seriously overcrowded situation. The bathhouses could no longer accommodate the increasing number of people. There was an infestation of fleas, which covered the bodies of the prisoners dressed in the dirty, ragged clothes, which they received after their obligatory disinfection. There were already several thousand Polish citizens within the prison building who had no idea what awaited them. They sat in their cells not knowing why they had been arrested, let alone how or when their misery would end.

After some time, a large number of "*Wlascowcow*" (a group of Ukrainians under the direction of General Wlasow who joined the Germans to fight against the Russians), were thrown into the prison cells occupied by the Polish people. This had been done intentionally to make all of the detainees even more miserable and frustrated. The hungry Ukrainians began to tear food from the hands of the poor prisoners already incarcerated there. The Ukranians had already spent a lot of time in various prisons awaiting some sort of organized transport to take them into the depths of Russia. They had a feeling of desperation equal to that of the Poles. Prison guards pretended not to see these battles for nourishment. The long festering hatred between the nationalities was very convenient for them. People from each group would leak information about their adversaries, and their wardens planned to use that information to their own advantage. This information would be used in the future to keep their workers in line.

Toward the end of February 1945, at about 3:00 a.m., one morning all of the prisoners were ordered to assemble outside of the building. Standing in the cold, holding their belongings in their hands, they knew that their stay in this prison was to end that night. Soon soldiers entered through the open gates holding dogs on leashes. Then the prisoners were surrounded by cavalry and herded out of the prison yard. The prisoners marched through the streets of their beloved city, clutching on to their beltless and buttonless pants. Despite the early morning hour, the residents of Wilno came out to bid farewell to the unfortunate detainees. They lined the streets along the roadways, crying and waving. Soldiers on horseback pushed back the jostling crowd of people toward the gateways of their homes, at times using whips on those who showed resistance.

This enforced march of the prisoners was a depressing and unforgettable sight to see. Up until now, such displays were only seen in movies depicting Egyptian pharaohs and their slaves. Cattle cars already waited at the train station. Handrails had been built on their rooftops so that the transport guards would be able to move about freely and safely. The armed guards were prepared to use their weapons at the slightest provocation or at any attempt to escape. The cars were still closed, and prisoners were told to kneel in the snow and wait for them to open. No one would dare to get up on the threat of being shot.

Finally the doors opened and fifty people were loaded into each car. There was no place to sleep or sit. The only furnishing in this cage was an iron stove that stood in the center of the wagon with a small pile of peat for fuel. In the back of the car a small pipe was fastened in the wall for urination purposes, while a small opening in the floor could be found for the prisoners' more serious bodily functions.

The doors loudly clanged shut, and bolts were solidly latched. This essentially imprisoned the passengers inside the car. In the semi-darkness of these quarters, a deadly silence spread among the gathered prisoners. They still had no idea where they were being taken. There were many different theories, but on one thing they all agreed, that this was going to be a long trip into the depths of Russia. Finally, with the sound of the locomotive's whistle and a banging of the buffers, the transport began its journey. Through the gaps in the wagon's walls, the prisoners looked at the railway stations of bigger and smaller cities they were passing by, trying desperately to orient themselves as to where they were being taken. The transport passed Minsk, Homel, and then pulled into the railway station in Poltawie. Now they were able to figure out that they were going to Zaglebia Donieckiego (a coal mining area).

The nights were horrible. The prisoners would lie upon the bare floorboards, freezing from the cold that would reach many degrees below zero. Sometimes, the train would stop for a short while, allowing army transports to pass through. Many of the transports were heading to the front lines, while some were returning back into the country, carrying wounded. The meals consisted of soup or canned pork, which was made in the USA. Again, the terrible thirst was a grave problem. There was no water to be had. The two weeks of traveling enclosed inside the train seemed like an eternity. They had been dirty and unshaven for weeks before this trip, and looked like the hopeless vagabonds they were.

Finally the transport stopped for the night in Dzierzynsk, an industrial city. The prisoners were now certain that they were being brought to work in the coal mines. After several hours of traveling farther, the entire transport was unloaded in the Woroszylowka railway station. Among the crowd of arrested, everyone searched uselessly for faces of those they knew – friends were unrecognizable to each other. Only by their voices were they identifiable.

The curious native people asked the guards whom they had brought to their settlement. From the sight of the arrested newcomers, the natives could not figure out their nationality. Naturally, they were informed that these individuals were Polish bandits brought to do work and that they should avoid any friendly relationships with them.

Immediately, everyone was rushed to a camp that was surrounded by barbed wire which had remained from past German prison camps. Buildings which had been intended for quarters, had been completely destroyed. They had broken walls, glassless windows, and no furnishings inside. Nothing had changed – the same coldness, the same dirt, and bare floors on which to sleep. Toward evening of that same day, a labor camp officer appeared, introducing himself as being the warden from the NKVD branch. In his speech he told the prisoners that they had been brought here to establish order and organization in the mining work camp which had been ruined by fascist prisoners of war.

"Your responsibility," he said, "will be to renew the buildings, as well as work in the coal mines. In this way you will atone for the damages inflicted on the Soviet Union. In the future, you will be able to return to your own country." The total number of those exiled was approximately twelve hundred people. Some of these were already working at renovating the labor camp buildings. The rest were engaged in clearing the rubble and debris of the ruined mine and taking out the coal from the lower panes. There was no way out of this situation but to show one's skills and competency as well as eagerness to work, with the hope that this would speed up release from the camp.

Within a short time, glass was installed in the windows and bunk beds were built. On the camp's square, people had constructed a concert shell, while near the barracks a barber shop and a bath house were erected. Within the mine, there was a new coatroom for the miners and a large wash basin. There was a new working mine shaft, of three hundred meters, and one of seven hundred meters nearly ready for operation.

The labor camp warden was astonished at the Polish efficiency. Satisfied by their work, he improved the quality of the food that was delivered from the camp kitchen. They brought soups, mostly made from cabbage, and sometimes with noodles, which were called "Italianska" by the Russians. Breakfasts and suppers were accompanied by bread and black grain coffee without sugar. Those prisoners who worked underground received one-half kilogram of bread each day. Despite the improved standards of conditions in the labor camp, the death rate among the prisoners was very high. During the course of several months, about four hundred of the prisoners that had been sent to the labor camp had died from various illnesses and accidents. The elderly, as well as frail young people were dying. The dead were quietly taken away during the night. Bodies were buried in old slag heaps next to the mine. A few of my brother's friends and acquaintances remained there, never to return to their homeland.

In August 1945, Tadek was released from this forced work and with an easy heart, he returned to Wilno. He no longer took walks upon the sidewalks next to administrative offices of Russian powers. With this observation, my brother concluded his tales of his time spent in slavery work. This had been a period of the war during which millions of people had lost their freedom or their lives, in a foreign country under the foot of the merciless NKVD.

After our family was reunited, Tadek got a job in a printing shop in the city of Chorzow, which was not far from the city of Gliwice. Our lives began to proceed quite normally, resembling what it used to be, at least for a while. Business at the garage where I worked began to pick up, and I began a steady job there as a driver. There was much to do. We took away the garbage from the district occupied by the college, delivered coal to the academic cafeterias in Katowice, at times delivered equipment needed by the schools, and did a variety of other jobs. Each day, all day, the trucks were continuously in use. Drivers were able to make money on the side by performing small tasks for individual customers. Private contractors were willing to pay a premium wage for having their wares delivered a short distance. Within a few weeks, I was able to buy myself a motorcycle. I was also buying gold rubles, and setting them aside for the future, assuming that these times of bonanza would soon be over.

I was worried about my relationship with the Communist Secret Police (U.B.). Several of my friends and acquaintances had been visited by official authority members of the U.B., who interrogated them about my past. Information was being gathered from all the places I had been. This was a fact that was hard to understand because from the moment I had left Wilno, I had not taken part in any political work. My lifestyle was visible and the fact that I had been a soldier of the Home Army (A.K) was a thing of suspicion to communist authorities. Proof of this fact was that my application for acceptance into officers' school was categorically rejected.

When I had been in the R.K.U. (recruiting office) I had seen, quite by chance, my papers marked in red pencil with an additional note stating, "A.K. member under observation." During the general recruitment of young men into the army, I had been considered as being qualified for front line duty. It was not pleasant to discover that I was now considered a third class citizen. It was not long ago that I had shed my blood for Polish freedom. In this situation, there was no hope for me to have a life and career in communist Poland.

This was a time prior to elections. A list of candidates for government service was announced. Premier Mikolajczyk had arrived from London. Posters had been hung all over the city calling for people to join the communist Workers Party. As part of the opposition, academic youths poured out onto the streets shouting: "We want Mikolajczyk! We want a Democratic government and free voting! Mikolajczyk! Mikolajczyk!" The shouting of thousands of citizens spread throughout the streets. Armed police and dense rows of Voluntary Citizens Reservist Police opposed the gathered crowd. Clubs and machine gun butts were wielded. Polish blood was spilled once again, the blood of people who demanded just a small amount of justice. These riots, which citizens staged in the hopes that something would change, were short lived. Leaders were arrested and Poland was quieted before the elections.

Throughout cities and villages, army orchestras played high-spirited hymns, demonstrating a falsely joyous mood. Streets were decorated with red colors, and many posters were hung, encouraging people to vote for List 1 – the Workers Party. Voting was coerced. Halls in small towns and villages were already prepared for this purpose. Crowds of depressed people were brought in by the truckload, and presented as "help" for the authorities in counting votes.

Over the sounds of the orchestra, the secretary of the local Workers Party delivered a grand speech praising the new orderliness in the country, and in support of a friendship with the Soviet Union. After concluding each sentence, the pack of gathered Moscowian thugs gathered around the microphone, and with thunderously applauded ovations, shouted, "Let the Workers Party live!" After the conclusion of the speech, the secretary claimed that there was no need to delay the time of voting. "All of us, like one being, will of course vote for the candidate of the party," he said. "Let whoever has different thoughts raise his hand."

There were a few brave souls who did this and were allowed to toss their voting cards into the ballot box of the opposing candidates, such as, Mikolajczyk's. Their names were noted and they mysteriously disappeared from their homes a short time later. The ballots were counted by party representatives. It was no surprise, therefore, that their candidates were unanimously elected throughout the country. We had encountered this Soviet system a long time ago in Wilno. Nothing had changed. The only thing that had changed was the nationality of the organizers and the land upon which the action was taking place. My friends and I sensed a sad future for us and our country under the rule of Moscow. We began to talk about the possibility of again leaving our homeland.

I was then reminded of the words of a Russian major to whom my mother had gone for advice regarding my leaving Lithuania for Poland. That good friend had told her, in trusting confidence, "Let your son go to the country where he will have a better life for several years. Later there will be the same kind of mess in that country, as we have in Russia."

In Gliwice, I had met a girl at a soccer match to whom I owe much gratitude. She showed a liking toward me. She came from a good Warsaw family – past owners of a paper mill called "Skiba." Christine always admonished me by saying, "Czeslaw, do you have the intention of staying a chauffeur for the rest of your life?"

Like water that can carve a groove into a rock, her words made an impression on me. After passing the entrance exams for the first year in college, I had to interrupt my work at the garage. The money I had previously set aside became very handy. I was more and more dissatisfied with the dominating powers in Poland, and I could not reconcile myself with the thought that I had fought for the freedom of Poland, and this freedom was very unlikely to be achieved. My friends, Mietek and Leon, were as dissatisfied as I with Poland's political situation.

We then decided to defect from Poland, a country in which we no longer saw a future for ourselves. The first thing for us to do was to change our place of residence. The city of Gliwice did not suit us or our families as a place in which to stay permanently. We had fond memories of the green landscapes, the rivers and the lakes of Wilno, our birth place. The dull smoky terrain of Slask was too depressing for us to think of spending our lives there. I had interrupted my studies, sold our furniture and with the complete agreement of our parents moved by the sea. In Gdansk, near the Baltic Sea, we were determined to somehow organize our families and assure them a place to live and work, before we would find a way to defect.

# In Gdansk
### (Czeslaw)

While riding the train to the coastal city of Gdansk, I thought about what my future might hold. I wondered when I would finally be able to find a place in which I could settle down and live permanently and peacefully. I was now, once again, traveling to a new, unfamiliar city, not knowing what to expect.

This time, I realized the seriousness of this decision because my mother and brother were with me, and I felt responsible for them. I took solace in knowing that the parents of my friend Mietek had already found an apartment in Gdansk. In September, Mietek's father had begun a job at the Academy of Medicine, and it was there, on the school's property, that he had found a place to live. His responsibilities were to supervise the heating system for the academic buildings. He had promised to employ my brother in the boiler room, filling the stoves with coal.

Mietek was waiting for us at the train station in Gdansk. We took a trolley to the Academy of Medicine. We were received very hospitably at the home of Mietek's parents, who let us use their very own bedroom. However, we were told from the beginning that our stay could only be temporary because of strict orders about strangers staying in an official apartment. This was understandable to us, and we were infinitely grateful for the help shown us at that time.

The next day, my brother and I went to scout out the lower part of Gdansk where I had the hope of finding an apartment among the houses that had been ruined by the war's activities. My lucky star, that had guided me my entire life, did not disappoint and helped me this time as well. On Chlodna Street, I noticed a three story brick building with a huge hole in the wall. This was what remained after an artillery missile had exploded there. After examining the entire house more closely, I found a partially abandoned five-room apartment, on the second floor. Two families already occupied two rooms and a kitchen. The next two rooms, worthy of pity, stood filled with the bricks from a knocked down wall. Beyond the hall in the bigger room, a floor was missing since the neighbors had used it for fuel in their stoves. There were no doors between the rooms. The windows were without glass and the ceilings had fallen in from missile explosions.

We felt fortunate to find a place in which to live, even though it required a lot of work. None of us realized how much work was in store, but we eagerly got started. My brother carried bricks from nearby houses that had been demolished. I mixed cement and stacked, and sealed the bricks so that they closed the hole in the wall. That kept out the cold wind blowing from the canal. As we were working we remarked that we now knew why that street carried the name "Chlodna" (cool) – our chilled hands confirmed the appropriateness of that name.

Next to be repaired was the ceiling. Once again a good friend from the past came to our rescue. We happened to meet Mr. Narkiewicz, a former neighbor from Mlynowa Street, in Wilno. He was the father of my close childhood friend, Janek. He was very kind to us and helped us get the materials we needed for our renovations. Mr. Narkiewicz was well established in Gdansk and ran a small bookbinding workshop. He showed us where cardboard was available, and with this we covered the ceiling.

I searched through junkyards and found a door and some glass to put into the windows. After sealing the rooms as tightly as possible, we turned to another serious problem. We needed heat. After more searching, we found an old, but usable, iron stove. This solved our problem perfectly.

After two weeks of intense physical work, and many hours spent searching for the materials we needed, we became the residents of our very own home. There was a common kitchen for the families living there. There was no bathroom as such. Outdoors there was a deep hole in the in ground, surrounded by walls, and a roof made from old boards. That was the bathroom facility. In all the old stone houses, the pipes in the bathrooms had burst from the freezing cold, and had not been repaired.

Proud of our accomplishment, we thanked the Fijalkowskis for their help and for their hospitality in the overcrowded apartment. After getting our suitcases, which were filled with everything we owned, we went to our own "palace." Without great difficulty, I found work as a welder in the Gdansk shipyards, where the first ore and coal carrying ship was being built. This is how we survived the first winter by the Polish sea. Gdansk was overcrowded with expatriates from Wilno, therefore, we met many people we had known from there, and we felt much more comfortable among them than we had felt among the people in Gliwice.

In the Spring, I received an offer to change jobs. There was a need in the Seaside Unifying Company for an installation technician to work rebuilding the Old City. Jan Piwcewicza's father notified me of this position. Jan had been my friend at the technical high school and he had also been my arms companion in the partisan unit. After interviewing with Engineer Duszkiewicz from Wilno, I immediately was hired for the job. The engineer assured me that I would feel as though I was among family since water supply system specialists as well as sewage system specialists from Wilno controlled the entire office. His words were not exaggerations. This was a time of pleasant, productive work during which I showed a great deal of initiative and contributed new ideas for improving the system of monitoring work performance and calculating the procedures of paying by piecework. The only cloud on the horizon was the continuously unsettling prying of the Communist Secret Police (U.B.). During a time when I was particularly busy at work, I received from the personnel director, a thirty-two page evidence report, which I had to immediately fill out. Over the period of several weeks, I would receive these same papers at home, which I also would complete and return. I frequently inquired as to the purpose of this, and I would repeatedly receive the answer that the previous papers had been lost. Mietek, who was also employed as a warehouse worker in the same company, was also called to the personnel office to immediately fill out identical papers. Apparently, the U.B. compared our lives, retaining these accounts in their institution's archives for future use. This had been the tried-and-tested Soviet system of the NKVD (Soviet Military Police).

When summer arrived, Leon, my friend and companion as we fled Wilno, came to see us. He had moved from his apartment in Slask so that he could be near Mietek and me. We were three true friends who were joined by an inseparable bond and innumerable war adventures. With the intention of escaping from the country, we began planning what we could do to confuse the U.B. agents, as well as the Borderland Protection Army and the Gdansk police. Our aim was to escape to Sweden.

Sweden lay beyond the sea, so that necessitated that we have a boat with a motor. That was as far as our plans went at that time. Up until then, we had never had any contact with the sea. Having lived near two rivers in Wilno, we knew how to swim like fish, but our knowledge about operating a motorboat was slim. This fact, however, did not seem to interfere with our intentions. To the contrary, being completely unaware of the power of the sea, we saw no problem in achieving our crazy goal.

We began building a boat of our own design. In our friend's garage we welded the ribs of the boat, which we then covered completely with thin metal. When the hull was ready, we put in some inflated tubes as flotation devices. Additionally, we welded on a keel to protect the boat from tipping over if we were to encounter large waves. Little by little, we added various individual items intended for comfort and safety for the long excursion. After the work was finished, the time came to load the boat onto the car so that we could bring it to the canal at Martwa Wisla. Shockingly, we discovered that the three of us could not budge it. This was something we had not considered. We eventually rounded up several people nearby, and with much struggling we were finally successful in transporting our masterpiece.

Once on the water the boat looked very manageable, and we were proud of our work. We then set out to determine a route for our escape. With every attempt, soldiers of the Borderland Protection Army stopped us, from the mouth of the canal to the Baltic Sea. After thoroughly examining our boat and checking its registration, they told us to return to Gdansk. Around the entire Martwa Wisla canal and next to the mouth of the river, there were army stations. Evidently they were expecting the arrival or departure of amateur illegal sailors. All of our work in constructing our boat turned out to be senseless and useless for the plans we had set out to accomplish. Therefore, we would have to find another way of transporting ourselves across the sea.

The three of us would sometimes sit in the boat in harbor, and rack our brains for a solution to our problem. Often while we were sitting and staring into space, we saw a man on the canal who seemed to be spending free time on the water. His boat had a very imposing motor attached to it. We watched this boat maneuver around the canal, and then come into shore. One of us jokingly said to the man: "With that kind of motor one could even sail across the sea."

He looked at us sharply with a gaze that seemed to penetrate. "I'm Dabrowski," he introduced himself. After exchanging names and clasping hands we saw our new acquaintance staring at our iron clad boat. He then asked us what we wanted to do with our battleship – start a war on Russia? By this statement, he let us know that he was not a follower of the ruling system in Poland. As our conversation developed, we admitted our plans to depart Poland.

As it turned out, we had come upon a fisherman who knew the sea and its vicissitudes. The government had confiscated his fishing cutter, and at the same time taken away his right to fish. He also was ordered not to sail into the sea. Enraged, as were we, with harassment by government officials, he also was looking for a way to leave the country. He could not accomplish this alone, and with joy, he accepted our proposition to set out together. His opinion of sailing across the Baltic Sea was positive, if we had good weather. In the case of bad weather, our chances would be very slim and we were to expect a quick drowning in the cold water.

Surprisingly, we were heartened by his words. We already had a boat, motor and crew. Now we needed to settle on a date and place from which we would set sail onto the sea. We determined the time unanimously – the fall – when during Indian summer, the warm wind blew from the south.

We chose the most suitable route for escape on a vague map.

According to that map, we could see that from Lake Zarnowiec, a small river flowed into the sea after crossing about ten kilometers across unpopulated areas. It meandered, turning through bordering marshes and meadows. It would be necessary to get more information, so that we could determine if the boat would be capable of navigating over the shallow river with equipment and four passengers. And, most importantly, would there be a border army post at the river's outlet?

I took it upon myself to check on the border stations, already having a plan in mind. I reminded myself that in one building in the Old City, in which we had worked on the installation of a sewage system, I had met a bricklayer who was an avid fisherman. This loyal communist always boasted about his successful fishing excursions. He would be the perfect companion to have in the area close to the border. It had been forbidden for anyone to cross this area without permission of the coast guard. His communist party book would save me a great deal of trouble in case the seaside patrolling safety officials stopped us.

The next time I happened to be at the site, I began to talk with the workers about fishing. I also spoke of what I thought was a wonderful place to catch fish. My friendly bricklayer, with the hopes of a good catch, suggested that perhaps we could go fishing together. I had been waiting for exactly such a suggestion. Right then and there, I made plans with him to set out together on a fishing expedition, to a place I had chosen from the map. Everything worked out as planned. We loaded our bikes onto the city bus, heading from Gdansk to the town Zarnowiec. From there, we rode our bikes farther along a path to Zarnowiec Lake, from which our river flowed. We then went along a country road in the direction of the river's outlet to the sea.

After traveling approximately eight kilometers, we stopped about two kilometers from the shoreline. The sun had already set and it was almost dark. We stayed there and waited until dawn, subsisting on cut water cane and whiskey we had brought along. We had promised ourselves that we would catch many varieties of fish in unbelievable amounts, as every fisherman does.

At daybreak, I left my companion by the lake and headed for the sea alone, supposedly looking for fish. I had told him that there were huge pike in his area, and that I would be coming right back. I was gone for half of the day. I had kept walking until I reached the sea, and I had met no one along the way. I did have a pleasant surprise, however. In the river's outlet, directly on the edge, lay an abandoned fishing boat, which probably was used just occasionally by those who lived in the nearby village. I looked it over thoroughly. It was an old boat but it was in usable condition. It still looked good enough to take for a trip on the sea. The amount of sand on the floor of the boat denoted that it had not been used for some time. This completely resolved the problem of transporting our own boat to the river and sailing in it to the sea.

After my discovery, I somehow lost my way, but eventually found my way back to my companion. I had spent half a day away, but for a very good purpose. Finally, I found my fisherman and asked him how the fishing was going. "Shit – not fish," he told me, showing me a few perch strung upon a rope. During the return trip home, his facial expression and disposition betrayed his feelings. I felt somewhat sorry that I had taken advantage of his gullibility and willingness. Yet, from my viewpoint, I was completely satisfied.

Now that we had decided what our escape route would be, there remained but one thing for us to do. We had to assemble the equipment we would need. We had to buy four twenty-liter canisters of gasoline. We had to get life preservers, and we had to rent a truck with a driver who would bring us to the lake. We still had some time until our designated date of departure, which was to be at the beginning of September 1949, and the time seemed to drag endlessly.

Finally the day of departure arrived. I had left the family home so many times, yet always seeing my mother's tears caused a hidden pain within me. I could never show my true sentiments. I would always pretend to be cold and unfeeling at the tragic moment of departure and separation. The last hug within the embrace of my brother and the shutting of the door behind me concluded those moments of emotion. This time, the gamble was very serious. If the expedition failed, a death within the depths of the Baltic Sea, or a very long jail sentence threatened us.

From the start of the day, things did not work out well for us. The driver, who was an acquaintance of ours, arrived several hours late with the rented truck. Next, we had to follow a detour around a bridge that was unexpectedly closed for repair. Eventually, we arrived at the place near the lake where a path branched out from the main road, and would lead us to the sea. Night had already fallen.

In the darkness, we unloaded our things, said farewell to our driver, and overburdened with supplies, we set out. I carried the motor, Mietek and Leon carried three canisters of fuel. Each carried a canister in one hand and one hung on an oar between their shoulders. Dabrowski carried the last canister, oars, life preservers and a little bit of food that had been prepared for us by my mother.

Before us lay a long dirt road, and when we walked, our feet stumbled over the bumps and potholes. It had been easy to ride our bikes over the length of this road during the light of day, but now the matter appeared entirely different. More and more often we needed to stop for a short rest, and our hands were numb and weakened from carrying our heavy things. My friends could not deal with the canister shifting on the oar. Sometimes all of the weight of the cans rested on one of them. In turn, the hard metal of the motor pressed into my shoulder, causing me increasing pain. We often exchanged the things we carried, but that still did not improve our situation. Our times of rest became longer and more frequent.

Everyone began to curse me, but I didn't have the slightest clue why. After all, I hadn't built this road which, seemingly, had no end. It was a good thing that in the dark we couldn't see how much of the road still lay ahead. Over and over my friends would ask if we were getting any closer. I lied to them because I myself didn't know exactly how much more of the road was before us.

It was almost morning when I finally recognized the turn into the place where my acquaintance had been catching fish. It had taken us almost all night to cover eight kilometers. There was no possibility that we could sail that day because it was still quite a distance to the abandoned boat, and in addition, we were completely exhausted.

We agreed to spend the day in hiding. We lay down within the thick rushes along the riverside. We slept like logs on the flattened swampy reeds, completely invisible from the nearby road. Swarms of mosquitoes and flies settled on our uncovered faces, biting us constantly. We patiently withstood the torment because it was actually nothing compared to the night on the road.

Around noon, Mietek came out of hiding and headed for the road, but we had no idea where he was going. He didn't come back to us. We waited impatiently until nighttime. We then decided to head out to sea without him. To go back from the seaside terrain was impossible. We cleaned any remaining sand out of the boat, secured the motor and loaded the boat with gas, then pushed it out onto the waters of the Baltic.

I had waited until then to announce that, unfortunately, I was not going to sail with them. I didn't want to leave Poland without my dear friend, Mietek. He and I had been close since our high school days. I stood on shore and listened to the whirl of the motor as my friends cast off. The boat continued to distance itself until the moment when all I heard was a swooshing sound of the waves as they crashed upon the sand of the water's edge. Lonely, I returned to the road, feeling depressed by this unfortunate situation. Two of my closest friends, with whom I had spent years filled with happiness, pleasant adventures as well as dangers, had disappeared from the horizon of my life. Leon sailed across the sea in an uncovered fishing boat, while Mietek was probably in the hands of the police. There was no other possibility. I would not allow myself to even remotely think that maybe he lay dead somewhere. There was no reason to think about that. He had neither money nor valuable items that would have enticed anyone to rob or murder him. Lost in thought, I didn't even notice when I had already come to the end of road.

In the early morning hours, I left Zarnowiec heading for Gdansk, wanting to be able to still appear at work so as to have some sort of prepared alibi. I was expecting the worst, knowing the methods of investigation used by the Communist Secret Police (U.B.). I didn't learn about Mietek's adventure until after he had been released from jail, a year and a half later.

This is the story he told. He had come out onto a road to stretch his legs after having slept several hours on the reeds. He happened to come upon the Volunteer Citizens Police Reserve patrol. This patrol was on the lookout for raiders who were assaulting and robbing the cooperative housing association in the small nearby city. From that very spot he was taken to the police post and accused of this criminal offense. He did not respond to these accusations, not wanting to expose his friends who were waiting for him. It was not until the next day that he admitted to the jointly planned escape. Officials of the U.B. and the Citizens Police drove away with him to the place of our overnight stay near the river's outlet. They saw our footprints and the impression of the boat on the sand. It was then that they finally believed his story, and Mietek was returned into the hands of the authorities in Gdansk.

Words cannot describe the joy, as well as uncertainty, that overcame my mother when the following morning, the son she thought she had said goodbye to forever, stood in her doorway. I gave her a full report on what had happened, and begged her to go to see Mr. and Mrs. Fijalkowski to find out if their son, Mietek, had returned.

Soon after, I was called to the personnel manager's office, where they questioned me about my friend who, for some days, had not shown up at work. I pretended to be very surprised and alarmed about his absence. I told them Mietek had been preparing to go fishing in Lake Zarnowiec. I was certain at that time that his fate was in the hands of the Communist Secret Police (U.B.) and that I would most likely be called there for interrogation.

I immediately went to see the director of our department, Mr. Duszkiewicz, hoping that he could help me in this most difficult situation. I admitted to my affiliation to the Home Army (A.K.) as well as my participation in the unsuccessful attempt to escape to Sweden. The director was a citizen of Wilno, and immediately understood my situation, and the threat of my impending arrest.

"Mr. Plawski," he said, "things are working out well because in a few days, diplomas for the best work leaders will be distributed. I will include your name on the list. I am certain this will benefit you during the time of investigation." I was summoned to the ceremonious distribution of those important certificates, which acknowledged the strenuous, intensive and faultless work accomplished in the rebuilding of the Old City in Gdansk. I walked up to receive my diploma. I had to ignore the sounds of laughter echoing here and there across the theatre hall in which this communistic circus of distinction and awards was taking place. The workers knew of my past and of my open aversion to the regime which was reigning in Poland.

About three weeks later, I received a letter from Sweden in which Leon asked me about Mietek's fate. By the appearance of the letter, it seemed that it had most likely been read by the police officials. From that day forward, I went to work with my newly possessed diploma in my pocket. I dressed, each day prepared in the event I might be arrested. This meant wearing heavy clothing such as boots, jacket, bulky sweater, even when the weather was warm. I knew that if I were to be arrested, I would be sent to Siberia to work for a long time, and the heavy clothing would become a necessity. The sight of me wearing this type of clothing caused both an interest and concern to my friends in the office.

The working team in the installation department was comprised of repatriates from Wilno. We constituted a close-knit group of people who had gone through the same types of losses, battles with the invaders and the period of disarmament of the Home Army by the Soviets. No one bragged about this, and people did not admit to being members of illegal organizations, yet it was easy to sense this by the similar behaviors and opinions, which bonded us together.

And so it came to be – a bitter moment, awaited with fear, but unavoidable. In the morning, the personnel manager came to my desk announcing, "Citizen Plawski, please go immediately to the unification of the coastal area and report to the office of Director Szminda, who has some very important business to discuss with you."

I knew what kind of business this would be. Until now, the director had never asked for me. I said goodbye to my friends, not admitting where I was going or why I was leaving. I only mentioned that I did not know when I would return. In the corridor, which led to the director's office, two agents were already waiting for me. "Are you citizen Plawski?" the officer asked me. Yes, I am," I replied. They grasped me under my shoulders and declared in a business-like tone, "Come with us."

"Where and for what?" I tried to gain control, but their reply was short as they simply stated that I was needed for interrogation at the police station. A car already stood waiting by the door. We arrived at our destination within a few minutes. The two agents showed the security officers, who stood immediately inside the entryway, their documents of authority. I was then taken to the second floor.

"Don't look around," came a command as we climbed the stairs. They instructed me to stand in the hallway with my face toward the wall and again commanded that I not look to the sides. Then the officers disappeared into one of the offices. I stood facing that wall, without moving, for half a day. The time dragged incredibly. Nothing was happening all around. From time to time, someone walked by.

Occasionally, from what I could tell by the sounds of footsteps, another detainee would be hurriedly led past me. At times, I heard doors opening onto the hallway. Someone would glance in my direction and then shut the door again within moments. However, this movement gave me an opportunity to judge the time of day. When the door opened, even so briefly, light from within the office fell upon the floor of the windowless hallway. In this way, I could tell that it was well past noon. The sun was setting, as this was the autumn season – the end of September.

Finally, I had waited long enough, and now something would happen. Under police escort I entered a room in which sat a young man behind the desk, pretending to be an important official of the law. "Sit down," he ordered me, pointing to a chair that was standing a short distance from him. "Keep your hands on your lap," he ordered. For quite some time, he pored over papers that were spread out before him. He looked at me penetratingly, as though he was looking for reasons for the terror-stricken look upon my face. *You fool,* I thought. *You have too little practice and experience to scare me and take me off balance.*

"Where is your friend, Leon Mamczyc, and the other one, Mietek Fijalkowski?" he threw the question at me unexpectedly. I answered truthfully, "I recently received a letter which told me that Leon is in Sweden. But where Mietek is, I haven't the slightest inkling. Whatever happened to him, no one knows. He left to go fishing and got lost, driving his family into despair, as well as me, because he had been my best friend."

At this, my pronounced agent got up from his chair and slowly came closer to me. "You pipsqueak – are you going to tell the truth or aren't you?" With this statement, he hit me across the face with his open hand, repeated this action across the other side of my face, and systematically beat me – once from the left side, and once from the right. I sat calmly, clenching my fists upon my thighs. I thought how wonderful it would be if I could stand up from the chair and return several punches. After all, in my time I had been a boxer. After a while, when his hands stopped trembling, he began to scribble something in his notebook, looking at the papers which lay in front of him. I knew that he was looking through some of my life histories that I had filled out during my time as an office worker.

"Now you must accurately tell me all about your life from the time you were young until the present time," he said. I began this confession, which I had already put together quite well in my mind. Wherever needed, I always gave the same facts about my life, only intentionally changing around the dates of when things actually happened. It was not wise to reveal in writing concrete proof of one's good memory.

The officer asked me the names of my superiors going back to the times of my being associated with various secret organizations. This was not difficult to hide as I knew only their code names. He wanted to know everything about the course of my life during the partisan impact. In my statement, I said I had revealed everything to the Liquidation Commission in 1945. I also said it was possible for him to gain information from there. He jumped out of his seat and again took his hands to my face. This time, his first blows gave me a nosebleed, and with a badly aimed blow he struck my eye. After unloading his anger, he left the room, leaving me alone.

I noticed that the officer had made small pencil marks on the pages of the papers he had on his desk. I knew he wanted to test me to see if I looked at the papers while he was gone. I sat motionless in my place knowing also that in the neighboring room sat several thugs waiting for any kind of sound or movement on my part. After a while, the investigator returned to the office and again began to write about the course of events according to my admissions about where and when I had last seen my friends. I emphasized again that it had been when they had left to go fishing on Lake Zarnowiec.

After he finished writing down my declarations, I was asked to sign the testimony. I did not. I first asked to have the statement read back to me in its entirety. And just as I had thought – there had been written, intentionally, a false ending which claimed that the last moment I had seen my friends had been when they were leaving for Sweden.

"I can't sign this," I said. "I didn't know that they wanted to escape from the country." For this statement I received a kick in my side, which caused me to fall off the chair. He rewrote that last statement, and was rewarded with my signature on the testimony. "You're a wise guy," he retorted as he walked me to the jail cell in the basement of the building.

After I had consumed a hot cup of grain coffee and a piece of plain, stale, dry bread, I lay for quite some time thinking about what would happen next. I wondered what fate had in store for me. Weary, I finally fell asleep, tossing and turning in an uneasy sleep on a pallet stuffed with hay.

The next day, I again waited impatiently to see some sort of action in this "house of justice," which was realistically a house of torture. Again in the afternoon, they led me to another room where three officials waited for me. Again began a questioning of how, what, where, and with whom I did things during the course of my life. Random questions were coming from all directions without giving me any time to think. Despite that, I was in no hurry to answer them. I asked them to wait a bit for my responses, as I wasn't able to concentrate due to the pain in my inner ear. After saying this, I held onto my ear on the side of my face where my eye had been struck. When they asked about the cause of my pain, I responded that they should ask the official who had beaten me the day before. This time, no one hit me. One of the officials, apparently more culturally advanced, told me that in the future I would most likely be sitting in jail. For now, due to the fact that I had done such a good job rebuilding the ruins caused by the war, I was allowed to go home.

Just as I had suspected, my diploma for being a socialist labor leader had definitely helped me. Before I left, they passed me a commitment to sign, stating that I would write a letter to my friend in Sweden, asking him for information as to who had helped him during his escape. I also had to sign that I would not reveal the names of my investigators or methods of investigation that I had endured in this bureau. I was threatened that if I were to reveal these procedures, I would receive a punishment of ten years in jail.

Oh, how beautifully the sun shone after I left that gloomy building! I did not even look back in its direction as I marched down Dluga Street. After returning home, I immediately grabbed my fishing pole and headed toward the water. I needed to sit quietly by the canal, and forget about what I had endured during the past few days in the U.B. office. I knew that Mietek was sitting in jail and I also knew that the evidence we declared covered everything perfectly. Otherwise, I would not have been allowed to go free. It was not until several months later that a court trial took place for the jailed Mietek. He faced the kind of judge who took into consideration the young age of the accused, and deemed that after the adventurous experiences Mietek had endured, he had just taken off for a trip to the sea to go fishing. The judge gave him a sentence of eighteen months in jail. Leon never wrote to me again, knowing that his letters would first fall into the hands of the police.

The following spring, after Mietek's trial, I went to the city's army prosecutor asking for information about visiting my friend. He asked how I was connected to the prisoner. "A cousin," I replied. "Get out of here, you bum, or else I'll put you in jail, too." This was the gracious reply that the communist Prosecutor gave me. I returned home quite depressed from the way I, a citizen of a free country, had been treated. I no longer had any illusions. The words "get out of here" became lodged in my mind and became the additional incentive I needed to leave the country.

Toward the end of the summer of that same year, I received, this time from the city Police, permission to visit Mietek. He had recently been moved from jail to a property where he performed forced labor during the remaining months of his sentence. We sat opposite one another in the company of a police officer who was listening to our conversation. Mietek looked quite well, but what was most important was the fact that he had not lost his vigor and will to live. During our friendly chat, I asked him whether he had any plans to visit "Miszka." This was another name for Leon that had been used only by us. "Oh, we've absolutely got to go visit him," answered Mietek. This response from my friend made me very happy. It was apparent that his jail stay had not frightened him too much nor had it taken away his courage and resolve. He still continued to think about escaping from the coast. I returned home from the visit, whistling aloud, which was something unheard of with me because I have never been a very musical sort of person.

Now I faced a new assignment – to organize the next sea expedition. I hoped that this time it would be more successful. The preceding trip had been planned well and it was only by coincidence that complications had prevented a successful outcome. It was understandable that we should repeat the same procedure, from A to Z. The process was not easy, by any means, and this time we must be particularly careful because we were under still tight observation by the U.B. I realized that our access routes to the sea would be watched even more carefully. The Army Border Protection units patrolled every convenient route to the sea. The authorities knew that in order to leave by means of the sea, suitable equipment would be needed, and most importantly, we would have to have a boat. Therefore, in my way of thinking, the bigger the obstacles, the bigger was the chance for the expedition's success.

I formulated for myself a plan of action:

1. To find suitable access to the sea.
2. To recruit two new crewmen.
3. To obtain money
4 To find and purchase a seaworthy four-passenger boat
5. To purchase an attachable motor, no less than ten horsepower.
6. To obtain four twenty-liter canisters of gasoline.

I began again from the beginning. I found a lake on the map that was inaccessible for mechanical vehicles. It was Lake Lebsko, into which flowed the river Leba. The Leba River flowed through the swampy terrain stretching from the city of Lebork, all the way to the sea. The lake was separated from the sea by a narrow strip of rugged tall sand dunes.

On the eastern edge of this lake lay the small town of Leba. This was a wild sort of area, which looked to be ideal for our plans of escape. For the next departure, I planned that we bring a boat and lower it into the flowing Leba River, which was near the city of Lebork. We would then sail with our equipment across the river to the next lake about forty kilometers away. We would be rowing to be as quiet as possible while crossing the lake. We would then bring the boat and equipment across the sand dunes to the sea's edge. In order to accomplish this, I had to examine the terrain to convince myself that the river was fit for navigation in a boat, and also that there were no border Army Posts.

I boarded a train, heading for Lebork. From there I walked with a fishing pole in my hand and a backpack on my shoulders, heading down the river. I wanted to assess the flow of the river and to determine whether there were any obstructions for a loaded boat. Furthermore, I had to orient myself so that I could estimate what the sailing time would be to reach the Lebsko Lake.

The road went along the river's edge. I didn't have the slightest idea how far I would have to go. According to the map, the distance was approximately forty kilometers in a straight line. Once I began my journey, I was convinced that the goal of my journey was simply unreachable. The river edges were covered with an overgrowth of thick bushes, lush and fertile grass, and an obstruction of trees and marshes which I had to circumvent. The river's corridor winded without stop, I had to sometimes wade through the water to head north in the direction of the sea.

As far as the eye could see, there was no human being anywhere. There was grass everywhere – lush grass reaching above the waist. Grass and prickly stalks of wild raspberries caught onto my pants, not allowing me to move forward. They tore at my hands and legs, and the bleeding lured swarms of flies and other bloodthirsty insects. Exhaustion overtook me by nightfall. After eating a hard-boiled egg, and taking a gulp of water from the river, I buried myself in a pile of flattened grass. For a change, I didn't feel anything biting me or crawling over my body, so I was able to get some sleep. It was damp and cold, but I was able to stand it until morning.

The next day, I continued my journey, not expecting that it would be any better than the day before. I marched myself right into a clump of bushes with thorns. It was there that I was attacked by huge horse flies that had been lured by my sweat and blood. I became agitated and had to get away from my attackers. I began jumping through those barbed bushes in the direction of the river. However, that did not improve the situation. The flies continued following me in droves, biting me unmercifully. As I ran in a frenzied panic, I snagged a fishhook attached to a fishing line, with my leg. This hook should have been reeling in large fish, not a person. I didn't even try to take it out. In pain, I jumped into the water fully clothed, going completely under water. Soon I managed to calm down, and drag myself back to shore. I then carefully worked the hook from my calf, leaving my leg bloody and sore.

Toward evening, I finally reached the lake region. I had set my compass toward the opposite side of the lake where I could see, in the distance, a small sandy beach. I plodded along another three miles to the distant town of Leba. This was on a Monday, during the month of August in 1950. The vacation season was just about over, so I had no problem in finding a place to stay for the night in a tourist home. After a much-deserved rest, I joined a group of tourists the next morning for a trip across the lake to a sandy dune area that was approximately four miles away. Walking along the sand, I began a conversation with the captain of the boat on which we had sailed. I asked him whether or not it was safe to walk along the coast. I didn't want to be arrested for being found on the coastal border.

"Don't worry about it," the captain replied. "There is no patrol during the daytime on this deserted place. It isn't until nighttime when they patrol the beach between the observational towers. With the exception of wild pigs and deer, there isn't a living soul here." According to his observations, the captain continued to explain with pride, "There is no road leading toward these hills."

I separated from the group of tourists, traveling along the sand between the hills. I reached the sea's edge, heading back to the lake, remembering each dune and the most accessible passageways among the hills. The winding road was about one mile long. It would be, however, much more difficult to traverse carrying our boat. I realized this was not going to be a pleasure trip. I returned feeling most fortunate that I had found a road upon which no one was traveling – with the exception of the howling sea winds.

Before leaving, I returned once more for an excursion to the dunes so that I would be able to accurately picture and mark that road in my mind. At the place where I had reached the sea's edge I saw, on the side of the hill, a dug out shelter with a roof and a bench. It was apparent that soldiers had rested there during their beach patrols. Just to discourage these soldiers from slacking off from their work, I took it upon myself to demolish the roof. I then collapsed the existing walls and broke up the benches.

I returned to Gdansk, thinking about the next task on my list, which was to find two individuals who would be eager to risk losing their lives or their freedom in this dangerous undertaking. This would probably be the biggest problem. After all, it was not possible to advertise about this in the newspaper. I could not publicly state that we were looking for two daredevils to accompany us in our escape from Poland.

Many of my friends agreed with my plans and expressed the desire to leave the country, but when they discovered that the trip would take place in a small boat, they said I must be crazy, and that was the end of the discussion. My circle of acquaintances in the coastal area was decreasing rapidly and I found myself not knowing where to turn. I knew many guys from the city of Lodz, and a great number of them were expatriates who had settled there from Wilno. Therefore, it was there that I planned to focus my attention in my search for a couple of courageous young individuals to accompany us. I went to the city of Lodz with this sort of hope, but the matter ended at a party where several bottles of vodka were downed. My friends really did not have any important reasons to leave the country. The commission of the Home Army's liquidation had summoned none of them. Many, also, had already begun their own families.

I returned to Gdansk a little depressed but still not losing hope for a better tomorrow. I knew I would simply wait for Mietek's springtime release from jail, and in the meantime, I hoped to meet someone eager to leave the country. During the winter, I received some unexpected news that my friend from Gliwice, Czeslaw Skiba, was coming to the coast – to the city of Sopot – and wanted to meet with me. He was the brother of Krystyna, my former girlfriend. He had come to the homeland from England where he had served in the Polish Air Force. Before the war, his parents had owned a paper company in Warsaw. He now wanted to manage a similar business in the free Poland. I remember that at the time of my departure from Gliwice, Skiba had complained that the Treasury Bureau was mercilessly applying back taxes to their expanding business.

I met with Skiba at the address he had given me. He had lost considerable weight since the last time we had seen one another. Apparently there was no place within Communist Poland for a former pilot. Aviation service on English territory was like salt in the eye for the Polish authorities. Skiba had been called for interrogation to the U.B. Public Safety Bureau. There he was asked ridiculous questions such as why he had come to Poland. They did not believe that he wanted to be with his family in his homeland. Russian flunkies did not trust people who had come from the West. They believed that these individuals returned to their homeland for the sole purpose of secret battles with the existing government.

Skiba immediately got to the point about what he wanted to discuss. He said he had heard from a mutual friend that we were planning to go to Sweden. "Can I join you?" he asked. "I know that Leon Mamczyc was looking for a fourth person to complete the crew of your expedition.

"You're late by one year," I told him with a laugh. "Leon is already in Sweden and Mietek is sitting in jail. But you can always join us. Actually, you came to us now like a star from the heavens. I am looking for not just one, but two individuals to join our planned escapades in the fall." I told him about our plans to depart in September and that we were currently planning and accumulating the necessary equipment.

"If you are serious about joining us, you'll need to contribute a serious amount of money. Mietek is currently in jail and I have already spent most of my savings. I still have to buy a boat and motor and I don't have enough money."

A handshake became our signed contract. He gave me a sizeable deposit and promised that I would receive the rest of the money when he returned to Sopot in the spring. His plans were to live there until the time of our departure. Next, he added that I shouldn't worry about a fourth enthusiast for our trip. He also had a friend who was equally harried by back taxes and had expressed a desire to escape. I did not give Skiba detailed plans of our escape, because during those times of Stalin's regime, it was safer to know less. A few drinks of a good cognac proved that we understood each other.

I returned home late that night. Along the way, I stopped at the Sopot Pier. Sitting on a bench, I looked at the sky, which was filled with millions of stars. Among them, I searched and found the brightly shining Polar Star. This is the star, which I had chosen as my caretaker and which was the one that had lit my way during the years of night marches in the partisan units.

I didn't waste time. The next day, I immediately went to a shipyard in Nowy Port to order a small boat. The boat builder who lived there promised to build a seafaring craft for me, modeling it after one of the smaller boats that he had on dry dock for the winter. With some great difficulty, the two of us hoisted it up a little, so that I could be assured that four of us would be able to carry it across the desolate wilderness and sandbars that separate the lake from the sea. He promised me that the boat would be ready in the spring. After I had given him a substantial deposit, I returned home, satisfied with the completed transaction and myself. Now I could peacefully await Mietek, and the summer when we would be able to test the boat on the water. To complete my assignments, I had to acquire an appropriate motor.

April 1951, was the designated time when Mietek would be released from jail. He had served a sentence for innocently walking out onto a road at a border zone. After being released from jail, he returned home looking quite emaciated, but in good spirits. His parents, who had waited for his release for eighteen months, were overjoyed. His poor parents were unaware that in a half-year's time they would once again be crying over his disappearance.

Soon, we went to the yacht shipyard, looking over the newly built boat, which appeared to be an absolute wonder – ideally made to our expectations and intentions. Barrel-shaped with a side two feet two inches high, five feet wide and eleven feet in length, it was well adapted to carry people to yachts anchored on the sea. All that it needed now was to be painted. We planned to pick it up in two weeks, and pay for it at that time.

I went to visit Skiba, who had already returned to the coast. He was living in Sopot and had promised to be our banker. I needed the rest of the money to complete payment of the boat and to purchase a motor. I informed him that we planned to leave the third week in September. We planned to meet one more time, at which point Skiba hoped to bring along with him our fourth crewman, Walter Drzewinski. Walter was planning to come to Skiba at the beginning of July. We all were to be on the alert for a departure any time in the middle of September. Our departure was dependent upon the weather. Indian summer usually held on from the middle of September to the beginning of October. With an assurance that all plans were set and everyone was prepared, I returned home to work.

Mietek was still not working. After being released from jail he went to Warsaw to buy the motor we needed for our boat. He returned smiling. To my questions as to what he had bought, he showed me a package wrapped in a thick paper, but he did not open it. "You'll see it on the water when we take our boat out the first time," he said to me with a secretive smile.

Indeed, we went to the shore, attached the motor to our boat, and steered the boat toward the Martwa Wisla canal. The ten horsepower motor worked like a charm. But when we completely released the gas, the front of boat was dangerously high above the water. Mietek had purchased the motor from a private owner after first testing it on the Wisla River. After a few hours on the water, we steered the boat to the edge of a small gulf, where we planned to leave it until the moment of our escape. We turned the boat over to a local fisherman for safekeeping. He promised to take care of it, for a good price. Until that time, none of us could have imagined that we would be the owners of an expensive boat, which was hidden twenty kilometers from Gdansk.

We returned safely to the city, stopping for a short while at a place where our metal boat still stood. We had sailed it practically every week, spending Sundays in the company of some girls we knew. We caught fish and swam in a nearby area. We knew that the captain of another boat moored in this area was observing us. We also knew that this captain was giving reports of our sailing activities to police officers, who were always suspicious of our intentions regarding another escape.

I continued filling out questionnaires at work, always the same questions regarding where I had been and what I had done in my life. I gritted my teeth as I tried to endure the harassment. I knew that this would not continue long. I took a week's vacation from work at the beginning of August. I told them I was going to a relaxing resort by a beautiful lake in Leba. It was a great time for a vacation, and other adventures.

I took a bus to Leba, and then headed to the place three miles away where the river flowed into the lake. I had to assure myself that I hadn't made a mistake in outlining the direction toward the sandy beach on the distant opposite side. Feeling tired, I fell asleep in a pile of cut grass. I awoke to the sound of a sharp scythe. I got up and wandered toward the landowner that was hard at work. I was pleased to note that he had a Polish army hat upon his head. This ex-soldier who was working in this wilderness certainly was not a Communist. Communists sat in offices or owned villas.

"God help us," I said to him, as was the Polish custom. The young man took off his hat, wiped his perspiring forehead, and asked me, "How did you get to this God forsaken place?" I told him that I was going to the lake Leba, and hoped to catch fish along the way. I added that I was already tired and hungry and that I was looking for a store where I would be able to buy some food for the road ahead of me.

"Sit down, sir," he said with an encouraging gesture toward a clump of yet uncut grass. Within the blink of an eye he unfolded a bundle which lay beside us, taking from it a piece of cheese, some bread and a pitcher with sour milk. He invited me to eat. From his behavior I was able to deduce that I had come upon a fellow citizen, a person from the east, an expatriate such as myself, torn from his homeland. He was happy when I told him that I was born in Wilno. "Please rest for a while until I finish cutting this piece of land – then I will take you with me to my home," he said.

I fell again into a deep and satisfying sleep from which I was awakened by the friendly shaking of my shoulder. I noticed standing opposite me, a wagon filled with fresh dried hay. We climbed onto the wagon, and rode through a nearby forest chatting along the way. I learned about the tragic war experiences of this young person. He had been taken from the terrain of Wilno to Siberia where he lost his parents. He survived alone until the moment of amnesty and later entered the communist Polish People's Army. He had survived battles on the front as far as Berlin. After the war he had received compensation for lost land and war services. He settled in this wilderness, among disapproving "Kaszubs" (native people in north Poland). Since he had been given a house and a piece of land, he and his family were assured a decent standard of living, but he never stopped missing the land he had left behind in the east.

It was apparent by looking at him that he was very pleased with having met up with a fellow countryman, and it was with pride that he showed me his very well maintained homestead. He introduced me to his wife and young son. In a short while, his wife invited us to the table for a supper she had prepared. After sharing the evening meal, he and I sat on a bench near his house, and told each other about our lives.

"Please don't go anywhere for the night," he said to me. "My wife has already prepared the guest room for you. Stay with us a few days. It's not often we have the opportunity to have such a pleasant guest in our home." Of course, I didn't refuse his offer. I truly felt like a part of the family with them, and I really didn't have anywhere else to go for the night.

The next morning, after an early breakfast, we went back again to that same field which he had planned to finish mowing the day before. I told him that while he was working, I would go to the lake to see if I could catch some fish. He didn't question me, yet it was quite evident that he didn't really believe my story about fishing. He just said that when I returned it would be faster and easier if I went by the road to get back to his farmstead.

The area was truly beautiful and this was an opportunity for me to spend the rest of my vacation quite pleasantly. Before I realized it, I had come upon the road and the bridge near the lake. The river's outlet falling into Lake Lebsko constituted quite a shallow sand bed over which we would have to drag our overloaded boat. At the end of this sand grew thick water rushes, hiding the view of the lake water. I got into the water and, hidden by the growth, one more time set my compass in the visible direction of the opposite edge of the tall sand dunes. I had to determine whether or not an area of overgrown grasses on the dunes was not longer than half a kilometer. I needed to find this place during the night, and I would have to swim about six miles of waterway. That was a difficult task, but I had deep faith that with the help of God, I would find the place.

I returned by way of the road toward the home of my new friend. He didn't ask me if I had caught any fish. It was apparent that he was wondering about my stay in the border zone. Whether he had figured out the truth, I really don't know. He pretended that nothing was unusual about my stay on the coast. I spent a few days at his home, and then we left in the morning, to go to the city by wagon. Our farewells, two strangers until recently, were very warm.

One more time I set out on a tourist trip to the dunes. The tour guide recognized me immediately and I had to pretend to be captivated by the wilderness and beauty of this forsaken wasteland. Just as I had done before, I separated from the group, knowingly going by the easiest and shortest route to the sea's edge. I had to be certain that I would not make a mistake at night in reaching the same place. Again I came across the ruined hiding place where the soldiers rested. I once again made it evident that an unfriendly assailant had paid a visit. I did this without any great anger, but just to make it unpleasant for soldiers to rest there. The time to return had come. With a last look, I bade farewell to the sea and returned to the tourist group already waiting for me.

The next day, I clambered into a bus and napped throughout the entire return trip to Gdansk. After returning home, I went to Sopot and became acquainted with the new person who was to accompany us on the expedition. He was Wladyslaw Drzewinski, a buyer from Bytom, who was also disgusted with the Treasury Bureau. I didn't really take to this older gentleman. He was short, middle-aged, of a frail build, and did not show much promise of being any great help in carrying heavy equipment. But, he was the one and only volunteer for the escapades, so we had no choice.

We all planned to be ready to leave sometime during the second half of September. I told them that everything was ready and we were waiting only for the right conditions. Earlier, I had arranged with a friend to drive us to our point of departure in his truck. I told him to bring two inner tubes filled with air, and four canisters filled with gasoline. Those items in the truck would not arouse suspicion and we had no other place to keep them. The promise of a large payment assured us that he would carry out the assignment.

A week before our planned escape, the newly purchased boat was registered at the Water Bureau in Tczew, so that we would have an official document in case our loaded wagon was stopped on the road. Registration far from Gdansk assured anonymity and kept the authorities unaware of the fact that we possessed another boat which was concealed.

The last days at home were depressing. My mother knew about the small "shell" of a boat in which we were planning to sail across the Baltic. She was sewing small pillows to protect our shoulders when carrying our heavy things. She also made small sacks for many articles that we had found both necessary and useful on our previous unsuccessful expedition. My mother cried tears of tenderness and desperation, expecting the worst sort of ending for this undertaking. I, too, was not feeling pleased about leaving both home and family so often. This had to finally come to an end.

# Stay in England
## (Teresa)

The Bajorski family stepped off the ship's deck onto the dock in Southampton, England, feeling a sense of curiosity mixed with anxiety. They stood, surveying their surroundings, and waited for instructions. They sensed an old-fashioned Anglo-Saxon orderliness and serenity around them. The family soon learned that they were to be transported to a transitional camp in Daglingworth. This had been prepared especially for the displaced persons from Africa. They were to stay in barracks, which had been quarters for the British soldiers during World War II. There they would remain until being assigned to more permanent housing. Their transportation had been arranged, and they would soon be traveling by train to Daglingworth.

After arriving at their new lodgings, the newcomers had nothing to do but settle in and relax. A month passed without any concern about food or housing accommodations. Meals were prepared and routinely served in the cafeteria. Teresa laughed when her mother tossed out the food they had brought from Africa – some very fatty kielbasa along with bread that had been dried before their departure.

A short time later, Emilia Bajorski learned that she was assigned to work in Gloucestershire. It was a camp for former army personnel from southern England. She was to be a waitress in the new restaurant that served demobilized British army officers. Homes for the families assigned there were already prepared. They would live in metal barracks, in which every family was allotted one room. Many of these rooms were still furnished with equipment remaining from when it had been occupied by military forces.

The trip to Gloucestershire was, as usual, by train. The Bajorski's came to feel that their whole lives were connected with the clanking of wheels over railroad tracks. After arriving at the station in Evesham, they were taken by bus to Springhill Hostel, a camp situated on a hilltop in a picturesque setting. The entire camp area, where they were to live, was surrounded by barbed wire that remained from wartime. The families felt safe and secure there, and also had a sense of freedom. They could see several roads leading toward the towns below, and rolling, green fields filled with wild flowers.

The Bajorski family found it easy to get settled. They were among friends from Africa, and therefore, were very content. Food was prepared and served in the cafeteria, and this became a place for friendly gatherings and conversations. Teresa was enrolled in the local camp school and Edek would attend the high school in Bottisham.

Emilia, had not forgotten her smeared check, which she still kept safely hidden. With the help of the camp director, who guided her to a local banker, she was able to redeem the check for cash. A while ago, she had considered it worthless, so this was a great bonanza for her. It was, to Emilia, a substantial sum of money. Teresa became the beneficiary of some of this newly acquired currency. For a few pounds, her mother bought her a used bicycle, which had been refurbished by a boy they had known in Africa. On many days after that, Teresa would speed around the camp on her new bicycle, breathing in the clean air and feeling free as a bird. Often she would stop along the way, get off her bike, and run through the green fields. She felt an energizing new sense of freedom.

Emilia was paid by check for her work. It was Teresa's duty to bring this check to a nearby bank to be cashed. She rode her bike downhill to a bank in the town of Chipping Campden. With the money in her pocket, she next stopped at the local ice cream shop. The ice cream was scrumptious and Teresa savored every bite. This was something she had only dreamed of when she was in Africa. After feeling satisfied by the ice cream, Teresa started on the trip home. She pushed her bicycle up hill, a distance of a few kilometers. Along the way she enjoyed gazing at the charming cottages, with their neat fruit and vegetable gardens. Often some of the English neighbors would call out to her, sometimes asking if she needed help.

During the summer, local gardeners came to the camp in wagons filled with strawberries. They would recruit volunteers to pick over the fruit, so that it would be ready to be made into jellies and jams. Teresa always volunteered for this job. She was allowed to snack as she worked, and she ate her fill. She loved eating the fruit, and the pay was incidental.

Teresa had always enjoyed singing and dancing, and it was with great enthusiasm that she signed up to join a theatrical group. This was organized by Mrs. Grosicka, a friend from the camp in Tengeru in Africa. Teresa was one of the most energetic and talented performers in the group. She careened and jumped like a young deer to the sounds of Polish folk tunes. All of the young performers had endured the same trials and deprivations, and they were basking in their new freedoms and opportunities.

Teresa had just turned thirteen. The camp educational counselor suggested to Emilia that she send Teresa to a more advanced secondary school. He suggested the Sisters of Nazareth secondary school in central England. This would be at considerable cost to the family. Emilia was reluctant because this school was quite a distance away, but she agreed. Teresa was not allowed to enroll in the local public school at this time because their term was already in progress.

One of Teresa's girlfriends learned that Teresa was going to leave to study at the Nazareth convent. She began telling Teresa about her own experiences of terror in that convent school. The girl had been physically thrown out of the convent school by the Mother Superior for the minor offense of having appeared in the chapel without an appropriate head covering. The young girl found herself outside the school's walls with no way of making her way back to where she lived at the camp. She had no money to buy a train ticket, and if it hadn't been for the kindness of some English people who befriended her, she would have had to walk the long distance home. The girl warned Teresa that Mother Superior Bonoza always showed great kindness toward a new student. Then after a short while, her attitude changed radically and she would incessantly persecute a new student for the smallest of offenses.

Emilia knew that Teresa needed the proper clothes for this new school, so she hired a local seamstress to make Teresa an elegant suit and dress. She bought Teresa a pair of beautiful patent leather shoes and some silk stockings. A helpful neighbor offered to accompany Teresa to her new school. Teresa dressed in her new outfit, and in the care of her neighbor, she was on her way.

Through the windows of the train car, Teresa could see the quickly passing fields covered in green and divided by neatly arranged stone walls. Here and there, she saw long lanes lined with towering trees. These led to a manor house surrounded by fruit orchards, far down the lanes. These residences, built from huge carved boulders, gave evidence of the power and wealth of the owners. They concealed a mysterious lifestyle, unknown to the young girl who had been raised in the forests of Ural and the jungles of Africa. Teresa was filled with fear and anxiety as she rode through this alien territory to an unknown destination. Horrible memories returned to her from the times she had previously spent in an orphanage. She remembered times of hunger and misery, as well as the separation from her mother, beloved aunt, and those closest and dearest to her. With these thoughts, tears came to her eyes, obscuring the beauty of the landscape through which she traveled.

The trip took half a day. The train stopped at the station in Pittsford, not far from the bigger city of Northampton. Teresa's caregiver hired a taxi and directed the driver to take them to the school. They drove down a seldom-traveled road that wound around a variety of abbeys belonging to the Sisters of Nazareth. Finally, at the end of the lane loomed the convent building, surrounded by huge trees. The grounds consisted of fruit orchards, and gardens. There were beautifully maintained paths lined with flowerbeds leading to more buildings. The chauffeur let Teresa and her guardian out in front of powerful oak doors fronted by stone steps.

Teresa's caregiver lifted the huge brass knocker, and let it fall. The sound reverberated loudly within the building. All was quiet, without a sign of life from within the building. Finally, the rustle of slippers moving along the stone flooring could be heard. The door opened slightly as the thin, pale face of a nun appeared in the twilight. "What is your business here, sir?" she quietly asked. "I've brought a new student to school," answered Teresa's companion. The nun then stepped aside and motioned them to enter.

"Please follow me," she said as she moved noiselessly down the dark corridor, lighted only by the narrow windows high in the walls. The nun brought the new arrivals to a door with the inscription "Reception Office." She knocked boldly and disappeared into the darkness. A voice from inside invited them in, and Teresa and her companion entered the large room. In the center of the room stood a huge desk. A very tall and thin Mother Superior rose from an armchair to stand near the desk. This was Sister Bonoza.

"Oh, my darling Teresa, you've finally come to us!" were her words of greeting. She had a smile on her face, a nose bent like an eagle's, and cold eyes which contradicted her smile. While saying these welcoming words, she was tenderly patting and smoothing her new student's hair with her bony hand. "Everything will be good here for you," she said to Teresa, "just like in your family home because, after all, we are all God's children." All Teresa could do then was thank her caregiver for accompanying her to the school. After hearing her words, the friend escaped discreetly. Teresa was then alone with the Mother Superior. Within a moment, like a chameleon, Bonoza changed her image.

"Follow me," she sharply ordered Teresa. With her suitcase in hand, Teresa quickly followed the long-legged nun down the narrow, cold corridors. It was difficult for her to orient herself in the complicated labyrinth, which led to the living quarters of the students. Sister Bonoza opened the door to a room in which stood two beds side-by-side. A narrow window let a small amount of light into the room. There was a table, two chairs and a wardrobe-type cabinet for clothing. An unpleasant damp chill hung in the air. There were no heaters or radiators, and the high ceilings enhanced the bleak atmosphere.

"Here you will live with another girl," announced Bonoza. "Now you can rest and familiarize yourself with the rules of our convent and school. These rules are hung right here on the door." The Mother Superior turned and left the room. Teresa immediately began to read the long column of regulations, which she would be required to obey. They were as follows:

1. No talking is allowed on the convent grounds. After leaving a room, one should keep absolute silence.

2. Shoes worn within the building must have soft soles and heels, so that footsteps cannot be heard along the corridor.

3. Letters to be mailed must not be sealed. They should first be slid under the door of Mother Superior's office. After her approval, they will be mailed.

4. Any monies must be placed into the convent safe to be used for expenses related to any costs incurred here.

5. You may not speak directly to the Mother Superior. You must approach her by a written note, to be placed under her door.

6. Every day after supper you must report to vespers with an appropriate veil upon your head.

After reading the regulations, Teresa collapsed on her bed. She felt confused and afraid. Teresa wondered how she would ever survive in this strange environment without the guidance and comfort of her mother. She awoke to the sound of someone entering the room. Teresa rose, and saw her new roommate standing just inside the room. The girls introduced themselves. They then began to talk and to tell each other a little about their past lives, and their present situations. Teresa's new friend began to whisper to Teresa about some of the various punishments inflicted by the despised Mother Superior. She said that the students, as well as many of the staff, thought that Bonoza was mentally ill, but that they had to tolerate her various antics. This nun made life in that convent miserable. Teresa was also advised not to put all her money in the convent safe. "You must keep some of your money for unexpected situations," her roommate said.

This sounded like good advice. Teresa hid a few pounds in the lining of her suitcase. Soon the girls' conversation was interrupted by the quiet sounds of bells calling them to supper. The new girlfriends walked into a large hall, which was divided into two sections. On one side of the room were tables and benches for the nuns, with similar furnishings for the students on the other side. As Teresa entered, all eyes turned in her direction. A new student was always of interest to the student body. But very quickly they all focused their eyes back on the modest suppers before them. Not even the sound of spoons scraping on the dishes could be heard. The girls communicated with each other in whispers. Immediately following supper, everyone gathered in the convent chapel for vespers. After church, the girls returned to their rooms to prepare themselves for the next day's lessons.

Breakfast was served in the same dining hall, and then the girls went to class. To get to the classroom building the students walked through the fruit orchards, which were among beautiful lawns and gardens. The gardens, which were tended with loving care by the nuns, were vast and beautiful. Upon arrival at class, Teresa was greeted in French by Bonoza : "Bonjour, Mademoiselle." "I'm sorry, but I don't understand this language," was Teresa's reply. "That is not of my concern. You must learn. All the girls speak French and you must do this, too," Bonoza replied.

Teresa was completely lost and couldn't concentrate on her lessons. There beyond the windows, birds flew freely, the sun shone brightly, and here she was confined within these school walls, listening to something she didn't understand. She was not accustomed to a life of regimentation. Teresa felt grumpy and very dissatisfied with her life at that time. She hated being closed up in that gloomy building. This frame of mind encouraged her to behave inappropriately.

Ignoring the command of silence, Teresa walked through the convent's corridor with the other girls and began to talk loudly. The Mother Superior was apparently waiting for the new, naughty student, to misbehave so that she could put her in her place. Teresa was telling the girls something they all thought funny, and they were almost choking with laughter. Immediately, Mother Superior loomed around the corner. "You must always remember, young lady, that we must maintain serenity within this temple of quiet and prayer," she said, pointing toward and hitting Teresa's forehead with her skinny, crooked finger.

That same day, Mother Superior came to the cafeteria during mealtime and loudly announced that there are individuals within the group who are not adapting to regulations and are also hiding money in their suitcases. It was apparent that while the girls were out of their rooms, she had done a search of their things. "At the same time," Mother Superior noted, "I must stress that only slatterns wear silk underwear. Therefore, I urge that individual to write a letter to her mother asking her to send her proper underwear."

Teresa knew that the Mother Superior was talking about her, and that for her own good, she would have to conform. Without any procrastination, Teresa turned over the remaining monies she had been hiding to the school's general cash area. She also wrote a letter to her mother, asking her mother to send her thicker stockings and more conservative underwear.

Teresa's hair was another distraction and point of contention between her and her authority figure. Her hair was unruly, fell in her eyes and tended to curl tightly. Sister Bonoza did not like to look at curly hair. She ordered Teresa to wet her hair and straighten it, which Teresa did. This dampness made matter worse, her hair curled more tightly, and Sister Bonoza had to concede defeat.

The girls knew about Sister Bonoza's psychiatric problems and therefore tried hard to not get in her way or provoke any situations. The annoyed Bonoza had the habit of releasing her tensions on the first person she encountered. However, the girls were adolescents and full of spirit. Sometimes, they too had to release their nervous energy.

During a break between classes one day, some of the girls got into a friendly melee. The floor became littered with scraps of paper, the blackboard was smudged with chalk, and the chairs were scattered about the entire room. Bonoza saw this disarray with horror. She ordered the supervising nun to bring a broom from the tool shed and to line up the naughty girls in a row. One by one, each girl had to kiss and bow before the broom, apologizing to the broom for her part in the mess. The girls also had to promise the broom that this would be the last time they did such a thing. The teacher received a reprimand and had to spend additional time in church, seeking God's forgiveness for the fact that she had not overseen carefully enough the orderliness of the school.

The unfortunate nuns never had a moment's rest. After their daily chores, when evening fell, they had to rise every hour and hurry to the chapel for prayers. The students often heard their quiet steps as they hurried to offer their devotions to the ever alert God. This life filled with work, constant prayers, and living in cold quarters with meager food, did not foster good health. There were many nuns who had serious illnesses that were in need of medical attention.

The only time that Teresa felt happy and comfortable was when she was able to be in the orchards. She loved the green serenity and beauty of nature. Her memories of Africa, and the freedoms she had experienced there, were still a very large part of her life. Winter came and brought with it rainy weather. This did not help Teresa's moodiness and feeling of despair. She sometimes thought about running away from that depressing place. Unfortunately, there was nowhere to turn for help and she had to try to adapt to those almost intolerable conditions. This life was so different from the way she had been raised. At the school, she found herself under constant suspicion and observation, and she could not express herself. Finally, she began to look forward to the end of the school year, and the long awaited summer vacation.

One day, while sitting on a bench in the orchard, she heard her school friend calling, "Teresa, your father has come!" Teresa sat, not moving from her place on the bench as she heard the girl's fabrication. After all, her father had been dead for several years. However, curiosity got the best of her, so she decided to head toward the office to see who was waiting for her. She immediately recognized the man who had brought her to the convent.

"I've come to take you home," he said. "You've been accepted by the public school. Go pack your things; I've already taken care of your release with the director of the school." Teresa suddenly felt as though someone had attached wings to her shoulders. She ran to her room, and hurriedly threw her things into her suitcase. She said goodbye to her girlfriends and hurried toward the building's exit. Sister Bonoza waited on the stairs, talking with Teresa's caretaker.

"Oh, my darling Teresa, you're leaving us so unexpectedly," Bonoza said with a desperate voice. She embraced Teresa with her bony shoulders. "We'll miss you." Please, you must write to us, at least a few words, to tell us how you are doing at your new school." She made no mention of Teresa's money, which remained in the convent cash box. Teresa didn't have the courage to speak up and demand it herself. She just wanted to get out of there as quickly as possible. The return trip went more happily and seemingly more quickly than the ride to the school. After all, Teresa was returning home! She truly felt sorry for the girls who remained at the school and who had no hope of escaping.

Teresa's family was ecstatic to see her and she had a joyous homecoming. Her brother had recently come home from high school for summer vacation. After a few days, Edek wrote a letter to the convent's board of directors asking for the return of Teresa's money. After some time it was returned to her. This closed an unhappy chapter of Teresa's life in the care of the Nazarene Sisters.

Again Teresa found herself to be free as a bird, spending her days enjoying the beautiful landscape surrounding her home. She again sped along on her bicycle and rode down to nearby towns to take care of her mother's financial business. She gazed at various displays in store windows and forgot about the time. She saw there wonders she had only dreamed about when she was a small child. Colorful balls and beautiful dolls from around the world, dressed in outfits of their homeland, filled the storefronts. Clothing and shoes lay behind glass windows within the reach of her hand. After having felt such deprivation as a child it was hard for Teresa to believe this abundance. As she had before, Teresa stopped for her ice cream treat, and fruit in round waffles. She pushed her old bicycle up the hill again, singing Polish songs. She wallowed in the vision of the rich greenness of meadows, overgrown with field flowers. Often, she would pick the most beautiful flowers and adorn herself and her bicycle.

Teresa was completely free, without burdens or responsibilities. Time sped past. Summer was quickly coming to an end. It was time to begin preparing for a new trip, this time to the public school. Teresa now felt no fear about leaving home. Nothing could be worse than her stay at the convent school. Teresa would attend a boarding school, with no cost to the family. It was time for the school year to begin, and about a dozen girls from the camp, carrying their baggage, climbed into the railway car. They were ready for the long trip to the secondary school in Diddington and a new experience.

It was much fun riding with such a large group of familiar girls. After the daylong trip, the train stopped at the station, and from there the girls were driven to the school. The school buildings did not look impressive. They consisted of metal barracks where army personnel had been stationed during the war. Thirty-two girls were quartered in one barrack. Other areas were designated for lectures, gymnastics and dining for the students. The teaching staff consisted of Polish teachers who had arrived from Africa. Many of them had been released from camps where they had lived as displaced persons in the Soviet Union. Teresa recognized many familiar faces among the group of students gathered there. They had all endured and survived the times of torture, illness and hunger in the orphanages of Uzbekistan.

It was the earnest intent of the Bajorski family to eventually return to live in a free Poland. Therefore, Teresa was enrolled in a school where classes were taught in Polish, with just one hour per day of English instruction. In Edek's high school, most classes were taught in English. There was a relaxed atmosphere at Teresa's school, and this was very conducive to learning. Here no students were poked in the forehead with a bony finger. In addition to concentrating on her studies, Teresa signed up for the theater group. This ensemble presented a variety of musical shows, and Teresa was able to show her singing and dancing talent. She became recognized for her outstanding performances, and this made her very proud and self-confident.

The teachers guided their students on many field trips throughout Great Britain. The girls visited mighty castles scattered throughout Wales. These castles long ago had protected noblemen from invasion by aggressive Scottish tribes and marauding Vikings. The palaces and cathedrals in London were awesome sights to these young women. As far as the eye could see, stately old church steeples stretched across the horizon. The roofs of these amazing buildings concealed within them treasures from all over the world. The students spent entire days visiting museums, theaters and monuments. They paused along the banks of the Thames River, and watched the huge cargo and passenger ships as they steamed into the harbor. These ships brought exotic goods from faraway lands, and many new immigrants planning to settle in the British Isles.

Teresa returned to her home for Christmas vacation. She was thrilled to find Aunt Jozefa there. Jozefa had not been able to leave Africa with the rest of the family. Those not closely related to army personnel had to remain in Africa until there was a need for their labor in England. Jozefa had finally been assigned to a job in a textile mill in Liverpool. She had been working there for a year, and had earned a short vacation. She did not yet speak English well, but managed to find her way to the Springhill Hostel, where the rest of the family lived. They had a happy, loving reunion, and talked throughout the night about their experiences since they had last been together in Africa. The sisters had never been separated before that time, and Aunt Jozefa had been like a second mother to Teresa and Edek.

Emilia shared with Jozefa a letter from their brother, Janek Maselek, who lived in the United States. He had suggested that the family immigrate to the United States and set up permanent residence there. All the temporary camps in Great Britain were being liquidated at that time and they needed to decide where they would live in the future. There was no doubt, and little discussion. The decision to go to the United States was unanimous. The family had no intention of returning to Poland while it was still under Russian rule. Emilia's brother, Janek, now called John, had lived in the United States for many years and he was well established there. He promised that he would find them housing and employment. The family applied to the American Embassy for visas and waited anxiously for their approval. Jozefa, now called Josephine, went back to her factory job, and prepared for her departure.

The Bajorski's were designated to leave in November of 1952. A tugboat loaded with passengers took them to the huge ocean liner docked outside the harbor. They stood with mouths agape looking at the tall upper decks, which were lit with thousands of lights visible against the backdrop of the dark ocean. The ship Liberty, on which they would sail across the ocean, was the second largest ship in the world, second only to the Queen Elizabeth.

The passengers climbed the stairs and walked down the labyrinth of corridors on this massive vessel. The Bajorskis were brought to their assigned cabins where, with great relief and joy, they fell on the freshly made beds. Their time of rest was short, as curiosity prevailed. They familiarized themselves with the schedules and safety rules and regulations. Soon Teresa and Edek, now Edward, set off to explore the ship. Standing on the upper deck, Teresa and her brother looked for the last time at the island where they had spent four years of their young lives. On that shore they had experienced a serene and orderly life, and been enabled to put behind them the sufferings experienced in the Siberian taiga and the wilds of Africa. With an enormous blare of its siren, and the raising of its anchors, the huge ship edged its way out to sea. The family was going to a new land, where they hoped to establish a permanent home. They were determined that their wandering days were over.

That evening they all went to the magnificent dining room for dinner. Elegantly dressed waiters threaded their way between the crowded tables to serve the passengers. There was a fantastic array of foods, and the servings were more than generous. The family feasted on several courses, appetizer through dessert. After dinner and a short stroll around the deck, they made their way back to their cabins for a contented night's sleep. Several days passed in this routine manner. Since it was November, the weather was cold and the ocean rough, so their time out on deck was usually short. November's cold and damp winds penetrated their clothing

The Bajorskis spent many evenings being entertained by shows in the concert halls or by watching other people dancing in the ballrooms. The last night before they arrived in port was one they will never forget. As the family was eating their evening meal, the dishes suddenly slid from the table and crashed to the floor. Chairs and tables slid across the room and smashed into the walls. Then the ship lurched again, and furniture and people were heaved in the other direction. The passengers let out screams of terror as the ship tossed about. Teresa sustained a minor injury to her hand, as it was crushed between the chair and the wall. The ship captain announced over the megaphone that a huge wave had hit the broadside of the ship, and that the passengers should prepare for a period of rough seas. A tremendous winter storm was heading their way from the direction of the United States. Within moments the crew cleaned up the debris and new settings were secured to the tops of the tables. The rest of the meal was completed with some difficulty as diners had trouble finding their mouths with their eating utensils. None of the passengers was seriously injured during this turmoil, although many were treated for bumps and bruises.

The night continued to be chaotic. Passengers had to be tied to their beds, and nearly everyone was seasick. At daybreak, the woozy travelers peered through the portholes and watched huge waves crashing against the ship. It seemed as though the ship could not withstand the pounding and buffeting it was receiving. Later the family learned that they had survived the largest Atlantic storm in over fifty years. Teresa promised herself that once she reached land she would never step foot on another ocean vessel.

Later the next day, they saw the outline of land as the ship entered the Hudson River. The ship moved into New York Harbor and saluted the Statue of Liberty with a blast from its horns. This was a very moving and exciting time for all of the Bajorskis. They stood on the upper deck, and searched the crowd on the pier, looking for Uncle John. They knew him only from pictures. After a time they recognized what they thought was his form, and shouted to get his attention. He stood with his wife, Helen, who turned and wildly twirled her scarf in the air. The family disembarked with much rejoicing. There was an emotional reunion of the whole family, but especially by the two sisters and brother, who had not seen each other for over thirty years

Uncle John drove the family directly to a well-known restaurant, *Mother Lionis*. Here again the family was treated to huge amounts of delicious food. They couldn't believe the abundance, and Emilia thought it wasteful. In England they had been served healthy food, but in more modest amounts. Uncle John laughed at her reaction. He was proud of this evidence of prosperity in his adopted land.

John then drove them to his home in Connecticut, about one hundred sixty kilometers north of New York City. He lived in New Britain, an industrial city that employed many new immigrants from Poland. The new arrivals were pleasantly surprised to be able to read some of the signs in store windows. Emilia knew that this would make shopping much more convenient for her than she had anticipated.

Emilia, Josephine, Teresa and Edward moved in with John and Helen. They needed to acquire a nest egg before they could be on their own. Emilia, now Emily, and Josephine were employed in a factory, which produced electrical kitchen appliances. Edward began his studies at a nearby university in Hartford, and Teresa, who was then seventeen years old, began high school in New Britain. They had both acquired a good basis in the English language, but found their new studies challenging in the beginning.

Emily and Josephine found communication difficult at first. They had trouble understanding the idiomatic Polish that was spoken by their neighbors. It was a version of Polish interspersed with English words. They didn't know whether they should laugh or cry as they listened to a radio program, which was broadcasting lively polka music featuring a soloist who was singing, "Who stole the kiszka (sausage)?"

Teresa signed up to sing with the Ignacy Padarewski Polonia

Choir in New Britain. It was there that she heard the pure Polish language spoken. The choir consisted of about fifty members, who were predominately new arrivals from England and Germany. They sang traditional Polish songs at district meetings, theatrical performances and concerts within the New England states. Teresa acquired many new girlfriends from participation in this choir – girls, who like herself, had lived through great hardships and deprivations in Siberia. These experiences served as a tight bond between the girls.

After about a year, the newcomers were financially ready to move to their own residence. They found a comfortable apartment in New Britain, and bought furniture and other necessities. Finally they had a place they could call their own, and they settled into a secure lifestyle. Edward graduated from the University of Hartford and became employed by the State of Connecticut in the Department of Revenue Services as a Deputy Commissioner. After graduating from high school, Teresa studied at a secretarial school for two years, and then took a position with The Phoenix Insurance Company.

After five years, came a moment of great happiness and pride. All of the family became citizens of the United States. For over twelve years they had wandered throughout three continents of the world, without having any country to call their own. From this moment forward, they had a new homeland, and a sense of safety and stability. They could now begin to build a new life and hope for a healthy and prosperous future.

# Through the Baltic Sea to the Land of the Vikings
## (Czeslaw)

The big day had finally arrived, September 25, 1951, when we were to at last attempt our escape to Sweden. This day became engraved in our minds forever. We hoped to realize our long and often thwarted plans to flee from Poland. A driver, with a large rented truck waited for us at our appointed rendezvous, along with four canisters of gasoline and two large inflated inner tubes.

I arrived first, at the predetermined hour, closely followed by Mietek. My friend was always reliable. Anxiously we awaited the arrival of Skiba and Drzewinski. Mietek and I were still unsure if they would actually participate in this escapade. After a while, we breathed a sigh of relief when we saw the silhouettes of our crewmen hurrying in our direction. From a distance, they looked like a father and son, since Czeslaw Skiba was tall and robust, while his friend was short and frail.

The time we spent exchanging greetings was short. We piled in the truck and were off to locate our sailing vessel, which we had entrusted to the care of a friendly fisherman. He and the boat were situated in the Wisla Canal, twenty kilometers past Gdansk. Each one of us realized the seriousness of the moment and there was no conversation among us and no smiles on our faces. We realized the extreme danger of this undertaking.

This was a period when Communist terror ran rampant in Poland. We were constantly under observance by the local police. The authorities knew of our repeated attempts to escape. U.B. officials kept watch over our original boat, which was docked in the canal's harbor. They did not know that it was of no use to us. We had constructed this boat when we were inexperienced boat builders, and unfamiliar with the existing coastal conditions. Sailing that boat out into the sea was impossible. Many army guards protected the outlets of the rivers and canals, and we would certainly be detected.

Now before us was a different road to conquer – one that was an eight kilometer wide stretch of land, that was very carefully watched by the border police. We drove to the distant town of Lebork, seventy kilometers away, where the Leba River rapidly flowed. After meandering about eighty kilometers among diverse meadows and marshlands, it flowed into the large Lake Lebsko. This lake was separated from the Baltic Sea by a narrow strip of tall irregular dunes, which had been created by the windblown sand. The terrain itself protected the approach to the sea, therefore, there was a strong possibility that we could avoid being discovered by the border patrol.

It was not easy, nor was it pleasant, for us to think of leaving our homeland forever. This was the country in which we were raised, and for which we had fought for many years. I could not rid myself of the image of my mother's head peering out of the window of our apartment as I was leaving home. I had not looked back, as I tried to contain my tears. I knew that this time it would be the last farewell – a return from this road would not be possible.

Eventually we arrived at the place where our seaworthy boat was stored. We paid the fisherman for being custodian of our vessel and, with lightning speed, loaded the boat and all our gear onto the truck. We, four adventurers, climbed into the truck and were on our way.

We stopped at the main train station in Gdansk. Mietek and Drzewinski got out of the truck. They took the dismantled ten horsepower motor. This was in accordance with our plan. We had to have an alibi in case the police stopped our truck while we were traveling. Our explanation would be that we were on vacation and setting out on a fishing trip. Having fishing equipment and a small three horsepower motor made a lot of sense, having a ten horsepower motor with us would cause suspicion. Mietek and Drzewinski planned to bring the big motor by rail to the station in Lebork, and then meet us at an appointed place by the Leba River. We were to rendezvous near a small bridge, which was in the dense thickets that covered the river's edge.

Our trip by truck went without a hitch. Our hired driver helped us lower our boat into the water. We paid him for his services, plus a hefty tip, which he was not expecting. "Gentlemen, make good use of your freedom," he said, waving his hand as he drove away.

We didn't have to wait very long for our friends to arrive with the motor. They raced up, agitated and panting. Mietek said that they had seen army members along the way, driving in this direction. However, since he and Drzewinski were able to take a short cut, they had managed to elude the soldiers.

We wasted no time. The boat was at the water's edge, and we all jumped in, shoving it out onto the water. We were carried forward by a rapidly, roiling current. The Leba River had snakelike turns and its edges were covered with a clumpy thicket. The river's current carried our small boat, into the depths of the sprawling meadows on the shore. The only thing we could see in the distance was a small herd of cows casually grazing on the rich grassy vegetation.

As soon as we found ourselves at a safe distance from the road, we attached the small outboard motor. This propelled the boat briskly toward the northern part of Lake Lebsko. The weather was magnificent, a true Indian summer day that enabled us to take off our shirts and delight in the sun's rays warming our bodies. It was an interesting sight to see – the small boat scurrying about the narrow yet rapidly flowing river. Our boat was heavily laden. It carried all our basic necessities, four canisters of gasoline and the bigger motor, plus four daring sailors. It was buffeted by the waves, and sometimes threatened to overturn, or at least take on a good amount of water. I had to be extremely watchful about the direction in which we were traveling. I tried to remember from my last visit the topography of the area. We had to watch out for immersed tree stumps and their roots since these could easily cause a disastrous accident. The river was fairly shallow, and only rarely did it have deep pockets that had been dug out by currents. Fortunately, the water was crystal clear, so we could easily see any impediments.

A few hours into the trip we encountered our first obstacle. A tree had fallen across the narrow river, blocking our path. As the water was rather shallow, we managed to jump out of the boat and stop it before crashing into the tree's crown. We had to remove our baggage from the boat, and put it on the shore so that we could push the boat across the branches. This took about an hour of diligent work. We then retrieved our gear, and were again on our way. The only other obstacle we faced was a very low bridge that required us to carry the boat and supplies across a country road, and then lower it back into the water.

By evening we reached a bridge over which ran a road leading to Leba. After sailing under the bridge, we were happy to see the growing rushes of Lebsko Lake. As quietly as possible, we sailed into a clump of reeds, which hid our boat from the side of the road. Hidden from the world, we assembled the motor and enjoyed a bite to eat. We were now faced with the daunting task of carrying all of our things over the expanse of dunes. We discarded everything not considered essential. Drzewinski tried to rescue some of the contents of his small suitcase, but the rest of us deemed that books and extra underwear were not critical necessities. "You'll be satisfied if you can manage to carry your own body across the shifting sands of the dunes," I said to him solemnly.

We could never envision what awaited us in the next phase of our expedition. Until now, this had been a trip with dangers and a few obstacles to overcome. It had been made somewhat pleasant by the beautiful fall weather we experienced. Now, as the sun set, its rays lit up the opposite edges of the tall hills with golden ribbons, adding glorious hues of yellow to the shifting sands.

Through the years, sand that had been blown about by the wind covered the pine forests, as well as the remains of a fishing settlement. Only the tops of chimneys stood above the surface of the sand. The entire opposite bank was overgrown with tall reeds. Among the thick rushes, only the sand that was at the very edge of the water was visible. We were waiting until sundown to start our voyage across these dunes and through these thick rushes. I carefully set my compass to the part of the seaside accessible for landing. We had to manage to get to this area in the dark.

Night fell. We pushed the boat through a clumpy thicket that surrounded us, and found ourselves on the open lake. Luckily, a full moon lighted the water, which spread before us. Our goal was to land on the opposite bank eight kilometers away. We all climbed in the boat, and I quietly lowered the oars into the water, rhythmically rowing in the designated direction.

I did not feel tired even though this was already my second night without sleep. My nerves had been tense from the moment I had left home and now, with this huge task in front of me, I didn't think about resting. My adrenaline fired my energy. There, across the water, was the open beach accessible for our landing. As I rowed I counted to one thousand, tensing the muscles throughout my entire body. After one thousand I began to count again. I repeated this procedure several times without stopping, and without resting. Fortunately, the glow of the moon lit the high hills in the distance. This enabled me to row in their direction without having to look at my compass.

After a few hours on the water, the boat finally poked its nose into the wet sand of the seashore. The matter of rowing the width of the lake was now behind us. Quickly we unloaded our baggage from the boat, hiding it in the nearby bushes. I divided the load we had brought as logically as I could. Mietek and Skiba took four canisters of gasoline. Drzewinski took two oars and the small motor, which was wrapped in the sails that my mother had sewn.

My share in this division of labor was to carry the large motor. Since I was somewhat familiar with the territory I moved ahead. Step by step, wandering between the dunes, we moved along the fine-grained sand. Our legs sunk up to our ankles in the loose sand, and it was with great effort that we were able to extract them. We were rapidly becoming exhausted. After every few steps, Drzewinski sat down on the sand, panting heavily. His physical condition could not cope with such extreme exertion. Skiba also finally announced that he, too, could not carry the gasoline any farther.

I did not want him to think that I was taking advantage, so I gave him my motor in exchange for his two canisters. He realized shortly after that the hard shaft of the motor was even more uncomfortable to carry, as it sunk into his shoulder causing unbearable pain. Finally it became obvious that we were all too unfit and exhausted to continue on in this manner. I suggested that we carry the items one by one. We left some of our things in hiding, and by working together we took one item at a time a short distance up the road, and then returned for another item. This was much less taxing on our bodies, but the amount of time expended was increased immeasurably. With relief, we finally reached the shore with the last of our items and heard the sound of distant waves as they hit the beach. We hid the equipment in the seaside growth of the nearest dunes.

It was now midnight, September 26, 1951. I was shocked to see Skiba and Drzewinski collapse on the sand as though they were dead. They didn't move a muscle. They were both totally exhausted from the arduous ordeal. It was obvious that they needed time to rest and recover before undertaking the next task. We now had to return to our starting point and then retrace our steps carrying the boat.

The minutes of rest flew by dizzyingly, as tends to be the case when there isn't much time to waste. With extreme reluctance, our group picked itself up, and began to slog back across the dunes. We dragged our feet, walking in the return direction toward the boat that we had left behind in the thick brush at the edge of the lake. I dreaded the thought that soon we would have to pick up the boat and place it on our shoulders. Would we be able to carry that two hundred-kilogram weight up the hill, and across the sand that engulfed our feet as we trudged across the dunes? This boat had carried us on a wonderful trip down the Leba River, and now we hoped to return the favor by carrying it almost two kilometers across the dunes to the sea. We had high hopes that it would once again be good to us and carry us across the sea to our eventual destination. We rested a short while, but under no circumstance could I allow my friends to relax very long. We needed to be far out into the sea before dawn, where we would not be visible from the observatory towers that were located on the shore.

With extreme exertion we lifted the boat from the ground and placed it on our shoulders. Fortunately my mother had made small pillows for us that we used as shoulder pads. These pads were a godsend in protecting our shoulders when we were carrying hard, heavy objects across the wilderness. We had already had experience using them in our first unsuccessful attempt at escape. Carrying this heavy boat was not easy, and our backs were breaking from the unevenly distributed weight of the boat. We sunk up to our ankles in the loose sands of the rough terrain. When we walked up hill, the boat rested its complete weight on those of us who were in the back, and then it shifted its full weight to the front when we went downhill. While on the hillside, the boat leaned on its sides, and we lost our balance, as our feet sunk deeply into the sand on that side. Rest breaks were now occurring more frequently. Our breathing was becoming violently strained, and our lungs were wheezing, desperately trying to get the oxygen they needed.

At that moment Drzewinski fell to the ground crying, and refused to get up. He also emphatically balked at continuing in our attempt to transport this cumbersome boat. Mietek, frightened and angered by this behavior, threatened Drzewinski, shouting that he would beat him into cooperating with us. After everyone quieted down, we rested for a short time, and then decided to change our method of moving the boat. None of us had the strength to go on as before carrying the boat on our shoulders. We decided to push it while kneeling in the sand. We slowly shoved it forward a meter at a time, and eventually reached the peak of the hill. Going downward was a great deal easier. The boat slid along the sand toward our desired destination. Unfortunately, beyond that hill was a second hill, then a third, as well as several others. There is an end to everything, however. Eventually, with great joy we again heard the swooshing of water, and from the last dune we could see the white foam of the waves crashing on the beach. Now we had to discern just where and when the army patrol would be walking between the observation towers. These were placed approximately four kilometers apart. We needed to wait for them to pass the area of the beach in front of our hiding place. This was a perfect time for us to relax get some much-needed sleep. We were completely exhausted from the ordeal of wrestling with the unwieldy boat.

After we had become somewhat refreshed, we saw the silhouettes of two soldiers slowly trudging up the beach. They were smoking and chatting, and passed by us heading west. We waited over a half-hour until they disappeared from sight. We then lowered the boat from the top of the dune and quickly returned to get the gasoline and motors, which we had previously hidden in the bushes.

I jumped into the boat, once again grabbing the oars. Skiba and Drzewinski settled quickly in the front while Mietek pushed the boat into the sea. He waded up to his waist in the water, and then hopped into the boat. I paddled quietly and rapidly, trying to propel us far from the shore as quickly as possible. We didn't want to start the motor too close to shore and attract the attention of the coastal army patrol. After having rowed a few sea miles, I attached the engine to the backside of the boat and filled the tank with gasoline. With great apprehension, I pulled the starter's rope. It wasn't until the third try that the motor started, and that sound was beautiful music to our ears.

The moment of great uncertainty and tension had passed. Luck continued to be on our side. After such a long trek through the sand and brush, the motor could have easily become clogged and unable to start. That would have been such a catastrophe since we were now visible by anyone in the observation tower. At this time we were one step closer to freedom, unreachable by the coastal security guards. It was now twilight, and before us was the mighty gray sea with swelling waves produced by the southern winds. Somewhere out in the north lay Sweden, to which we hoped to sail in our small shell of a boat.

Our fear of the officials was not yet a thing of the past. We noticed a string of lights that was rapidly approaching from the southwest. They were nearing us rapidly, and cutting across our path to the north. We were overcome with horror. We thought that soldiers in the observation tower had spotted us and were in pursuit. I revved up the engine and turned directly to the east hoping that the boats would bypass us in the dark. When they were a short distance away, I turned off the engine, and we waited in silence until they sailed by. With relief, we confirmed that they were not small navy boats, as we had feared, but just a fishing fleet, heading for the northern part of the Baltic Sea. This time our engine caught on without any false starts, and we sped up our race with time. Dawn was nearing, the sun soon lit up the sky. Fortunately for us, the sandy hills from which we had just departed were no longer visible on the horizon.

We sailed northwest in accordance with the setting of our compass. We had to be sure that the tides or winds would not carry us to the right side of Oland Island. In that case we would sail northerly along the shores of Sweden, and that would be a disaster. So far, all was going well. A gentle wind assisted the engine and boat, which were being carried along on the friendly waves. When we were already about forty miles from the border of Poland, we noticed a huge ship sailing from the west in the direction of Gdynia. It slowed down as it passed us. The ship's crew gathered at the railing, and gazed at us steadily. They must have been curious about the four men in a small boat, slowly cruising north. They saw a three-meter shell climbing the waves of the Baltic Sea on its way toward land, which was still about two hundred miles away. We passed them while keeping directly on our course, and soon we were out of sight.

The weather was excellent; the last days of Indian summer. The sun warmed our clothes that were thoroughly wet. We had removed some of the articles of wet clothing and dried them in the warm rays of the sun. Drzewinski found some sort of sandwich in his pocket and shared it with us, dividing it into four pieces. This was the last of our food provisions and it was consumed with lightning speed. After we had imbibed a few gulps of alcohol that had been thinned with cherry juice, we were in a much better mood.

We recounted our good fortune and accomplishments. We were lucky to have avoided being arrested. We had conquered the arduous travel across a formidable terrain. We were also fortunate that everything so far had gone according to plan. Before us now stretched the endless waters of the Baltic Sea. Overtired from the stress and hard labor we had endured, my friends, one by one, began closing their eyes for a much-deserved nap. The rhythmic droning of the motor rocked them to sleep. Unfortunately for me, since I was in charge of staying our course, I could not sleep. The water spraying me from the sea helped to keep me refreshed and invigorated.

It came time to refill the tank with gasoline. I woke Mietek and asked him to lift the canister, while I started the flow of the fuel by sucking it up through a rubber hose. This was not a pleasant activity in a boat that was rocking wildly on the waves. As I sucked on the tube it was impossible for me not to ingest some gasoline, and it made me ill. Since no one else was familiar with this operation, it was left up to me. Mietek, was a great help, in spite of his weakened condition, and he gladly did anything I asked of him without any excuses or complaints. It was quite obvious that he was excited by our successes and anxious to do anything to bring this expedition to a happy conclusion.

During the afternoon of that same day, I anxiously noted the increasing size of the waves that were being driven by the strong wind. In the evening, the southern wind began to change direction and was blowing more from the east. For us this was a fortunate thing as we did not want to sail toward the north. The water seemed to change color as the sun sank in the west. It now appeared navy blue with white streaks of foam on the crests of waves. Guiding the boat over these tumultuous waves became increasingly difficult. I had a hard time keeping a steady speed as the rushing water attacked our boat from the rear.

We had prepared ourselves for the coming night and more inclement weather. We secured two canisters, which were already empty, under the bench together with the air- filled tubes. They were tied with a rope and would hopefully assure the boat's floatation even if a bigger wave were to pour water inside. We were now experiencing stronger winds and lowering temperatures. We began to shiver in our wet clothing.

Skiba and Drzewinski were wrapped in the canvas sail and lay hunched over in the front of the boat. They were terrified of the boat's pitching on the huge waves. Mietek, shivering from the cold, occupied himself at times by bailing out water from the boat. Often larger waves would hit the side of the boat and their foam splashed in soaking us even more. It was getting really dark, which made it very difficult to judge the direction and size of the waves. The smartest thing to do would be to travel without the use of the motor. I removed the motor, wrapped it in a canvas sail and laid it at the bottom of the boat, where I hoped that it would remain dry. We connected a small sail, which would carry us wherever the wind chose.

Then began a horrendous battle with the waves. They attacked our boat from behind, and with their white foaming crests tried to flood our small vessel. The raging sea was trying to swamp us. "Poseiden," the almighty God of the sea seemed to be looking for companions in his underwater kingdom. However, he didn't know that he was dealing with stubborn, determined individuals who tightly held onto the broadside of the boat. We had full faith in our own luck and endurance during the time of his anger.

In the middle of that dark night, probably somewhere around three a.m., we saw some lights in the distance. After a short time they disappeared. We surmised that these lights were from Oland Island, which lay in the north. We passed by Oland Island, as the mighty winds had pushed us toward the west, in the direction of Sweden. Luckily, this direction was in our favor because it saved us from traveling the length of the rocky Swedish coastline. Apparently I had mistakenly set my compass too much in the northern direction.

Before dawn, when the stars in the heavens had already paled, sleep overcame me. For a short while, I unguardedly closed my eyes. The sound of splashing water pouring into the boat, which was then riding sideways against the coming waves, woke me. Mietek, who also had fallen into a short sleep, woke and grabbed a pail and began to bail out the water, which had already accumulated in the boat's bottom. This was a warning, and we would get no further sleep at this time. Impatiently we waited for some show of light from the eastern sky. Being in complete darkness on an angry, stormy sea was a horrible experience especially for inexperienced sailors such as we were.

At daybreak, the sea began to calm down a little. As the sun rose, the winds began to subside, and the white crests of the uncontrollable waves began to dissipate. I placed the smaller motor on the stern of the boat and slowly we began to sail in a northwestern direction. That was another horrible journey. Our small boat had to climb very tall embankments of water and then fall into the depths of the sea just moments later. We thought that we would never manage to conquer the next wave. We all began to get seasick. Our empty stomachs had begun to shrink, and quickly emptied themselves.

Finally, at about noontime, after thirty-two hours on the water, we saw a point of land on the horizon. With hope for an ending to our trip, we sailed in that direction. At first, only the outline of a lighthouse was visible. After a while, we were able to recognize the Swedish flag as it flew high atop the lighthouse, which stood upon a small island of rocks, like a solitary mushroom in the forest. However, for us this was already the Promised Land. This was a land that we hoped would accept us across its threshold. It was the land to which, only under the supervision of the Blessed Mother, were we able finally to sail.

We were finally approaching the rock, and I had to sail around it, looking for a place to tie the boat as well as an entrance to the rocky shore. We were still a few meters from the rock when Drzewinski jumped out of the boat into the water. He had misjudged the depth of the crystal-like, clean sea. He thought that the water was already shallow in this area. Terrified, he shouted, waving his arms as he plunged into the depths of the offshore waters. This incident made us realize that the unfortunate fellow did not know how to swim! He had dared to sail across the Baltic Sea in a small boat knowing that he could not survive if the boat capsized. Luckily he was able to grab onto an oar that Mietek handed him, and happily climbed back into the boat which he had been so eager to abandon earlier.

A two-person Swedish lighthouse crew had noticed the boat with four sailors nearing the island and came to meet us. Skiba turned to them and, in English, explained who we were and from where we had sailed. Since the watchmen were representatives of the Swedish government, he asked them for asylum. They helped us pull the boat onto a secure spot. Our new acquaintances invited us into their building. They helped us to remove our drenched clothing and dried it by a warm stove. We blissfully savored the hot tea that was given to us.

At this time, the lighthouse crew, named "Utklipan," informed the border patrol in Kalskrona that they had four escapees from Poland who had landed on their island. After waiting a few hours, a water police torpedo boat cruised in. They were to take us displaced persons to a port in Kalskrona. As we sailed toward the northwest Swedish seashore, approximately forty miles away, I finally fell asleep. This was my first real sleep in three nights. I awoke as we were docking at the quay where the area police were already waiting for us. They greeted us kindly, asking where we had sailed from and when we had left our country. They told us that government representatives would be coming the next day to ask us more precise questions about the route of our trip and the reasons for our escape from Poland.

We drove by car to the city, where a police officer took us to the police station. Within a short time, a dinner from a local restaurant was brought to us. After we had eaten, the police commander, seeing how tired we were, suggested that we rest. Despite the fact that it was still quite light outdoors, it was already evening. He apologized for the fact that we would have to spend the night in the cell of the police station, however he assured us that the door would be left open so that we would know that we were free individuals and not prisoners. We were very appreciative of his tactfulness. For the first time in years, we felt truly free – not threatened by arrest and communist police harassment.

We four exhausted travelers immediately fell into a deep peaceful sleep. We were comfortable on clean bedding, and although our cell was barred, we knew that we were at last free people. We had left our homeland and the life that we had known. We had distanced ourselves from our dear families and friends so that we could breathe the air of freedom.

The next day, immediately after breakfast, we were driven to Cytadel, which was by the Oceanside in the western part of Sweden. There we were to wait for our political asylum. Our stay in Cytadel would be about two months, during which time we would be investigated. After the investigation was successfully completed, we would be given jobs in districts designated by the authorities. After receiving political asylum, all fugitives were required to live in a prescribed town, with no thought of moving around. Cytadel was an old fortress, which lay by the Baltic Sea with a view of Denmark across the strait. A high wall made of red bricks surrounded it. This was a lovely area in which to take a scenic walk in one's free time.

Each of us had a designated work time in the kitchen to help the cook prepare meals as well as clean the kitchen area. Most of our spare time was spent trying to learn the Swedish language. For a while, we were not allowed to move away from our designated area or to form friendships with other fugitives who were already staying there. After talks with officials from the Swedish Immigration Bureau, the situation changed and we were allowed to mingle with the others. With surprise, we found out that we were not the only Polish people that were staying in this fortress. After several days, other fugitives came to visit us. One man introduced himself as Edward Woronowicz. He told us that he had sailed over to Sweden with a cruise organized by the Higher School of Sea Commerce in Sopot, Poland.

Strange things occur in life. A few weeks prior to our escape, I had been in Gdynia. Sitting there on the pier's edge, I watched some young people preparing their yacht for a sea trip. I was envious that they were able to sail out of the country on a decent boat. I also thought about what awaited in our future when we found ourselves out on the waters, far from land. What sort of chance would we have in our small shell of a boat on the open sea? At that time, I had paid particular attention to a person with unusually shiny metal teeth. He had smiled broadly, showing teeth made of stainless steel, while he was talking with other crew members of the yacht. That had been this very same Edward

Woronowicz. During our conversation, another fugitive from Poland came forward, Kazimierz Lemanski. This meeting brought us much joy and in a short while, a sincere friendship formed between us.

After a few months, we received certificates testifying that we had been granted political asylum. We were then supplied with new clothing and informed that we would be working in the A.S.E.A. – an electrical motor factory in Vesteros. From our future wages at the factory, we were required to gradually pay off our debts for the wardrobe we had received. We were informed that we were not allowed to stray anywhere far from the city in which we would be living. We also had to report each month to the area police.

We were transported to Vesteros and assigned to live in the private home of an old tailor, Bartfel. This man welcomed us very sincerely, communicating with us with a very elementary knowledge of the German language. He introduced us to his wife, Gertruda, explaining to us that they had just married a few years ago, and telling us also that he loved his wife very much. I was to occupy one room on one floor with Mietek, while Skiba and Drzewinski bunked in another.

On Saturday, filled with curiosity, we set out to explore the town in which we were to spend the first part of our stay in Sweden. This city of Vesteros is located in central Sweden near a large lake whose canals connected with the Baltic Sea. Despite the sunny November weather, it was very cold. We walked around for a couple of hours, and after a modest dinner in a local restaurant, returned home. The friendly homeowner greeted Mietek and me and gave us the address of the factory office where we were to report on Monday to begin our jobs. The question of our upkeep was also explained. We were to receive breakfasts and dinners from coupons, which we would buy in a cafeteria near the factory. We were amazed at the organizational efficiency of the authorities, and how well prepared they were to admit and care for fugitives from communistic countries.

Skiba and Drzewinski were informed that they would soon work at another factory in a neighboring town. They were assigned their lodging in that town, and soon moved away from Vesteros. This was the time that our paths diverged, and Mietek and I eventually lost contact with our fellow adventurers.

In the early morning hours of the next day, Sunday, we were surprised by a visit from the lady of the house. Gertruda came to us with a tray filled with a variety of cakes and hot coffee. Gertruda offered these treats to her new tenants who were still lolling in bed. "Var so good. Please, help yourselves," she said with a smile as she poured the hot coffee into cups. It was so comforting to us, who were deprived of family love and warmth, to feel the sympathy of a stranger.

We were excited to begin our new lives in our new environment, and on Monday morning we hurriedly dressed and headed for the cafeteria where our breakfast awaited us. We bought coupons for the whole month, and then enjoyed our meal. Milk, coffee, cocoa, various cheeses, oatmeal, eggs and blueberry preserves were all spread out on a large table for us hungry workers.

After breakfast, we checked in with the authorities, and were then taken to the locker room. We each received a towel, a piece of soap and cream for our hands, and assigned a locker for our belongings. Everything around us was immaculate. It was so pleasant to look around and see the workers decently dressed in factory overalls. The bell rang, and we were taken to the lathe department where we were introduced to the master craftsman who gave us our assignments. Working on a lathe was no problem for me, as I had already received practice in this type of work at the Mechanical Secondary School.

The day went by with the speed of lightning. A bell announced the nearing of the end of the workday. We cleaned our lathes and the surrounding area of oil and chips. A hot shower revived us and invigorated our physical and mental state. We were then ready for the dinner that waited us at the cafeteria. There was an abundant amount of food. A wide variety of foods was placed on the table and we could eat as much as we desired.

After returning home, we tried talking with our landlords in Swedish to assist us in learning the language as quickly as possible. We felt that this was vital in our new circumstances. Weary from the day's events, we finally just turned in to get some rest. We had a lot to think about and discuss. We compared the prosperity of Sweden, which had enjoyed one hundred years of peace, with the desperation in our poor homeland of Poland, which had been harassed by invasions of enemy superpowers.

We continued to work in the factory for months, and tried to adjust to this new life in a foreign environment and to learn the language. Letters to our own country were the only means of communication with our loved ones, whom we missed very much. During this time, we established contact with our friend from our first escape attempt, Leon, who had already left Sweden and was now living in Canada.

As to attempting to make contacts and promote friendships with the fairer sex, I must relate what I consider to be an interesting situation in which I found myself. I was shopping in a local store and began a small flirtation with a pretty sales clerk. This pleasant conversation in my broken Swedish lasted quite a long time, assisted by gesturing with my hands and the use of a pencil. Soon, however, several other girls who worked there came up to us, laughing at my attempts to make myself understood, and to get a date. Finally, toward the end of the conversation, Inger, the girl with whom I was talking, gave me her address on a piece of paper. She also wrote the day and hour that she expected me at this address.

I returned home very satisfied with my success. I was forming and practicing in my thoughts, with my rather modest knowledge of Swedish, how our future conversation would go. On the day of our appointed rendezvous, I arrived at her door and rang the bell. After a while, the door opened slightly and I found myself, eye-to-eye, with a huge Swede. Confused and looking up at the over two-meter tall figure, I uttered some sort of invented last name and turned on my heel, running down the staircase. I hadn't taken more than several steps down the sidewalk, when I heard a window opening on the first floor. Following this, a male voice was calling my name. It was somewhat mutilated but still recognizable as my name. As I turned my head, I saw the same Swede waving his hand and inviting me to come back. I had no other way out of this. In the past, I had exhibited courage and dexterity in various critical situations, therefore, I thought I would be able to get out of this situation unscathed as well.

I soon found myself in quite an elegant apartment, face-to-face with Hercules. Luckily for me he was smiling. He apologized that his wife, Inger, was taking a shower and couldn't greet me, but that during this time we could get to know one another. Right then I found myself sweating as though I were under a hot shower also. I hadn't known that Inger was married and I couldn't understand this situation. Soon, she came into the living room – the refreshed lady of the house, introducing me as her "foreign" boyfriend. The conversation somehow did not go smoothly. I had nothing to say and no way to say it anyway. I found it difficult to swallow the food that I was offered. I had been raised in a country where such relationships were not even considered. I remained there, out of politeness, for a good while, but I was certainly relieved when I finally got myself out of there and onto the street.

When I next visited the store, Inger explained to me that her husband is not a jealous person and tolerates her having male friends. From then on, I avoided that store. I was in Sweden too short a period of time to get involved in such situations.

Living in the home of the old tailor, Bartfel, we noticed that the national flag was hung on the flagpole outside of the house. Some days it was lowered and other days it was raised, seemingly for no particular purpose. Curious about this, we asked our landlord on what occasions was the flag raised. "Are there so many holidays in Sweden that need to be celebrated so ceremoniously?" we asked. "Each time I am able to satisfy my Gertruda, I must let my neighbors know about it," the old man smiled and said to us with pride.

Every so often, the old man asked us why we didn't bring over some girls to join us for the night. This was not his curiosity, but rather only a discreet observation of foreigners and an understanding of their sexual drives. We lived, two to a room, and we would never even consider inviting girls in for nighttime flirtations. In Sweden, however, this was very natural, and something that only after some time were we able to understand. Relations with the opposite sex were very natural and no one hid this sort of thing. Girls themselves would propose to boys such called "company." After a certain time, they thanked them for the time spent together and peaceably went on their separate ways. They continued in this manner to look for their ideal mates for the future. Therefore, we were expected to adapt to this sort of system so as not to be considered perverted oddballs.

Often, we would talk about these topics with other Swedes, giving our opinion that this was a slackening of family morals. They claimed that in current times adults had no control over the youth and they preferred that their children took care of their love matters at home rather than somewhere in the bushes with an unknown partner. In this way, the adults felt the young people had a greater chance of avoiding venereal disease as well as accidental pregnancy. As can be seen, everyone has his own reasoning and we couldn't deny them this. The saying is "If you find yourself amongst crows, you must caw as they do."

Our time in Vesteros was spent primarily on learning the language, working in the factory and going to dances which took place every Wednesday. Sometimes we were discouraged by being rejected for the last dance, which was announced by the orchestra. We had no idea that the girl who agreed to the last dance gave the boy the chance to walk her home and he would receive coffee and cake in bed for breakfast.

Our social lives were usually tied in with a group of Poles in the area with whom we had become acquainted. Sometimes we had visits from new friends from Stockholm. We were pleased, as well as proud, that someone living in a higher station in life remembered us. These were older political and army emigrants. They treated us to dinner and discussed with us political topics and our times spent in Poland.

One of these men was Mr. Michael L. It wasn't until some time later that he revealed a secret to us. During one of his visits he admitted that he was a representative of a secret organization called "Freedom and Independence." The purpose of this group was to continue the fight against communism. He told us that this organization consisted of members of the former National Army and Polish Home Army (A.K.) under the direction of the government in London. He didn't have to talk very long to persuade us to join. We always had hope for a future war and a return to our homeland. We were told nothing else about the plans. To our questions he merely answered that, for now, we should continue working as we had been, and that we would be informed at the proper time. "From this moment you are soldiers of this organization, and must be obedient to future orders. Currently you find yourselves under our care. In the organization's ranks, I present myself under the code name "Swenson," and you may have contact with me only in a dire emergency by using a private telephone number," he told us.

Nothing changed in our lives after we entered the ranks of this organization. We continued working in the factory, making great strides in our prowess at work. Shortly, two new lathes arrived from Germany. In spite of the jealousy of the older Swedish employees, the new machines were turned over to Mietek and me. The manager of the department assessed the work of the two young Poles. Our accurate work, our independence in setting up the machines and sharpening the lathe knives, were very pleasing to him. The Swedes performed these tasks mechanically, which resulted in a loss of production time. Our prior completion of a Mechanical Secondary School plus our inborn ability in this field gave us a head start in our current trade.

This type of life might have been enough for normal people. Our nerves and energy however, demanded the stimulus of a more adventurous life. Our years spent in the woods, our constant hiding from arrest, and frequent attempts to escape from the terrain occupied by our enemies, were activities on which we fed. This monotonous factory work made us more tired than previous more physically taxing efforts. At first the changes to our life propelled us along, but now we were getting bored. Impatiently we waited for any kind of news from the Freedom and Independence organization. We wanted to be active in this group, and contribute something that would give us a feeling of importance and worth. In this way we could be purposely working toward Poland's freedom from oppression.

# Undercover In West Germany
(Czeslaw)

Finally, in 1952, Mietek and I received the long-awaited news from the organization, stating that we were to go to West Germany to take a course in telegraphy. We had no idea what thoughts were behind this, and we didn't ask any questions. This was an opportunity for change and we were very pleased.

We were to go to Germany by way of Paris. We had received our passports and visas to France, and were told to wait for further orders concerning our departure. Everything had been taken care of for us. All we had to do was pack our clothes and devise a story to tell our friends why we were suddenly leaving Sweden. After getting our orders, we were to board a plane heading for France. We were told that we would be met at the airport by someone who would recognize us by the particular way we held our newspapers.

These plans were followed exactly. At the airport in France we were approached by an elderly man who asked us if we were there to see our uncle Anthony. Our prearranged response was "No, we've come to see our aunt Agatha." After exchanging these passwords, we followed the gentleman out of the airport. He gave us a new password to be used at our destination. We all climbed into an awaiting automobile, and were on our way. The driver sped through the streets of Paris like a madman, often glancing around to see if we were being followed. He stopped in front of a store that sold men's shoes, and pointing toward the door said in Polish, "please go in there."

We went inside the store, demanding in Polish that we be given a pair of women's suede shoes. Without a word, the owner of the business led us to an adjoining room of the store and told us to wait there. After about an hour, another man appeared and told us he would be driving us to an apartment where we could rest. So far, during the course of these meetings, the individuals were very guarded. They did not reveal their last names to us nor did they ask for ours.

The apartment to which we were driven was on the first floor of a very nice brick building. It was decently furnished, but it was also quite apparent that it lacked a woman's touch. This was obvious in that the sink was full of dirty dishes, pots and pans. Apparently, people very similar to us had lived there previously. The man gave us his telephone number but emphasized that we were to use it only in time of emergency. He gave us the keys to the entrance door and an impressive wad of francs. "Live comfortably and happily while in Paris," he told us. "You'll be living here for several weeks. If you run out of money, call the number which I've given you, and someone will deliver more to you."

After the man left, we counted through all the banknotes that he had given us, realizing that he had given us the hefty sum of eighty thousand francs. This whole adventure so far had seemed like a fairy tale. Mietek and I were in Paris, we had somewhere to live, and we had plenty of money for our expenses. Two close friends found themselves in this metropolis of the world, on an unexpected vacation. This was certainly better than working in a factory at a lathe machine. At that time, we had no thoughts about when the vacation would end, and if we would have to pay for it.

We spent many days touring the city. We visited an innumerable number of historical monuments and museum exhibits, and saw the works of many famous painters and sculptors. During the evenings, we trudged about the winding streets, becoming acquainted with the secret nightlife of Paris. Throughout the night, music and singing could be heard from the many cafes. Crowds of people sat at the tables of the sidewalk restaurants, eating late meals. In all this commotion and hubbub, we became aware that we were not completely on our own. There was a covert group of people from the organization in our vicinity.

They observed us from a distance, watching to see whether or not we were making contacts with any foreign agents. This sort of investigation did not disturb us because we had nothing to hide.

We were able to handle everything very well even though we didn't know French. By using hand gestures we succeeded in communicating our needs, as well as buying everything we desired. It was obvious that residents of Paris had a great deal of experience in understanding foreigners.

This was for us a very carefree time. It even seemed a pity to lay down at night to rest. There was so much to explore and see within this ancient city that had always been a gathering spot for artists, as well as aristocrats from around the world. If only we could have stopped time, forgot about the hard times we had lived through, and not had to think about the future. If only we could have always remained in that jocular frame of mind, enjoying the beauty and charm of that city.

All things do come to an end, and our time of bliss was soon over. After we had been in Paris for one month, we received a telephone call and were informed that on the following morning we were to leave Paris. We quickly prepared for our departure. This time, we were driven to a property that was located far from other housing developments. Uncultivated fields and scanty forests surrounded it.

We were greeted there by a plump, elderly gentleman who introduced himself as a former captain in General Anders army. He ran the farmstead, together with his pretty wife and two young children. We were supposed to stay with them for an indeterminable length of time, sticking close to the buildings and terrain of this estate. He didn't mention an affiliation with our organization, but we assumed the entire family received payment for caring for new volunteers in the fight against the communistic regime. It was obvious, from the delicate appearance of the proprietor's palms, that his hands had not seen physical labor on a farm. A new car stood outside. It was not a model that could have been purchased from monies earned by harvesting crops from such barren soil.

During dinner, which had been prepared by the lady of the house, two unfamiliar men appeared and seated themselves at the table. Mietek and I learned that the men had arrived there by illegally escaping across the border of Poland. The younger of the two told about his stay in

Poland where he had been sent to make contact with a member of the organization. He had not been able to make the arranged contact, so he had hid near the outskirts of Warsaw without having anywhere to stay. He had slept in bushes at the edge of the Wisla River. Neither one of the men revealed his last name or any specifics regarding his underground work. Everything was veiled in secrecy. The others did not try to form any closer relationship with us, and that was also quite fine by us.

The time we were spending at this estate began to drag. There was nothing to do besides shoot from air guns at huge rats that were found eating scraps around a garbage container found in the nearby woods. We would spend many hours target practicing on those moving targets. This was both a pleasant and practical pastime. This skill might prove useful in our unpredictable lives.

After several weeks of this idleness, we became increasingly bored and began to gripe a bit. Apparently this must have had an affect, because within a short time, we were taken on an excursion. We were driven to Versailles, which was about forty kilometers away. It took us an entire day to tour this splendid palace, which was the king's summer home. Next, we were taken to a small lake where we swam for a while in water that was not very clean. After these two outings, our touring stopped, and we continued to wait, not too patiently, for the next move. Whenever we questioned how long this situation would last, the answer was always: "Please be patient. The time will come for everything."

That time came unexpectedly. We were given new documents and visas, which would take us to West Germany. In addition, we were given rail tickets and information regarding whom we were to meet and where we were to meet them. We were driven to the railroad station in Paris, arriving there a short time before the train to Germany was to depart. Mietek and I reserved seats by the window of a car in first class so that we would be able to observe the beautiful scenery as we went northward through France and the Alps. The scenic splendor one can enjoy while traveling from France to Germany is beyond description.

The railroad tracks were situated on the rocky mountainsides in snake-like turns, hanging over deep precipices. The clatter of the train's wheels, along with the grinding of the metal as it rubbed against the tracks, spoke loudly of the speed with which we traveled. Every so often we plunged into a dark tunnel which led into the interior of the mountains. After a while, the train exited the tunnel, and we were blinded again with the brightness of the sun's rays. The hanging bridges trembled under the heaviness of the locomotives and wagons, bearing with effort the speeding weight.

The train stopped at the German border. Customs guards entered the car, checking our right to cross the border as well as the legality of the items we were transporting. We handed them our passports. They looked at them, saluted and left the compartment. This was a formality, a responsibility fulfilled by the German powers. It wasn't until after they had left that we noticed that our passports now contained diplomatic visa stamps. By that time, we were already on West Germany territory, not far from our intended destination.

At the train station in Frankfurt, we again provided a password to an awaiting gentleman, and received the required response. We were driven in an elegant private automobile to the home of people who were in the organization's upper hierarchies. There we were informed of the course on which we were about to embark. The camp, where we were to be trained, was led by past officers of the Polish Army, the well-known "Cichociemnych." These soldiers had been paratroopers during World War II and had been dropped on Polish territory, which was occupied by the Germans. We were to be taught many skills. We were to familiarize ourselves with Morse code, and learn to jump by parachute out of airplanes. We were to be trained to become commanders of partisan units, and learn how to use explosive materials for the purpose of sabotage. We were also to be trained in marksmanship, close-combat fighting and survival techniques. We were to parachute onto Polish terrain during the outbreak of hostilities between the Soviets and the United States. This entire plan was not something with which I was in agreement. I had no intention of fighting those citizens who had remained in Poland, some of whom might be my relatives or friends. I was a Pole and I would never be an enemy of any of the Polish people. Therefore, I categorically refused to take part in the overthrowing of Polish land. If I were to take any part in this course of action it would have to be in the province of Wilno, which had been seized by the Russians.

I saw dissatisfaction on the faces of the leaders. They didn't tolerate opposition from subordinates. My biggest trump card was that I was familiar with the eastern terrain, since I had spent summers there in the Polish Home Army (A.K.). Therefore, they expressed their agreement with my thoughts and promised that Mietek and I would be assigned an operation on the terrain that was occupied by the Soviets.

After a few more weeks, we were notified that a selection of candidates for the planned operations would soon take place, and persons not accepted would have to return to their places of residence. We left Frankfurt, driving by car to Mannheim. There, we were driven somewhere outside the city limits to a one-family house. This was an important moment of time that would determine our immediate futures and whether or not we would be admitted to this secret organization.

After a while, I was shown to a room, which had a green rug and walls painted the same color. For the first time, I met American agents. I was shown an apparatus called a lie detector machine, and I gave my voluntary consent to be examined by this machine. I had sensors attached to my head, chest and arms. I was asked a great diversity of questions. Sometimes these questions were funny or naive, while some were quite serious. I was asked about my affiliation with the Communist party and my willingness to participate in the organization of a world revolution. An inky needle made a graph on the roll of paper in the lie detector. After the examining procedure was completed, I was taken into a separate room, which was for those individuals who had passed the testing and had been accepted for the course. I no longer had contact with those who had been rejected. Yet I was very happy to see that my friend, Mietek, had also passed the examinations and was in the room with me. From that moment on, the eleven of us who passed the test were known as "Combat" unit.

The next day, the entire group of us who had been accepted for training was driven to other quarters where the lessons began. We were sequestered in a house, and we walked around with headphones on our ears, not removing them even for sleeping. The tap of the Morse code continuously rang in our ears. In the beginning, we had no comprehension about what we were learning, but slowly we began to decipher the individual letters, and afterwards words, then finally given sentences.

During the day's rest periods, we had to write communications ourselves, practicing with our fingers to gain the required speed in writing the code. We had no contact with the outside world. Letters written by us were turned over to censorship and disappeared after they were checked over. None of us ever received any response to those letters.

After a month's torture of wearing the headphones, Mietek and I, and seven other students, were driven by automobile into the depths of the forest, to a camp surrounded with a tall wire fence. This was the American army's terrain under the vigilantly watchful care of three American sergeants who spoke Polish and were from some kind of special army unit. It was there that we met our new chief, Captain "Cichociemnych," from London, who used the code name "Richard." We also met a few instructors from various fields of sabotage units.

Among the group of instructors, I recognized an acquaintance from Sweden, John Winiarz, a former soldier of the Polish Home Army from the "Jedrusia" unit. He was then using the code name "John." I was dubbed, "Roman," while Mietek became "Blazej." We were not allowed to use any of our real last names.

We began intensive army training. Before dawn each morning, we performed extensive exercises after which we ran for several kilometers. After a short break during which we took a shower and shaved, we went to breakfast that was prepared by a Bulgarian cook. The food was fantastic! We were able to eat whatever satisfied our appetites. After breakfast, there were lectures. Following that, we went out onto the grounds to practice partisan fighting, close combat fighting and to learn how to set up landmines.

Every day there was something new. We practiced attacks on army columns with American soldiers participating, sneaking through borderlines that were protected by guards, and constantly sending and retrieving Morse codes. Every so often we drove into the city and pretended that we were being followed, and that we had to escape from alleged secret police agents. These exercises were performed with the participation of American Secret Service employees. During these exercises, it was fun to observe the German population, who, sometimes with terror in their eyes, watched us running about. We had to jump on or off speeding streetcars or buses without paying for a ticket. None of the conductors had the nerve to demand payment from us. The exercise routines ended in a good restaurant where at dinner we would receive an immediate assessment of our efforts.

Every so often we received passes to go to the city of Heidelberg. During such times the men would do everything they could to spruce themselves up. They would bathe, scrub their teeth, and even take pills that they thought would give them extra stamina. One of our men, Karol, had an enormously strong and beautiful voice. He sang so loud that the windowpanes shook under the influence of his high tones. He himself was not tall and would put inserts into the heels of his shoes so that he would appear more imposing. Before we left to go into the city, he would make an impressive roll from paper and insert it into the front pockets of his pants. During our stays in varying restaurants, he would approach the orchestra, asking them for permission to sing on the stage. During his artistic display, he would turn in such a way that would highlight this roll – naturally this was false advertising.

After the war, single German women felt the shortage of middle aged men. Therefore, it was nothing unusual that after such a concert, Karol would receive letters, discretely brought to him by waiters, which invited him to tables that were occupied by women who were longing for love. The guy got an abundance of food and drink, not having to spend a single mark from his own pocket. We would be bursting with laughter, observing the unsuccessful attempts by these women to win over admirers for the night. We knew that at a designated hour we all had to be at a gathering point and Karol would have to leave the disappointed ladies.

Mietek and I were very surprised by an accidental meeting in Mannheim with our friend, Edward Woronowicz. He had also arrived in Germany, having been sent to work through the same organization. He was occupied in a different underground cell that was sending mail to Poland, and until now, we had not had any contact with each other. Pieces of mail from the organization that contained large dollar amounts, as well as medicines sewn in pillows, were taken from an international train's wagon. This train was traveling from France, through Germany and Poland, to Moscow. Such pillows rode to Poland and were exchanged for others returning back to France through Germany. The number of the train car and the compartment were given by radio code to the appropriate hands of people in the organization.

The winter of 1953 began with preparations for parachuting. However, we didn't use airplanes. We practiced jumping from high towers and that was as far as we got. The course ended. The certified Chief Colonel of the Polish Army flew from London, giving us promotions to officer cadets with assignments waiting for us in the event of war. Mietek and I were to become independent commanding officers of partisan units on the land which lay northeast of the city of Wilno. The entire celebration was enjoyed with a very good cognac and Mr. Colonel, half-unconscious, left the training site. The camp emptied as we all left for the vicinity of Munich.

After completing the army training, the time for relaxation and a comfortable life followed. We received the same pay that was earned by American soldiers, and a car was at our disposal. This gave us the opportunity to explore the beautiful Bavarian mountainous terrain. Mietek and I felt that we could live like this forever.

This bliss ended violently. One morning there was general scurrying around by people from the organization. Three American Agents who were in charge of our "Combat" unit came and transferred us to a new location. For safety reasons we were forbidden to leave our homes. Hand weapons were distributed for self-protection. When we asked what had happened, we received the sad news that the Public Safety (UB) unit in Poland had uncovered the existence of the organization and there had been mass arrests of its members. After a few weeks, the group working on German soil disbanded. We were given the choice of entering the American Army or of returning to our former places of residence.

Before making a definite decision, we asked for advice from an interview agent who spoke Polish well. Sitting at dinner with drinks, for which we paid highly, we asked the man for his honest advice as to what we should do next. "Gentlemen, he said, get out of here as soon as you can. If you want to have some sort of private life, go back to Sweden. The army here will assign you wherever they wish and you will have no choice. You know the Russian language as well as Polish, and people with such skills are needed in the secret service."

We listened to his advice. After receiving some overdue pay, in dollars, and airline tickets for a return trip, we found ourselves flying to Stockholm.

# Return to Sweden
(Czeslaw)

After landing at the airport in Stockholm, Mietek and I no longer wished to return to the manufacturing city of Vesteros. We felt that the capital city was much too beautiful to leave. We settled in Huddinge, a small city that was about ten kilometers away from Stockholm, at the home of an old Swedish woman who owned two houses. She eagerly took us in, having hopes that we young people would be of help to her with managing her estates.

We needed to find work as our monetary funds were getting low. However, this was not an easy thing to accomplish. For reasons unknown to us at that time, we were being turned down for jobs despite the fact that we had the necessary qualifications to execute the work. This condition lasted for quite some time.

Each month we exchanged our dollars for day-to-day living expenses such as the payment of rent, the purchase of railway tickets, and the small pleasantries that were necessary when one is single and young. Slowly, the unadulterated truth began to reach our dim-witted minds that we were still continuing to be under the shoddy care of our organization. Even though we were no longer part of this organization, some of their representatives, in cooperation with the Swedes, were still trying to control us. They were pressuring us to exchange our American dollars for Swedish money, thinking that this would give them more control of us. We were wrapped up in an invisible web from which we could not escape.

Our money was just about depleted, and we had been searching for employment for a long time. Finally, Mietek and I both got jobs as welders in a factory called Skanja-Wabis. We had to travel about twenty kilometers, by train, to the small city of Sudertelie. This was not really the kind of job we had wanted. We weren't used to such dirty, monotonous work with diesel pipes. We often returned home with burns on our hands, complaining about the job that was not in our chosen field.

Mrs. Rab, the homeowner of our abode, promised to help us find better work, this time in our chosen field. She bought a Stockholm newspaper and began calling various institutions in answer to the ads they had placed searching for draftsmen. When she called these individuals, she gave them her highest opinion of us, and told them that we didn't drink alcohol or smoke tobacco. At times, we were able to hear in the telephone conversation that this sort of thing was unusual in those times and that it was difficult to believe. We knew that the major obstacle to our employment was that we didn't know the Swedish language. Finally, though, we received a positive answer from the director of a builder's automated brickyard office. He agreed to interview us. It helped that we knew German as the director spoke it fluently.

I agreed to accept the conditions of the job with minimal pay for a period of three months. After that period, the pay would be adapted in accordance to the kind of work that was being performed. My friend, Mietek, declined this job offer because he already was assured a job in a hydraulic pump factory with a considerably higher pay.

I was fortunate to finally be employed in a clean environment, doing what I had done before leaving Poland. I had no doubt that I would be able to handle everything on this new job well since I had inbred mechanical ability. Drafting was something I was familiar with from school as well as the work I had done in the office of hydraulic water supply systems in Gdansk.

I thanked Mrs. Rab for her help and I assured her that I would live up to the high recommendation she had given me. After three months of working at my new job, my pay had doubled. Engineer Jensen, the head designer, expressed his recognition of my good work as well as my structural knowledge in the area of machine building.

Life was good. I was learning Swedish and the customs that reigned in the country of past Vikings. I always had an appreciation for other people. Some Swedes may not have liked foreigners, but they never showed this and were instead always honest and kind. It appeared that Mietek and I lacked nothing. We had good jobs, we lived in the beautiful capital of Sweden, and we certainly couldn't complain about the good looks and favors of the girls. Yet somehow, our nerves couldn't reconcile with the peaceful and monotonous lifestyle. Every time we met with friends, we would spin dreams about far away trips over vast, extensive oceans and yet undiscovered lands.

Kazimierz Lemanski and Edward Woronowicz were two of these friends. They were eager for adventures in foreign lands, and expressed their willingness to join Mietek and me in whatever we decided to do. We had lengthy discussions about this, and at last, the four of us decided to gather together all of our earnings and buy a boat. We did just that, and decided on a fifty-year-old sailing yacht. Our intentions were to remodel it and set sail on it for a trip around the world. Kazimierz Lemanski was to be the captain of this sailing vessel since he already had sailing experience from when he lived in Poland. Edward Woronowicz also had knowledge of sailing on the seas. He belonged to a sailing club and had escaped to Sweden together with Kazimierz, when they were participants in the same race. Mietek and I, after having traveled the Baltic Sea in the small shell of a boat, were no longer afraid of the vast waters. At that time, and after what we had previously experienced on the water, we felt that we were well prepared for all further adventures on the sea.

Purchasing the eighteen-meter yacht was the easiest thing to do. Our problems started as we began to wonder where we would store the yacht over the few summer months and throughout the long winters. We needed to find a marina that would take our boat in storage. Summer in Sweden is quite short, and as a result, winter lasts for a full six months. We had to immediately think about taking the fifteen ton giant out of the water after removing the two huge masts. It would not be easy to find a dockyard that had a ramp and a large lift. The biggest problem was that Mietek and I had no money to pay for storage of the yacht, or for having it hauled ashore. Here Lemanski came to our rescue. He came from a family with some amount of money, and had a resource to which he could appeal.

Finally, after some extensive searching, we found an appropriate shipyard. It was quite far from Stockholm, on a small, almost deserted island. The storage of the yachts was overseen by Estonians. They told us that our yacht was one of the last to be accepted, and would be left on the rails of the lift over the entire winter because of its huge size. Also, it would be the first yacht lowered into the water in the spring so as to free the lift for launching the other boats. These conditions forced us to complete all the maintenance work we needed to do on the yacht in the early spring before the sailing season began. We would have to travel by canoe to the island no matter what the weather.

One day, after I had bought some groceries, I was rowing against the wind toward the island. This was not an easy thing for one person to do. As I neared the shipyard, I carelessly caught a finger of my right hand against the wooden broadside of the canoe. A huge splinter dug deep into my finger, and broke at the top of my skin. After a while, my finger became swollen and began to turn purple.

I pulled into the island in pain and in fear that I might developed a blood infection. It was impossible to even consider returning to Stockholm because the wind had become stronger and a canoe trip would have been impossible. Like it or not, I had to play surgeon to remove the splinter. I washed a sharp knife in alcohol, tied my finger above the splinter with rope, and drank a glass of whiskey to gain some courage. I also prepared a pair of pliers and a clean bandage to wrap around the wound. The decision was not easy. To cut one's own body caused pain even before one touched the knife. Yet there was no other way out of this situation. I didn't want to entrust this surgery to my friends since I was the one who had completed a first aid course while in the Polish Army camp. After completing the deep cutting, I pulled out the piece of wooden splinter using the pliers, and poured whiskey on the bleeding wound. After this surgical procedure, and feeling a bit drunk from the alcohol I had consumed, I laid down to rest. For a while, I didn't think about the work that needed to be done around the yacht. I didn't lie there for long, however.

A two-inch opening needed to be drilled in order to join the shaft of the propeller with the motor. It was necessary to puncture eighteen inches of oak, which had hardened with time and water. From the inside, the opening had to exactly target the articulated joint installed within the motor. We had undertaken a job that the shipyard specialists had refused to do. We were successful in accomplishing our goal splendidly. After looking over the work, the shipyard's supervisor shook our hands with respect.

Winter was approaching quickly. We struggled to remove the masts, as strong, gusty winds blew around us. It seemed that the winds were always gusty in this country, so we had to cope with it. Our boat remained on the island, covered with a borrowed tarpaulin made with a waxed coating, waiting through the long winter for four lunatics to return and complete the never-ending work of rebuilding her.

Now all that remained to be done was to formulate the plans for our upcoming trip, and to get some more money. The hair upon our heads would stand up straight when we began to count the essential costs we would have in preparing our boat to be lowered into the water. We needed a sealing paste, oakum, tools, waterproof paint mixed with copper (which was exorbitantly expensive), white paint made of linseed oil and a polish for the masts and cabin. We also needed brushes for painting and turpentine in which to wash them. We needed all these things in large quantities because, after all, this was a floating house that had not been renovated for many years. Unfortunately, we had gathered only enough money to purchase an old boat.

Spring arrived unexpectedly. It was time that the boat needed to be lowered into the water. Once again, we had to begin intensive work so that the boat would look sharp as well as sail smoothly. Supplied with warm clothing and enough food for several days, we sailed toward the island where our yacht stood. We had to spend the nights aboard her, so we wouldn't waste time traveling back and forth to the shipyard. Our day's work lasted more than sixteen hours. During the spring and summer in Sweden, daylight lasts twenty-four hours a day. It's difficult to even describe the amount of time we spent in renovating the old boat. Our hands froze from the early morning cold. Then after the sun set, we would be huddled over the damp pallets, trembling throughout the entire white night trying to fall asleep after a long day of hard work.

Such is the sailor's life when he doesn't have rich parents or a fat bank account.

And so, during the entire month of April and through half of May, every Saturday and Sunday, in the wind and cold, we spent our time working like Siberian slaves. These difficulties we endured with the hope of a future free life floating along the ocean waters. It wasn't until we lowered the yacht into the water and set the masts that a feeling of relief from all the work came over us. We sailed our "Smuga" (the name we gave our yacht), to the sailing harbor in nearby Stockholm. Small defects left to be fixed remained put aside until summer, as sailing chores are never totally completed.

Sailing is a beautiful and pleasant sport, especially for guests who can just relax and enjoy. However, crewmen have everlasting work. The boat must be prepared for sailing and following the voyage, must be cleaned and protected for the next use. Guests who become seasick tend not to have such a pleasant trip, and their illness makes it uncomfortable for the other travelers, and for those maintaining the boat.

We took many of our friends, most of whom were not familiar with the water, sailing on our boat. They were surprised that there were no toilets on the yacht. In answer to what was to be done was "belt it out straight into the water." It was a funny sight to see the faces of people as they held onto the mast's cable with their rear ends sticking out over the waters of the Baltic Sea. In such a situation, so as not to make the ladies feel uncomfortable, everyone was told to turn their heads and admire the sky and clouds. Modern luxuries cannot be expected on a fifty year-old boat, and once our friends realized this, many of them refused future invitations to sail.

We had many pleasant moments on the waters of the Baltic Sea. The summer flew by with incredible speed. Again came the time to plan what work remained to be done to the "old lady" (the yacht) next spring. There were many projects. An additional motor needed to be installed. Also, an outflow cockpit needed to be built so that during times of high waves, water would not enter the inside of the boat. Storm-proof sails had to be sewn and containers for sweet water needed to be installed. Springtime painting and maintenance were normal yearly tasks, and not worth adding to our list.

Our financial situation presented itself as increasingly worse. After all, with the exception of the slave responsibilities we had in maintaining the boat, we also had other pleasantries in which we were interested. It was not possible to leave the pretty Swedish girls alone or give up the sport of skiing. All of this claimed our hard-earned money. We saved on everything we could, such as living two to a room. We also tried cooking our own meals. Washing the dishes, however, was tiring, so after a short while we returned to eating at the cafeteria.

Then our travel plans changed drastically, and were put off indefinitely. Mietek found himself a young, divorced Swede, named Britt, who came equipped with two young children. His enthusiasm for ocean traveling diminished to zero. Apparently sailing in bed was more pleasant for him, and took place in a warmer atmosphere. Time passed quicker than I could imagine and after a year had elapsed, Mietek invited me to be a witness at his wedding. The young couple was determined to immigrate to the United States in order to try their luck at life beyond the ocean. Meanwhile, I really didn't want to separate from Mietek who had been my closest friend from our early school years. Following his example, I filled out papers at the embassy, requesting a visa to go to the United States.

We couldn't divide the yacht we owned in half. Two sailors were leaving Sweden while two remained flirting with native girls. The renovated boat was put up for sale. Apparently news of our leaving for the United States spread rapidly among the sailors. Many were interested in buying our boat. They waited until the last minute to make an offer, knowing that we would be desperate to sell and lower the price. At the very last moment, a few young amateur sailors came to us and bought the boat for a meager amount. We barely gained back the cash we had invested in buying the supplies for refurbishing our yacht. Our work over the renovation and nights spent in the cold and dampness were not included in the price. The Saturdays and Sundays that we had spent in hard labor, scraping the old paint and repainting all went for nothing.

After a few months, I received a letter from the Embassy. I was granted a visa to leave. I was assigned to pick up my visa at a particular time. This was a most inopportune time for me because I had already planned and reserved a place for a winter vacation. I went skiing anyway, and ignored the notification. After returning home, I found a letter from the ambassador, inviting me to a meeting and expressing that people wait years for visas while I had not come to pick mine up. I had decided that I was really not too eager to leave Scandinavia. At the meeting with the ambassador I expressed this sentiment. The fact that I did not have the money for an airline ticket influenced my thinking as well.

The ambassador was a woman who apparently wanted to get me out of Sweden. She promised that I would get a free trip to the United States, under one condition, that she not have to search for me all over the country. Another runaway from Poland had taken advantage of the visa that was supposed to have been mine. "You have the chance to visit the United States," said the ambassador. "If you don't like it there, you can always return here. The next flight is scheduled for July, and until that time, you have the opportunity to stay in the area and calmly pack your belongings." Meanwhile, Mietek, as a married man with a Swedish wife was placed on the Swedish list and had to wait for a family visa before he could depart for the United States.

It was a little sad to have to bid farewell to the friends I had made in this magnificent country that had given us the feeling of freedom and prosperity. I was again to go into the unknown, to another land where I had no family members and knew no one. I did not know the English language, and had no guarantee of work on this new continent, but I did have two hundred dollars in my pocket.

# New Britain – A Polish City in America
### (Czeslaw and Teresa)

As the plane headed west, it shook from the vibration of its four motors. After several hours of flight, the sound of passengers screaming, "Fire in the engine!" awoke me from a short nap. The captain's announcement came over the microphone, stating that indeed there was a fire in one engine and we would have to alter our route and head toward Iceland as soon as the fire was extinguished. By activating the fire extinguisher and redirecting the plane downward, the fire in that engine was put out. We finished the remainder of our trip on three motors at a significantly slower rate of speed. There was complete silence in the plane. In spite of the fact that the captain assured our safety for the rest of the flight, prayers could be heard from frightened women. The final hours of the flight were long and tense.

With great relief we saw the outlines of islands, and after several minutes of further flight, the American army airport in Reykjavik came into view. We could distinguish ambulances and fire engines waiting alongside the landing area, and this sight was quite disconcerting to us. Yet the plane landed smoothly and successfully and settled itself securely on the landing strip, to the great relief of all on board. Stewardesses quickly opened all of the exit doors and encouraged us to deplane rapidly. It was feared that the engine fire would re-ignite.

A civilian official informed the gathered passengers that due to the damaged engine, we would be guests at an American base until the plane was repaired. A new engine had to be brought from America and this would take about four days. Throughout this time, we were assured of receiving lodging and meals from the Air Force kitchen. A bus was made available to the stranded passengers so that we would be able to sightsee the entire island of Iceland. This was a most pleasant opportunity to look at the interesting and still active volcanic island.

The next day, we boarded the bus, complete with a tour guide who was familiar with the island. This island, which was covered in lava, without any large vegetation, was most interesting. The only visible green growth was some moss located in lower lying terrain. There were many visible hot water streams coming out from within the deep layer of lava. Built upon some of the larger springs of hot water, were small greenhouses. These greenhouses were heated by water vapors, which smelled like rotten eggs. Inside we saw small trees and vines growing in this northern country. On them were unripe oranges and grapes.

Our tour guide was enthusiastic about the ideal life on this island. He assured us that there was absolutely no unemployment. For the entire island, there was only one policeman, and even he had little to do because criminal activity here was nonexistent. Sometimes this officer's only task was to walk a tipsy inhabitant to the police station and place him in an unlocked cell. There was no military service. Americans would send their own M.P. in the event of any disturbance in the city. The weather was extremely diverse. Within the course of a day, one could see the sun, then some cloudiness, and quickly thereafter, rain and cold. A few hours later this was followed by the return of sunshine across the skies. The one and only unpleasant thing was the scent of fish drying in the open air. The fish were hung on lines and waved unsteadily in the constant wind.

After returning to the base, we noticed an American soldier wandering around. Eventually the young man gained courage and spoke to us in broken Polish: "I am Polish and I would like to invite you to the movies on base, but I have one request. I would like the two girls who were passengers on the plane to keep me company, sitting by my side." These girls he spoke of were about sixteen or seventeen years old. So, with their mothers' agreement and the assurance that we would look after their young daughters, we took off to see two American western films, which featured John Wayne. It's difficult to describe the whistling that was going on by the gathered army audience at the hall. Soldiers occupied hundreds of seats and one of them now entered accompanied by two young women. The young man was proud that he, a young Polish soldier, was in the company of these attractive young ladies. We learned from him afterwards that girls from Iceland tended to avoid the companionship of soldiers in consideration of the feelings of their countrymen.

As had been promised, the new engine arrived from America and was mounted onto our airplane, which was again ready for departure to the United States. It seemed the passengers had forgotten about their moments of fright, and were reminiscing about the fascinating tours they had been on throughout this interesting volcanic island. Our flight took off without incident, and we were happily on our way again.

During our flight, we saw the coast of Greenland, followed by a part of Canada, with wooded areas along the shores of Nova Scotia. Beneath us was North America. As far as the eye could see, there was the greenery of woods intersected with strips of lakes and rivers. There we saw the beautiful and wild landscape of the state of Maine. As we flew farther south we began to see small population settlements joined by a system of roads extending in the midst of a dense growth of greenery. Shortly, along the shorelines appeared larger cities. We flew over Boston, and after several more minutes, we were over New York, which was our destination. Beneath us we saw a jungle of buildings. As in a huge forest, there grew structures that seemed to touch the sky. Manhattan, with millions of rushing automobiles on its streets, throbbed with the life of the largest metropolis of the world. The airplane circled a few times around the huge airport, waiting for permission to land. Finally, with a jarring of its wheels, it sat upon American soil.

At the airport, a representative of the Polish Immigration Bureau was waiting for the arrivals, and transported the entire group to a hotel in Manhattan. Along the way, he explained that we were assured of a night's sleep accommodations as well as meals. Tomorrow morning, before eleven a.m., we must leave the security of the hospitable hotel and were on our own. "As free people in a free country you can do whatever pleases you. We, from our side, cannot help you any more," he told us. Those words felt like a bucket of cold water poured on our heads.

We had to adapt to our new conditions, forgetting about the Swedish arrangements and care.

At night, a curiosity to acquaint ourselves with life on the streets of Manhattan overcame our tiredness from the trip. We went out among the droves of people moving in various directions through crowded and littered roadways and sidewalks. This was a shocking impression after the cleanliness of Stockholm. Store displays were filled with diverse products, which lured the eyes of passersby. Everywhere were neon lights flashing colorfully, advertising products and inviting the curious inside bars and recreational taverns. Many girls of frivolous conduct stood on street corners encouragingly exhibiting their charms. We returned to our hotel rooms with an uneasiness – how will our freedom look tomorrow?

In the morning, after a hearty breakfast, our little group of travelers clutched their suitcases and stood on the sidewalk near the hotel's entrance. No one seemed able to make the decision in which direction to go and for what reason. This moment was interrupted by the appearance of a man that looked like a wise guy, full of self-confidence. He wore knee-high boots despite the July warmth and had a baseball cap on his head. He called out loudly as he approached us: "Who wants to go to work in a machine and airplane engine parts factory in the state of Connecticut! I'm looking for young, single people familiar with factory work."

Excitedly I raised my hand as a sign of my interest in his proposition. I was willing to take any kind of job. Behind me, few additional volunteers were to be found. "Take your suitcases and come with me to the nearby railway station," he said. Stunned by the bustling movement we followed our rapidly striding new leader, who soon stopped and bought tickets at the ticket office and put us into the train wagon. It was then that he deemed to introduce himself. "I am Stefan. We are going to a state in New England, to a factory whose owner is of Polish-American descent. I am his right-hand man and take care of all personnel matters related with recruiting people for work." With astonishment, I looked at this amazing individual. The man looked more like a laborer than the assistant to the owner of a large establishment. I kept my thoughts to myself. I was satisfied that I had found a place to settle in the new land, being that I did not speak English, and I had no friends or relatives on this side of the ocean.

After several hours of travel, interrupted by stops at various stations, the train reached our destination. "We're getting out!" shouted Stefan. We are just at a small stopover I thought, because what I saw could not possibly be the train station of New Britain, Connecticut. I was wrong.

We stood on the platform wondering what would happen next. We didn't have to wait long for a company car to arrive. We were escorted into a Cadillac, in which we were transported through streets filled with crowds of people. With surprise, I looked at the signs of stores and offices. They advertised products and services in Polish. The trip didn't last long. He stopped his car on Washington Street, an area in which mostly Poles resided. He brought me to a three-family house, in which single workers from area factories lived on the first floor. The landlady and owner of the house showed me a room where I was to live, and for which, together with kitchen privileges and cleaning services, I was to pay ten dollars per week. I was to share the room with another guest who worked on the night shift in the same factory. The room had modest but sufficient furnishings. Stefan, left me there and said that he would return for me the next morning to take me to my place of employment. I unpacked my suitcase and took over my allotted half of the bureau space. In a nearby store, I did a modest amount of food shopping. Tired from the events of the day, I decided to take a rest and ponder what tomorrow would bring.

I awoke to the noise of an opening door and the footsteps of my roommate, who had come home to rest after his night shift. I couldn't speak due to my surprise. I could not believe my very eyes! On the other side of the room stood Jan Winiarz, whom I had met in Sweden. He and I had become friends and had spent a year together in West Germany at a parachute training camp.

*"Jan!"* I said. *"Do you have to make so much noise and awaken your buddy?"* Now he, in turn, rubbed his eyes unbelievingly, as he was seeing me after a three-year separation. We had not seen each other since the end of the Cold War and the liquidation of the secret Polish organization. I had returned to Sweden while he left for the United States. We had not corresponded, and didn't know what had become

of each other. Now, suddenly and unexpectedly, we met on the other end of the world, bunking in the same room. There was no end to our talking about our experiences since our last meeting.

The next morning Stefan appeared and took me to the factory. I had already learned a lot about this factory from my friend Jan. He had been employed there from the time he had arrived in America. Stefan brought me to an office, and introduced me to the owners, Henry and Michael Budney. After a short conversation about my experience regarding metal-turning machines, I wanted to show my certifications from school as well as from work in Swedish factories. Michael waved his hand dismissively: *"I don't want to look at any papers,"* he said. *"In an hour, I will know all about what you can do."*

Next, I had to go through in-depth questioning by a former officer of the Polish Army. He had the responsibility of eliciting information of my former life, and my experiences going back to my youth. This procedure made me uncomfortable. These investigative inquiries had occurred much too often in communist Poland. I didn't know why he was asking these questions and who had requested this information. I had to find out.

At this plant, was a Mr. Joe G, who worked as a completed parts controller, and at the same time was assigned to hold talks with new employees and answer their questions. I went to him and asked why I was being interrogated. This did not please Joe, and he answered that if I wanted to work in this company, which produced parts for army airplane engines, I must answer all given questions. I had to adapt to these demands and concealed only my stay at the training camp in Germany, which was at that time a tightly kept secret. I informed them that I had worked in a garage near the American army base for which I had been given a certificate. My belonging to the Polish Home Army and my escape from Poland was sufficient proof that I was not a communist sympathizer. I was hired to work at Atlantic Tool. In the beginning, I was a lathe operator, with the promise that with the first available opening in the engineering office, I would be moved there and employed as a draftsman.

The factory crew consisted of very interesting and diverse personalities. In this workplace, one was able to meet a former farmer, working beside high officers from the Polish Army. None of them had any other kind of trade or profession, and were now working with materials used for engine parts and machines. After three months, as I was promised, I was sent to the draftsman's room, and immediately received orders to construct a lathe knife. After a few hours, the office manager looked at my work, and said with a smile *"good job."* I stayed in that office for the next several years.

Michael Budney, whom every employee addressed as *"Mike,"* liked to keep me busy with assorted jobs around his properties. I was, if I may so express myself, his personal draftsman. I did land surveying mainly on the border of his woods in Goshen. I did drawings of a motel in Niantic, summer homes, as well as additions to the factory. Sometimes, I received orders to go to the farm he owned and draw pictures of various breeds of cows. They were described in a catalogue by how they looked and where they were from. At that time, I sat on a rock that lay in a field among grazing cattle, drawing them with the black and white patches on their heads, sides and backsides. Photographs were not accepted in these catalogues which confirmed the dates of birth as well as the cow's ancestry.

Some people maintain that cattle do not have, and are not capable of showing feelings or interest. However, my experience makes me feel quite the opposite. One day, I could not get rid of a two-year-old cow. She circled around me, licking my clothing, putting her head on my shoulder, her saliva streaming from her mouth onto my clothes. Hitting it across the face and trying to drive it away didn't help. Driven by love, it kept returning to the poor draftsman who was trying to carry out his employer's orders. Finally, all wet, I had to stop work for that day. Toni R., who worked with me, was laughing hysterically as he watched me running away from the advances of the young cow. I demanded to be given help the next time, explaining that I was not able to draw animals when they were on the move, as well as I.

Michael sent a few boys along with me to hold the cows while I worked. However, this was not an easy thing for them to do – catching a calf on the open terrain.

One of the boys seemed to think he was some sort of Polish cowboy and came up with a seemingly good idea. He used a tractor ventilator belt as a lasso. Reaching a big calf, he threw the belt around its neck but he did not estimate the strength of this creature. The calf jumped up, and with speed, ran off into the far distance, followed by the pseudo cowboy stumbling and being dragged behind. A loud bellowing cry from the man echoed across the field of grazing cows. The calf was galloping on the grass, which was covered with manure, trying to free its neck from the man and belt that had been twisted around it. Not until some friends had blocked the way of the frightened animal was the roper able to free himself. After this experience, he was green and smelly. Only after he jumped into the small pond with his clothes on, did he regain the look of a human being.

I could not find suitable social company for myself in New Britain. People living in this city seemed to devote their time and energy to earning and saving money, which they needed for the upkeep of their families, and hopefully for the purchase of their own home. Being a young person recently from Europe where I had a very adventurous existence, it was difficult for me to get used to this way of life. Therefore, I spent my free time on trips to various parts of New England.

Skiing was one of my great pleasures, and I was very happy when winter arrived. In the state of Connecticut, there are many areas suitable for skiing, and I enjoyed my favorite sport quite frequently. At one time, this pleasure concluded with a serious injury, and could have been even worse. Skiing fast on an unknown trail, I hit ice that had been mixed with some springtime sand, and I went up like a rock shot out of a sling. I did a complete somersault in the air and fell on the surface of some packed snow, on my right side. The impact of the fall was unusually strong. I took a deep breath and lost consciousness. When I finally opened my eyes, I saw people from the Red Cross approaching with a stretcher. A girl from the life-saving services was hitting my face calling, *"Do you hear me?"* Still not quite fully conscious, I nodded my head yes. Placed on a sled, I was transported down to the rescue station. It was determined that I had no broken bones. After drinking a cup of black coffee, and taking a short rest, I returned again to the slopes. I still didn't feel quite normal, and as I was skiing, I began to feel nausea and dizziness.

I decided to quit skiing for that day, and headed back home. On the drive back, my right leg began to feel numb. I started to see the street lights as though through a fog. With difficulty, I reached the city of Hartford where I entered a restaurant to get a drink of club soda.

Using the bathroom there to urinate, I was alarmed at the sight of nearly black blood flowing from within me. It was then that I knew that my kidneys, which had been chronically ill during childhood and by some miracle had healed since, had now become seriously damaged. With difficulty, using only my left leg to press on the gas pedal, I managed to drive the approximately twelve miles back to my New Britain home. The landlord had heard my car and came out to greet me. I was happy to have assistance getting into the apartment and onto my bed.

The next morning, I couldn't stand the pain and asked to have a doctor come to the house. At that time, there was a physician in New Britain who spoke Polish. He was an old practitioner who had learned his profession in an army surgical assistant's school. He had come to the United States after WWI, and here, due to a shortage of doctors, obtained permission to practice medicine in New England. I knew him from work, as he took care of injured workers at the factory. Doctor L. touched my stomach and prescribed some kind of tablets to relieve the pain and said, "Do not worry, after a few days in bed, this illness will go away."

It did not go away and I wallowed in pain. I felt as though I was swelling inside my body. My landlord disturbed by my condition, called an ambulance, which took me to the hospital. I was taken on a stretcher and placed in a hallway, beside the window of the admitting office. The hopeless procedure of admitting an unknown sick person into the hospital began. Dr. L. couldn't admit anyone to the hospital because he was not an authorized doctor. It was necessary to find a doctor who was qualified and willing to admit me. A hospital nurse asked about a family doctor, but I of course had no family here. So began the search in the telephone book for a doctor who spoke Polish, and who would admit a young skier to the hospital. During this time, I was lying prone on the stretcher, crying out in pain.

Finally, after a very long search, a doctor of Polish descent was found. He came to the waiting area, and introduced himself as Dr. Kralewski. He asked me whether I would agree to his being my physician, and when I nodded my head that I would, he turned me over to the care of the hospital. This was not the end of my suffering. In vain, I asked for a drug to help relieve my pain. I was told that I would have to wait for another doctor, a kidney specialist, who was coming shortly. Soon I was approached by a tall man known as Dr. Gonti, a doctor of urology. He immediately gave me a shot of morphine and ordered that I have an exploratory operation to determine the amount of damage to my kidneys.

After regaining consciousness, I had the pleasure of conversing with the doctor, who informed me that he was giving me three days for the bleeding in my kidneys to stop. "Your right kidney is beaten and looks like a beefsteak," he told me. "It's very swollen and more than likely I will have to remove it." The next three days were terrible, not only because of the pain, but also because of the knowledge that I would perhaps need yet another surgery and lose such an important organ.

With impatience and fear I awaited the doctor's visit. Finally, Dr. Gonti appeared. I could see the smile on his face. It felt as though a rock had lifted from my heart. "You should consider yourself lucky, Czeslaw," Dr. Gonti said, "I have just returned from the operating room where I removed the damaged kidneys of a young boy who will have to rely on a dialysis machine for the rest of his life. You, however, seem to be improving and I'm giving you a few more days in the hopes that your bleeding will stop. With each day I felt better, and noticed that my urine was gradually taking on a lighter color. After ten days, I was able to return to work. My skiing, however, was put on hold for the next few years.

Leon was the leader of the workers who cleaned up the metal chips that accumulated near the machines. He was a simple person, with an exceptional amount of strength and energy. However, he suffered from annoying hemorrhoids, which hindered him in his work which he performed with pride. Not having a car, he asked his friend, Heniek K. to drive him to a doctor for a consultation in hopes of alleviating his pain. The aforementioned Dr. L saw him. After explaining the purpose of his visit, he was told to remove his pants and lie down on the table in the office. *"You,"* said the doctor as he turned toward Heniek, *"Sit on Leon's back and hold his hands tightly on the top of the table."*

Immobilizing Leon in this way allowed Dr. L. to use his knife to cut Leon's swollen, bleeding hemorrhoids. After that the Dr. stuffed a piece of bandage soaked in iodine into his rectum. During this surgical procedure, Leon kicked his legs back and forth as though he were in a bicycle race, yelling all the while from pain. He sounded like a wolf during a winter night's full moon. *"OK, Let him go,"* said the doctor to Heniek, and he obediently freed Leon from his grasp. According to Heniek's story, his friend was in such pain that he jumped up and ran down West Main Street while still fastening his pants. The poor guy didn't even wait for his driver to give him a ride home.

Personally, I was the witness to a similar procedure performed on another employee of the same factory. Leon was not alone in his anguish. Sometimes, I liked to break the monotony of work by dropping by the office of the old doctor for a little conversation. Once during our talks, the foreman of the drilling department came by, complaining of a bad cold. The doctor sat him on a chair, turned back his head while holding it by the hair, and stuffed a wad of cotton drenched in iodine up his nose. With a stick, he turned the cotton within one nostril, then the other nostril, constantly holding the rebellious patient by the hair. After finishing this procedure, the ungrateful Matt S. forgot, in his hurry, to thank the doctor who had demonstrated such helpfulness. The ungrateful guy slammed the door hard as he ran back into the factory.

Sometimes lacking proper knowledge of a language can lead to embarrassing situations. One day, Michael called me into his office and asked if I had seen an aluminum-cast bird somewhere around the grounds of the factory. I recalled having seen the cast of a large rooster in the precision drill parts warehouse. I said I had seen it and I knew where it could be found. I then received the order to deliver the item to the motel site that was being built in Niantic. I was instructed to give it to the workers, telling them it was from Mike and that they should mount it in the fountain being built. I took the company car and carried out this order to what I believed was perfection. The next day Mike burst into the office shouting, *"What are you trying to do, make me look crazy?"* The workers, as instructed, had apparently mounted the figure of the rooster in the motel fountain. It seems that it was a flamingo that I should have delivered, not the rooster. How was I to know that there was more than one bird in the factory? If he wanted a flamingo, he should have told me so. A rooster is a bird, you can't argue that.

The Atlantic Motel was built on a hilly area, which was situated at the intersection of a highway that went from New Haven to Providence, Rhode Island, and another, which led from western Connecticut to the

Atlantic Ocean. In all probability, the hotel's location foretold good profits to come based on tourist traffic during the summer season.

Starting up a new business is always difficult, however, and it usually requires a certain period of time to develop a good reputation. Mike was not in the habit of waiting for better times. He expected his investments to bring him immediate earnings. Therefore, he took advantage of the fact that Atlantic Machine and Tool had grown rapidly and its earnings had increased dramatically. He began to send departmental bosses to production meetings that were held at his motel. These meetings were pretty much accepted by governmental tax institutions as being necessary to the development of the industry. These meetings also produced income for the Atlantic Motel. Simultaneously, the costs incurred resulting from these meetings minimized the factory's taxable income, and this was profitable to the owners of the company.

Within the motel was a large conference hall with a bar and restaurant in which, after these meetings, guests were able to eat a bountiful and free dinner. Buses would leave the factory grounds filled with various departmental bosses and other deserving employees. These people through their honest work were helping Mike build his large businesses. Two conditions that Mike demanded from the people who took part in the meetings were that their behavior was impeccable and their usage of alcohol was moderate.

Every Saturday, there were dances at the motel to which departmental bosses came with their wives. At that time, everyone cautiously drank beer and black coffee and the wives were shown a good example of how their husbands behaved at such organizational functions. Mike sometimes sympathized with those who craved something stronger, and often called some of them up to the bar to be treated to a drink of hard liquor. Naturally, no one wanted to be left out and they began to compete with each other to have a drink with Mike. Mike called out to the bartender: *"Pour me some from my own bottle."* This was a bottle designated just for him. I knew about this bottle. The bartender was my friend. I was often sent to the motel to do various work, and I once asked him for a drink from Mike's bottle and I was given tea. The wives calmly watched the group gathered around the bar, secure that if their husbands were drinking hard liquor at least the factory owner was as well. These meetings and dances ended when another firm bought the motel, convinced that the Atlantic Motel had a large number of steady and loyal customers.

The factory grew quickly. When the three Budney brothers opened their company during the 1950s, it was housed in a small building in Newington. Michael occupied himself with technical problems related to the building of machines and tools as well as the production of airplane engine parts. His brother, Henry, took over the title of managing director of the office and personnel matters. The youngest, Ted, dealt with the planning, construction and maintenance of the factory buildings.

After several years, benefiting from army orders resulting from the Korean War, the factory expanded and the crew grew from a dozen or so employees to about two thousand five hundred. The Budney brothers did not rest on their laurels. They invested company earnings in the purchase of land on which they built motels and smaller factories that worked in cooperation with Atlantic Machine and Tool. They also invested in working farms. These brothers were an exceptionally well-matched group of business owners.

Henry Budney traveled all over the country, looking for land that was listed for sale. He was very driven. He mixed pleasure with business and achieved huge successes. Among his possessions was a summer home, which he had built by the Susina River in Alaska. This was an amazing place for catching salmon that were heading for the river springs to spawn during the early spring. The large Susina Mountain, part of which Henry owned, was hunting grounds for large animals. In a recreation hall which he built in Newington, Henry possessed an entire building of various exotic mounted animals which he had hunted during his trips in the United States and all over the world. While hunting in Alaska, he had the opportunity to shoot the second largest polar bear ever sighted. The standing twelve-foot male polar bear was really an impressive sight.

Henry knew about the thousands of Polish immigrants who were waiting for visas to the United States. Therefore, he established contact with the Polish Office of Immigration. He assured work in his factory for Poles who came to America. He became their sponsor and therefore enabled their quicker arrival in America. Henry was responsible for bringing over to the United States hundreds of families who had been in refugee camps scattered throughout the world and who did not want to return to communist Poland.

Teddy, the youngest of the brothers, was thriving as a result of the large expansions of the factory. Operating heavy machinery was his favorite pastime. He ran on all kinds of heavy equipment as though on a racehorse, pushing it to its maximum power. This reduced costs considerably, as he worked alongside other construction workers and inspired them to put forth their best effort. It also dispensed with the need for hiring outside construction companies.

There were many family members of the Budney's who worked in various departments of their factory. Without a doubt, all of the workers were thankful to the Budney brothers for their help in giving them a good start in life as well as for the opportunity to earn good money. Mike's whole life was involved in the factory and the fields of his farms. Today, despite the fact that he is ninety-eight years old, he still runs his factory of 150 employees and operates a bulldozer in his free time for "relaxation."

While thinking about the people I met and the relationships I had with them at this place of work, I must reiterate that this was a very colorful gathering of immigrants from Europe. After the end of World War II, the Polish Army was demobilized and many Polish citizens were deported to Germany. They did not wish to return to an occupied communist Poland, and turned to the United States for refuge. Here, in a new environment, a wide variety of people stood at the machines side by side. Army officers worked next to landowners and intelligentsia worked next to farmers. They all reported to a new general, the owner of the factory, Michael Budney. This man controlled this gathering of people from all over the world with an iron hand. They listened to him and did honest work, which is something that a great majority of these individuals had not done until this time. This remarkable organizer and great tradesman recruited a crew of Polish immigrants, and gave them the opportunity to settle in this country and learn a new trade. It was not an easy task to make them adapt to orderliness and a twelve-hour work day. He was able, however, to help even the most stubborn and helpless people overcome their inadequacies. This motley group became an organized work force, which took great pride and satisfaction from their work. They were doing an important and demanding job in producing parts for jet airplane engines.

Michael Budney was born in America, yet he never forgot the native tongue used in the home of his parents. Sometimes it was funny to see the sight of a former senior army officer standing straight at attention, listening to the litany given in Polish by Michael: *"You stupid sheep! Don't you know that you have to measure a piece after every operation? See you've created a piece of scrap and this is a waste of money."*

Sometimes Mike would walk through the factory corridors surrounded by a conglomeration of his workers who were used for various chores that had no connection with the factory. *"You, Tony, take the car and go to Goshen,"* he said. *"Plant fruit trees there around the pond. And don't forget to fertilize them so they will have better fruit. You know how to do that, you said so yourself, that you did it for a German gardener."*

*"Leon,"* he said, turning toward a factory painter. *"Get going with Kazik to paint my cabin. You'll find paint on the shelf in the barn. While you're there, make sure Joe brings the bull to the cow because she is ready for him."*

Next, he called to the overweight Gracek, saying: *"You take the tractor and plow another section of land. We'll plant more corn because the cows need more feed for the winter. That big tractor you were driving already needs fixing because the shovel for digging cracked when it was hit against a rock."* It was here that he turned toward John, who was walking behind him, a welder, busy as usual with digging in his nose with a dirty finger. *"When you're finished with that job with your nose, toss a welding tool in the truck and go and fix the damage to the tractor before Gracek breaks it a second time."* Like Napoleon Bonaparte who positioned his army all over the battlefield, Mike dispersed his brigade of helpers to work throughout the various places he owned. Included in his properties were motels, private homes, farms, iron foundries, as well as thousands of hectares of forests with fishponds that required continuous nurturing. Mike Budney was a successful farmer, considering the fact that he operated his farms quite inexpensively by the use of inexperienced workers.

After taking care of getting his workers dispersed to their variety of jobs, Mike would disappear for the moment into his office. From there he summoned by phone his right-hand man George B., who was the head of factory productions. After a short while, George's booming voice carried across the megaphone, informing all those who were involved to go immediately to the office for a meeting. Like a stick placed in the midst of an ant colony raises panic among the ants, so all the men immediately left whatever they had been doing. This caused nervous movement throughout the entire factory. The bosses who were being called quickly grabbed their notes, for it was not imaginable that any of them should not know the actual production amounts. All numbers had to always agree, and Mike had a phenomenal memory. He knew perfectly well about even the smallest orders for engine parts. After this type of meeting, Budney would usually buy himself a coffee from the machine and disappear back into his office for a while.

The group that was sent to the farm in Goshen was satisfied to find itself in the free open air without any supervision, and began working however and whenever they chose. Their job was to paint the interior of the summer home. First they were to thin the paint, but before that they relaxed themselves by sipping on some high quality liquor which Mike had left on the shelf. Mike was not a huge proponent of alcohol, but he always had a large reserve of the best whiskeys nearby. Leon, Gracek and Kazik appreciated this good quality, and time flew by for them. Leon became quite inebriated and disappeared from sight. Kazik jumped into a truck and drove off to find some girls. The drunken young person was looking for companionship, so that he could conclude this difficult working day within the embrace of some plump shoulders. Gracek, with a cigar constantly in his mouth, stepped out for a walk, taking in the mountain air. Goshen lay in a hilly terrain with thick trees surrounding it, about fifty miles from the factory.

After finishing his work, Mike called his cousin Ralph and suggested that they go horseback riding at the farm. He called me as well, telling me that he had some work for me to do. We left without hesitation. Before we realized it, the Cadillac had stopped in front of the cottage in Goshen. Michael wanted to see the newly painted walls in the house. The walls, however, didn't seem to have changed color, and the inside of the house looked like it had hosted a wild party. The table was covered with empty bottles. Mike quickly ran out of the house, bellowing loudly for his working crew. After a while, the quite drunk Gracek appeared, stumbling in our direction on somewhat uncertain legs.

Understandably, Michael was furious. He began calling the frightened worker all kinds of the worst profanities.

*"Instead of working you were all drinking my whiskey!"* Mike shouted.

Frightened by the shouting, Gracek fell to his knees, and on them, went from Mike to Ralph, who stood nearby, and back again. *"Mr. Mike,"* Gracek said. *"For the love of God, I didn't touch that whiskey. Those sons-of-bitches Kazik and Leon drank all of it."*

Throughout the entire time of this conversation, Gracek drew upon his fat cigar, which he held in his left hand hoping to kill the wafting smell of alcohol coming from his mouth. Gracek figured it out well that when he was on his knees, he was closer to the ground and the fact that he was unstable on his feet was less visible that way. He blamed the whole situation on those not present, hoping to soften the temper of his boss.

And so what was the property owner to do? He got up on his saddled horse, and with Ralph accompanying him, went off into the woods. From afar, I could hear as he complained, *"Damn, they knew what to drink – they drank my best whiskey!"* Mike liked and understood his old Polish workers, and shortly this incident was forgotten.

In my opinion, the Budney brothers should have received some sort of recognition from the Polish government for the services they had provided for so many Polish people. They had supplied the means that enabled thousands of Polish immigrants from all over the world to settle in the United States. After the end of World War II these people had no homeland of their own, and nowhere to turn for help in starting a new life. They came from all over the world to Atlantic Machine with the knowledge that they would be employed and have a place to live. These new arrivals to the small town of New Britain and Newington were welcomed into what seemed to be a second homeland. They were among fellow Poles who spoke their native language and maintained the same customs as in Poland. They were even able to send their children to schools on Saturdays to learn the Polish language. On Sundays, they were able to pray in churches, which held Polish Masses, and after death, they were able to lie among their own countrymen in a Polish cemetery. These were invaluable resources to these displaced persons.

Throughout the year, the new settlers awaited the coming Christmas holidays. In the factory, as well as in the homes, preparations were made for the celebration. The Christmas spirit was evident throughout the factory days before Christmas. Little by little, women began bringing prepared holiday foods to work. Here and there in various hidden corners under machines could be found bottles of "Wodka." On the day of Christmas Eve the workers cleaned up corners of the rooms and set up tables covered with decorated holiday tablecloths. Everything was done supposedly in secret from factory owner, Michael Budney. He, in turn, did not emerge from his office until the moment work was completed, usually in the afternoon after a five-hour day. When everything was ready, the workers invited the owner for the mutually shared traditional Polish custom of "the breaking of bread".

After a while, the sound of thousands of workers humming Christmas carols could be heard throughout the factory. They were singing Christmas carols that had been known to them since childhood. The owners of the factory, along with the office workers and the entire work force, were singing old Christmas carols as of one voice. They forgot about their class differences and that they were in a foreign country. Everyone felt completely at home as though among his or her own family. These moments of good will and camaraderie will remain in the memories of our people always. Today, despite the fact that this factory has been in operation for many years and that Michael Budney is now ninety-eight years old, this same custom still exists in his place of business. And certainly, despite occasional complaints about slightly lower salary rates, a sincere gratefulness for this old Polish man will continue to be held deep within the hearts of thousands of people.

Despite the fact that I had lived in the United States for several years, I could not adapt to the philosophy of life which seemed to dominate. Americans seemed to always be chasing the almighty dollar, and I wished to enjoy a more free spirited existence. I always thought about returning to Sweden. I missed the times when I was younger and Mietek and I spent so many carefree hours on the waters of the rugged Scandinavian coastline. Now occasionally, Mietek, his family and I would go on excursions together. I would take them in my car and we would visit areas rich in thick, green forests that grew in the surrounding hills. Sometimes we would go to the ocean, which was just about fifty miles away from where we lived. Yet things were not the same. Unfortunately, Mietek's wife was homesick for the Scandinavia she had left behind. She was also troubled by an ear problem and that interfered with her acclimatization to her new environment. Within a short time, they decided to return to Sweden. I was now left alone and without the friend with whom I had spent about twenty years of my life.

I began to feel bored in the city. Having my life revolve around twelve-hour days spent working in a factory was not my idea of a good life. The greatest enjoyment I had was those beautiful summer days spent fishing in the nearby Farmington River or at the ocean. During the workweek, I could look forward to Saturday evenings when I would go to dances at local dance halls. I liked to dance, and this gave me the opportunity to make new friends with the fairer sex. But more and more often, I thought about returning to Sweden or moving to California where my friend, Leon, lived. He flooded me with letters bragging about the climate and the beautiful western coast of America.

I was at a crossroads, not knowing what to do with myself. I realized that if I went back to Sweden, or joined Leon in California, I would return to my former life of seeking adventure. Years were quickly passing and I sensed that I should think seriously about my future, I needed to normalize my lifestyle and think of permanently settling down somewhere. My major asset was that I had a good job in my own trade and I was well liked by my superiors. This gave me stability, but I was troubled by the fact that I was lonely and had no true companion. Previously I had chased fun and adventure, and thought that these were the most important requirements for a happy life. However, I had just turned thirty-two years of age and slowly I was maturing and the voice of reason began to take control over my sense of adventure.

One Saturday, as usual, I set out to a dance held at the Haller Post Veteran's Hall in New Britain. I met an acquaintance from work, Miss Loda Kaczalski, who immediately snatched me forward, telling me that she would introduce me to some young ladies who occupied a table by the orchestra. Without too much interest, I followed her, so as not to seem rude. At the table sat eight girls, among whom were Loda's two sisters. After being introduced to this group of young ladies, I decided to ask a tall brunette to dance. She graciously accepted my offer. I was soon holding in my arms a charming young woman who reminded me of Helen Kurcewicz from the stories of author Sienkiewicz's "Fire and Sword." The slender girl danced lightly, like a butterfly in air. I was enraptured with her good looks and graceful movements. The dance proved to be very successful. I entertained my partner with conversations in which I told her about my plans to return to Sweden, and asked her about where she came from in Poland. She was not too eager to tell me about her past. She only told me that she had arrived from England to live at her uncle's and that her name was Teresa. It was unfortunate that out of politeness I had to also ask the other young ladies at the table to dance.

When I later danced with Teresa again, I asked her for a date, but she replied that she didn't have time for any kind of relationship. I didn't want to give up on the intended date. I asked her for her telephone number, and she replied that I could find it in the telephone book. I asked her last name and she replied that it's listed directly by the phone number. She's a joker, I thought, but I didn't press her, surmising that she had a willingness to continue our friendship, but was playing hard to get.

A few days later, I was cruising in my car along Broad Street, in hopes that somewhere I would see one of the young ladies from the last dance and I would be able to find out from them Teresa's address. I had luck! In my rearview mirror, I saw my girl walking along the sidewalk, burdened with a bag full of groceries. I pulled up to the sidewalk and proposed that I could drive her home so that she wouldn't have to continue carrying that heavy bag. After a moment's thought, she got into my car. Naturally I did not go in the direction that she had told me to go. I had to make good use of the moment while the bird was in the cage. Despite her complaints, I drove her to get some delicious ice cream on the other side of city. After this snack, she didn't want me to drive her directly home, saying that she still had to finish some shopping in a nearby store.

I knew then that the girl did not want to divulge to me the place where she lived. Therefore, obediently, I let her out where she instructed me. I then drove to the end of the street where I stopped so that I could see what direction she would go after finishing her shopping. Teresa came out of the store, and after looking all around her, quickly entered a six-family home close by. In this way, I found out where the circumspect lady lived. I did not finish an investigative course in Germany for nothing.

A few days after our chance meeting, I went back to the house on Horace Street and began to search for Teresa's apartment. I began from the top. I knocked on the door at the third floor and a voice invited me to enter. I then faced a kitchen full of strangers. Soon I happily met the proprietor of this apartment, who happened to be an acquaintance of mine, Frank Czajka, from the factory. He asked what had brought me to this house. I answered that I was looking for a young lady named Teresa, whose last name I didn't know. The smile upon Frank's face puzzled me. I did not know that he was the husband of Teresa's Aunt Jozefa. *"You've come a little too high up,"* Jozefa told me. *"Teresa lives one floor below, on the same side of the building,"* I thanked her and went down the stairs one flight to the floor below. I knocked energetically on the door, and upon hearing an invitation to enter, I did so.

An older woman, who was obviously Teresa's mother, stood by the stove. Teresa, wearing a white apron, was drying dishes. They both froze in their tracks as they saw in their kitchen an unknown and uninvited guest. Teresa was dumbstruck with surprise to see the man whose acquaintance she had been so cautiously avoiding. She stood there silently, not knowing how to behave in this most uncomfortable situation. I was not going to take defeat, so I walked up to the older woman and introduced myself, and at the same time turned to Teresa, reproachfully saying, *"So you had agreed to go to the movies with me and you are still not ready?"* *"I never agreed to go to any movie with you,"* she replied. A small argument began to see which of us would prevail. This was interrupted by Teresa's mother. *"Ask the young man into the living room,"* she said. *"After all, we shouldn't keep him standing in the kitchen."*

I sat down comfortably on the sofa, having no intention of leaving it any time soon. Slowly, a conversation unfolded. There was no shortage of topics. The young lady had obviously softened in her intentions to avoid the persistent stranger. At that time, I learned her last name, as well as the history of her entire family that was taken to Siberia in 1940.

Her brother, Edek Bajorski, arrived soon after and the evening passed in a very pleasant atmosphere. It was interesting to hear about the family's losses and the trials they had endured over the years of occupancy in the forests of Siberia, as well as the frightening trips to southern USSR, Iran, India, Africa, England and finally the United States.

After the conclusion of the conversation and before I was about to leave, I cautiously asked Teresa's brother if he had anything against my return visit. By this move, I didn't allow the possibility of a negative reply by the proud girl. After all, it was quite visible that she had lost her feelings of antipathy for me. As I later discovered, the main reason for her reluctance to develop our friendship was my stay in Sweden. Apparently, I had told her too many details about the customs and relationships that were prevalent there.

From that time forward, I was no longer lonely. Teresa introduced me to members of a choir to which she belonged. I met many interesting and outstanding people. I had come upon much good fortune. I finally found a worthwhile person with a beautiful character and outstanding beauty. It is not unusual, therefore, that my interest in her changed into more serious feelings of love, which led me to a serious cost resulting from the purchase of an engagement ring.

And so, what Hitler, Stalin and Polish President Bierut, with his pack of puppets from the political regime, couldn't accomplish, the small hand of Teresa easily did. Metaphorically speaking, she placed a colt's bridle between my teeth, taking away my desire to kick around the world, trying to find a doubtful happiness. We were married by Teresa's uncle, a Dominican priest, who had come to the United States to raise money to support a monastery in Poland. He did not forego the opportunity at this occasion to pour a great deal of holy water behind my collar. I suspect that this had been agreed upon with the ever-cautious Teresa.

Our future life evolved in a normal way. I received a promotion at work, as a supervisor's assistant in the engineering department, while Teresa enriched our home by gracing it with two beautiful daughters, Alice and Elizabeth. We bought a house, so that we would have a permanent place to live. We learned that the upkeep on our own home gave us the opportunity to spend many hours at work during what might have been free time, but this we thoroughly enjoyed. We have continued to live in our same home comfortably for forty-eight years.

It was understandable that I missed the members of my family who were still living in Poland. Since Poland was still under a communist regime, it was impossible for me to safely return. It was not until 1973 that my mother and brother finally were granted permission to visit us in the United States. They were here for three months, and we enjoyed and appreciated every minute of our reunion. That was their only visit to this country, although in later years Teresa and I were able to visit them in Poland. My mother lived to be ninety-nine years old.

Our two daughters are college graduates, and they are married with families of their own. Alice and her husband, David Mathieu, live in Connecticut, and have two children. Benjamin is a junior at Connecticut College, and Lauren is a freshman at George Washington University. Elizabeth and her husband, Jim Novitsky, live in Michigan. They have twin daughters, Emilia and Rebecca, who are nine years old. They are budding gymnasts and the joy of the whole family. One can say, therefore, that we are a most fortunate family and that we now enjoy an ideal life. That is certainly true.

However, something is still lacking for us. What is missing is the remembered sense of peace we felt from the sight of our homeland, with wheat fields billowing in the blowing summer wind. We also miss the smell of blossoming spring lilacs, and the chirping skylarks flying high over the harvested fields. We always will feel like weeds pulled from the soil of the homeland, which despite the best of conditions cannot completely acclimate themselves to a new environment.

That is what our poet, Adam Mickiewicz, wrote about one's homeland:

"You are like our health,
How much we value you, only he who has lost you will know,
Today, your beauty and splendor
I see and write about, because I long for you."

The End

Wilno-Downtown

Wilno-Wilja River

Roman Plawski pseudo. "Tonko"

Zofia Plawski Pseud. "Kania"

Tadeusz Plawski Pseud. "Bak"

Czeslaw Plawski Pseud. "Majster"

Nr. 1.                    W I L N O     15. VII. — 21. VII. 1942.

\* \*

Podejmujemy nasze wydawnictwo w chwili osobliwej, kiedy ucisk okupantów osiąga swe szczytowe nasilenie, — kiedy hitleryzm w przeczuciu swej nieuniknionej klęski wyładowuje na bezbronnej ludności krajów okupowanych swój jad nienawiści nacjonalistycznej w coraz bardziej brutalny, bezwzględny i bestialski sposób. Dziesiątki tysięcy rozstrzeliwanych i mordowanych bez sądu, — setki tysięcy katowanych po więzieniach i obozach koncentracyjnych, — miliony deportowanych do pracy niewolniczej w przemyśle wojennym Rzeszy — oto realizacja „Nowego Ładu" hitlerowskiego w Europie.

Ludność polska Wilna i Wileńszczyzny znalazła się w podwójnie ciężkiej sytuacji: krwawa brutalność niemiecka i, wysługująca się każdemu okupantowi nikczemność litewska podały sobie prawice w zamiarze całkowitego nas wyniszczenia. — Ogłodzenie miast i wsi przez bezwzględny rabunek rekwizycyjny żywności, — masowe usuwanie Polaków z pracy, — uznanie nas za bezpaństwowców, a w związku z tym przymusowe wywożenie ludności polskiej w wieku od 17—45 lat na roboty w niemieckim przemyśle zbrojeniowym, — branka młodzieży męskiej do służby pomocniczej w taborach na froncie — oto metody, które ten podwójny okupant względem nas stosuje.

Ale ni naszej nieugiętej postawy nie zdoła złamać, ani zachwiać naszej wiary w zbliżającą się chwilę wyzwolenia. Nadejdzie wkrótce dzień obrachunku. — Winowajcy naszych krzywd i cierpień poniosą zasłużoną i surową karę. Choć wrogie hordy zalały naszą Ojczyznę, — choć pod ich butem jęczymy w chwilowej niewoli — lecz ducha wolności i godności w Polakach nie zdołą złamać. — Quislingów, Lavali czy Kubliunosów nie wyłoniliśmy dotąd i nie wyłonimy nadal. Ciągłość naszego bytu państwowego utrzymujemy poprzez nasze przedstawicielstwo narodowe i bohaterską armię polską na obczyźnie oraz legalny Rząd Polski w Londynie, dzięki którym sprawienie Polski na forum międzynarodowym niepomiernie się wzmocniło. — W oparciu o naczelne Władze Polskie w Londynie w stosownym momencie chwycimy za broń i na gruzach wrogów odbudujemy Niepodległość naszej Najjaśniejszej Rzeczypospolitej, — na wolności, sprawiedliwości społecznej i poszanowaniu godności ludzkiej opartej.

To też pismem naszym pragniemy zadokumentować wrogom, że śmy w walce nieugięci.

Zadaniem naszego wydawnictwa będzie: — chronić społeczeństwo polskie przed zalewem wrogiej propagandy, — przed sączeniem jadu zakłamania i zwątpienia przez zaprzedaną Niemcom legalną prasę polską; — wobec zakazu słuchania zagranicznych audycji radiowych, informować o sprawach polskich i podawać istotne wiadomości o przebiegu wojny wg. komunikatów polskich z Londynu i Ameryki, — wskazywać nieświadomym lub chwiejnym właściwą postawę walczącego Polaka; — wreszcie piętnować i zwalczać każdy przejaw serwilizmu, ugody czy zaprzaństwa w łonie własnego społeczeństwa.

W nadziei, że dobrze przysłużymy się wspólnej, drogiej nam wszystkim Sprawie — oddajemy ten numer do rąk Czytelnika.

                                        R E D A K C J A

First edition—'illegal leaflet'- 1942

Squad of Young Polish Partisans

In Field March – Capt. "Jurand" and 1-st Storm Platoon

Mietek Fijalkowski Pseud. "Czarnota" Czeslaw Plawski Pseud. "Bej"

Camp "Tengeru" – Tanzania, Africa

Teresa and Edward in Pakistan

Bajorski family in Africa

Young Girl in Tanzania, Africa

Masai Warrior – Africa

Garden Worker – Camp "Tengeru" – Africa

Teresa with her bicycle – England

Teresa in High School – Diddington, England

Escaping Crew (Skiba, Drzewinski, Fijalkowski & Plawski)

Sand Dune in Leba

Boat used to escape

Czeslaw beside service "Jeep" – Camp "Combat"

West Germany – Camp "Combat From left: "Julian" "Czeslaw" and "Zenon"

Ski Training – Bavarian Alps Czeslaw and Edward

My Service Car – West Germany

Michael Budney

On Yacht – In Stockholm Fiord

End of Adventures

50 Years Together

Daughter Elizabeth's Family

Daughter Alice's Family